NorthStar

LISTENING AND SPEAKING
Advanced

SECOND EDITION

Sherry Preiss

Series Editors
Frances Boyd
Carol Numrich

Longman

NorthStar: Listening and Speaking, Advanced
Second Edition

Pearson Education, 10 Bank Street, White Plains, NY 10606

Pronunciation consultant: Linda Lane

Development director: Penny Laporte
Project manager: Debbie Sistino
Senior development editor: Paula H. Van Ells
Vice president, director of design and production: Rhea Banker
Executive managing editor: Linda Moser
Production coordinator: Melissa Leyva
Senior production editor: Kathleen Silloway
Production editor: Alice Vigliani
Director of manufacturing: Patrice Fraccio
Senior manufacturing buyer: Dave Dickey
Photo research: Aerin Csigay
Cover design: Rhea Banker
Cover art: Detail of Wandbild aus dem Tempel der Sehnsucht\dorthin/, 1922,
    30 Mural from the temple of desire\there/ 26.7 × 37.5 cm; oil transfer
    drawing and water color on plaster-primed gauze; The Metropolitan
    Museum of Art, N.Y. The Berggruen Klee Collection, 1984. (1984.315.33)
    Photograph © 1986 The Metropolitan Museum of Art.
    © 2003 Artists Rights Society (ARS), New York / VG Bild-Kunst, Bonn
Text design: Quorum Creative Services
Text composition: ElectraGraphics, Inc.
Text font: 11/13 Sabon
Text art: Duśan Petricic
Listening credits: see page 271
Photo credits: see page 271

Wandbild aus dem Tempel
der Sehnsucht ↖ dorthin ↗
Paul Klee

Library of Congress Cataloging-in-Publication Data

Preiss, Sherry
    NorthStar. Listening and speaking, advanced / Sherry Preiss.—2nd ed.
        p. cm.
    Includes index.
    1. English language—Textbooks for foreign speakers. 2. English
language—Spoken English—Problems, exercises, etc. 3. Listening—
Problems, exercises, etc. I. Title: Listening and speaking, advanced. II. Title.

PE1128.P68 2004
428.3'4–dc21

2003044731

ISBN: 0-201-75574-2 (Student Book)
       0-13-143911-1 (Student Book with Audio CDs)

Printed in the United States of America
7 8 9 10—CRK—09 08 07 06
4 5 6 7 8 9 10—CRK—09 08 07 06

Contents

Welcome to NorthStar

Second Edition

NorthStar leads the way in integrated skills series. The Second Edition remains an innovative, five-level series written for students with academic as well as personal language goals. Each unit of the thematically linked Reading and Writing strand and Listening and Speaking strand explores intellectually challenging, contemporary themes to stimulate critical thinking skills while building language competence.

Four easy to follow sections—Focus on the Topic, Focus on Reading/Focus on Listening, Focus on Vocabulary, and Focus on Writing/Focus on Speaking— invite students to focus on the process of learning through **NorthStar**.

Thematically Based Units

NorthStar engages students by organizing language study thematically. Themes provide stimulating topics for reading, writing, listening, and speaking.

Extensive Support to Build Skills for Academic Success

Creative activities help students develop language-learning strategies, such as predicting and identifying main ideas and details.

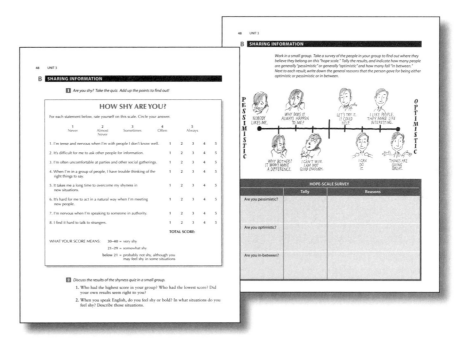

High-Interest Listening and Reading Selections

The two listening or reading selections in each unit present contrasting viewpoints to enrich students' understanding of the content while building language skills.

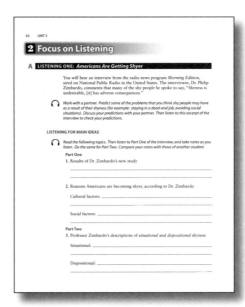

Critical Thinking Skill Development

Critical thinking skills, such as synthesizing information or reacting to the different viewpoints in the two reading or listening selections, are practiced throughout each unit, making language learning meaningful.

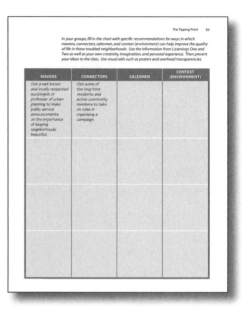

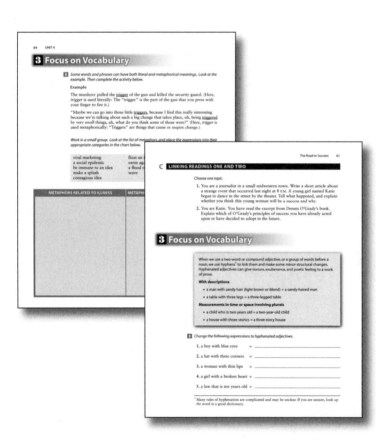

Extensive Vocabulary Practice

Students are introduced to key, contextualized vocabulary to help them comprehend the listening and reading selections. They also learn idioms, collocations, and word forms to help them explore, review, play with, and expand their spoken and written expression.

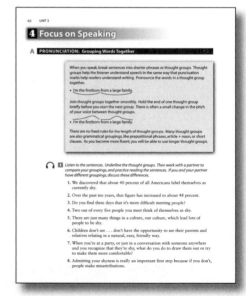

Powerful Pronunciation Practice

A carefully designed pronunciation syllabus in the Listening and Speaking strand focuses on topics such as stress, rhythm, and intonation. Theme-based pronunciation practice reinforces the vocabulary and content of the unit.

Content-Rich Grammar Practice

Each thematic unit integrates the study of grammar with related vocabulary and cultural information. The grammatical structures are drawn from the listening or reading selections and offer an opportunity for students to develop accuracy in speaking or writing about the topic.

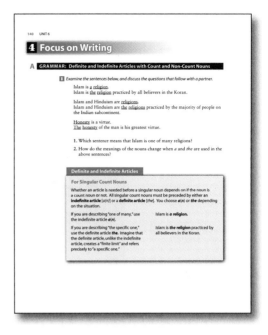

Extensive Opportunity for Discussion and Writing

Challenging and imaginative speaking activities, writing topics, and research assignments allow students to apply the language, grammar, style, and content they've learned.

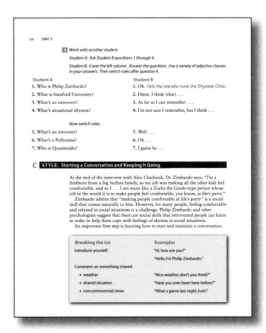

Writing Activity Book

The companion *Writing Activity Book* leads students through the writing process with engaging writing assignments. Skills and vocabulary from **NorthStar: Reading and Writing,** are reviewed and expanded as students learn the process of prewriting, organizing, revising, and editing.

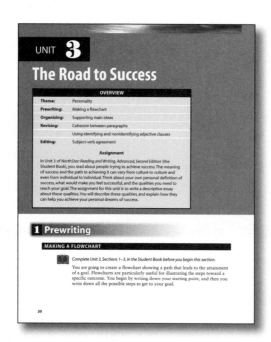
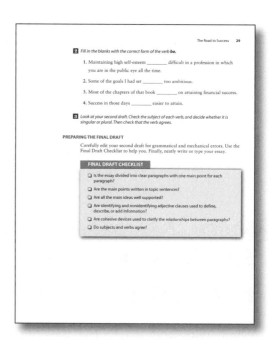

Audio Program

All the pronunciation, listening, and reading selections have been professionally recorded. The audio program includes audio CDs as well as audio cassettes.

Teacher's Manual with Achievement Tests

Each book in the series has an accompanying *Teacher's Manual* with step-by-step teaching suggestions, time guidelines, and expansion activities. Also included in each *Teacher's Manual* are reproducible unit-by-unit tests. The Listening and Speaking strand tests are recorded on CD and included in the *Teacher's Manual*. Packaged with each *Teacher's Manual* for the Reading and Writing strand is a TestGen CD-ROM that allows teachers to create and customize their own **NorthStar** tests. Answer Keys to both the Student Book and the Tests are included, along with a unit-by-unit word list of key vocabulary.

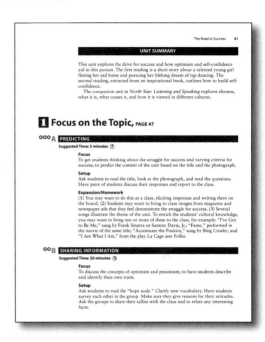

NorthStar Video Series

The *Northstar* video presents authentic, engaging segments from ABC broadcasts including *20/20* and *World News Tonight* as well as documentaries, cartoons, narratives, and interviews correlated to the themes in *Northstar, Second Edition,* containing two to five minute segments for each unit. Packaged with each video is a Video Guide with complete scripts, vocabulary for comprehension and background notes to enhance the accessability and enjoyment of the material. Worksheets for the video can be found on the *Northstar* Companion Website.

Companion Website

http://www.longman.com/northstar includes resources for students and teachers such as additional vocabulary activities, Web-based links and research, video worksheets, and correlations to state standards.

Scope and Sequence

Unit	Critical Thinking Skills	Listening Tasks
1 **The Internet and Other Addictions** Theme: Addiction Listening One: *Interview with an Internet Addiction Counselor* An interview with a psychologist Listening Two: *Time to Do Everything Except Think* An interview with a commentator	Distinguish between notions of addiction and compulsion Infer word meaning from context Recognize personal assumptions about technology Infer information not explicit in interviews Compare and contrast differing viewpoints Support opinions with information from interviews Hypothesize another's point of view	Take notes on main ideas and supporting details using a graphic organizer Interpret a speaker's intent by analyzing tone and word usage Relate listenings to personal experiences, values, and opinions Identify connecting theme in two interviews Identify emphasized words in speech Locate a support group through telephone inquiries
2 **Celebration, Florida: Disney's Utopia** Theme: Utopian Movements Listening One: *The Celebration Experiment* An interview with a scholar of American Studies Listening Two: *Living in Celebration* An interview with a resident journalist	Recognize personal assumptions about community Classify information Infer word meaning from context Infer meaning not explicit in a text Hypothesize scenarios Compare and contrast viewpoints Make judgments Analyze relationships between ideas	Identify main ideas Listen for details Interpret a speaker's attitude and tone of voice Relate listening to personal values Take notes on supporting details using a graphic organizer Synthesize information from two interviews Decipher words spoken with reduced pronunciation Listen to a movie
3 **The Bold and the Bashful** Theme: Personality Listening One: *Americans Are Getting Shyer* An interview with a professor of psychology Listening Two: *The Pollyanna Syndrome* A commentary	Measure and compare personality traits Rank shyness factors Infer word meaning from context Analyze word usage Re-evaluate assumptions in light of new information Critique an argument Hypothesize another's point of view Interpret song lyrics	Take notes on main ideas Listen for details Interpret speaker's attitude and emotions Relate listenings to personal experiences and values Identify thought groups in speech Compare and contrast intonation patterns Take a dictation

Speaking Tasks	Pronunciation	Vocabulary	Grammar
Make predictions Express and defend opinions Paraphrase a cartoon Act out a scripted conversation Use new vocabulary in a guided conversation Use gambits to build on other's ideas Use appropriate verb structures or gambits to respond extemporaneously Simulate discussion sessions at a psychology conference Conduct a survey Report survey findings	Highlighting important words	Context clues Definitions Synonyms Idiomatic expressions Word forms	Wish statements: expressing unreality
Make predictions Summarize ideas Practice expressing conjecture with gambits Role-play a conversation using new vocabulary Use opening gambits to voice opinions Play the role of a discussion leader Simulate a town meeting Present a two-minute movie review Conduct an interview and report results	Reduction of *as, has,* and *is*	Context clues Synonyms Definitions Analogies	Noun clauses after verbs of urgency
Make predictions Express and defend opinions Construct and perform a dialogue Use new vocabulary in extemporaneous responses Describe one's personality Use gambits to express uncertainty, to break the ice, and to maintain a conversation Role-play small-talk conversations Role-play interviews Present research on phobias	Grouping words together	Context clues Word definitions Synonyms Idiomatic expressions Vocabulary classification	Identifying and nonidentifying adjective clauses

Unit	Critical Thinking Skills	Listening Tasks

4
The Tipping Point
Theme: Trends
Listening One: *The Tipping Point*
  An interview with the author
Listening Two: *Tipping Points in Fighting Crime*
  More excerpts from the interview
	Interpret graphs
	Identify influences on personal behavior
	Analyze a case study
	Critique an interviewer's strategy
	Correlate personal observations to Tipping Point Theory
	Critique the Broken Window Theory
	Define problems and propose solutions
		Interview a classmate and record responses
		Summarize main points
		Listen for details
		Interpret a speaker's attitude
		Relate listenings to personal experiences
		Identify stress patterns
		Listen to and comment on a public service announcement
		Take notes in outline form
		Research a successful product at a local company

5
Feng Shui: Ancient Wisdom Travels West
Theme: Cross-cultural Insights
Listening One: *Interview with a Feng Shui Expert*
  A conversation with Kirsten Lagatree
Listening Two: *Feng Shui in the Newsroom*
  The expert redesigns a space
	Interpret quotations
	Evaluate environments according to the theory of feng shui
	Support opinions with information from the text
	Distinguish between common sense and superstition
	Infer word meaning from context
	Plan a space conforming to feng shui principles
	Develop a logical argument for and against an issue
		Explain main ideas
		Listen to summaries to complete a chart
		Identify supporting details
		Interpret speaker's attitude and tone
		Relate listening to personal environment
		Take notes using a graphic organizer
		Synthesize information from two listenings
		Identify patterns of stress reduction in speech

6
Spiritual Renewal
Theme: Religion
Listening One: *The Religious Tradition of Fasting*
  A news report
Listening Two: *Describing Monastic Life*
  An interview with an admirer
	Interpret quotations
	Challenge assumptions and stereotypes of monastic life
	Infer word meaning from context
	Analyze introductory statements and word usage
	Classify language related to religious practices
	Hypothesize rationale for various religious practices
	Evaluate appeal and benefits of spiritual practices
		Restate main ideas
		Listen for details
		Identify main ideas
		Listen and take notes on language usage
		Relate listening to personal preferences, experiences, and values
		Identify vowel patterns in speech

Speaking Tasks	**Pronunciation**	**Vocabulary**	**Grammar**
Make predictions Express and defend opinions Simulate a neighborhood advisory committee meeting Act out a scripted interview Use metaphors to make a point Use introductory expressions to extemporaneously restate information Develop and present a public service announcement Collaborate on a plan to change a trend Present research findings on a successful product	Stress changing suffixes	Context clues Word definitions Synonyms Metaphors	Adverb clauses of result
Summarize information in a jigsaw activity Express and defend opinions Act out a scripted interview Use new vocabulary and discourse connectors in extemporaneous responses Use gambits to emphasize a point Role-play a meeting Conduct an interview and report results Report research findings on phony cross-cultural products	Reductions with the auxiliary *have*	Word definitions Synonyms Context clues Word forms	Spoken discourse connectors
Make predictions Brainstorm motivations for spiritual renewal Express and defend opinions Summarize a reading using new vocabulary Use new vocabulary and expressions for hesitation in extemporaneous responses Act out a scripted interview Use gambits to tell an anecdote Simulate a community meeting Plan and present a five-minute speech on monasticism	Vowel alternation	Context clues Word definitions Synonyms	Count and non-count nouns and their quantifiers

Unit	Critical Thinking Skills	Listening Tasks
7 **Workplace Privacy** Theme: Business Listening One: *Interview on Workplace Surveillance* Interviews with workplace specialists Listening Two: *Managers and Employees Speak Out about Workplace Privacy* Two opposing points of view	Infer meaning not explicit in text Compare and contrast cultural norms of privacy Establish personal standards of privacy Support opinions with information from the text Hypothesize another's point of view Speculate on outcomes of a case Analyze two cases Compare and contrast word usage and meaning Extract logical arguments from the text to defend a position	Listen for main ideas Listen for details Interpret speaker's intensity of feeling Take detailed notes using a graphic organizer Relate listening to personal values Integrate information from two listenings Listen for correct stress in verbs and nouns Listen for logical arguments
8 **Warriors without Weapons** Theme: The Military Listening One: *Warriors without Weapons* An interview with a scholar of the Geneva Convention Listening Two: *Michael's Ignatieff's Views on War* More excerpts from the interview	Infer information not explicit in the text Evaluate personal understanding of a text Infer word meaning from context Draw conclusions based on information in an interview Illustrate abstract concepts with concrete examples Support opinions with information from an interview Make judgments on controversial issues Hypothesize qualities of an ICRC recruit	Take notes on main ideas Listen for details Listen closely to interpret meaning from word usage Interpret speaker's tone and attitude Relate listening to personal values and opinions Listen for specific information in classmate responses Complete an aural cloze Categorize vowel sounds Listen to a public service announcement and take notes
9 **Boosting Brain Power through the Arts** Theme: The Arts Listening One: *Does Music Enhance Math Skills?* A news report Listening Two: *Music, Art, and the Brain* An interview with a science journalist	Compare and contrast information Infer word meaning from context Evaluate proposals using criteria set forth in a report Hypothesize alternative ways to boost intelligence Judge the value and benefits of teaching the arts Analyze the pros and cons of education proposals Frame arguments for and against an issue Write a persuasive letter arguing a point of view	Listen to student summaries and take notes Listen for main ideas Take detailed notes using a graphic organizer Relate listening to personal experiences and values Take notes on listening Paraphrase main ideas of listening Classify sounds
10 **Television and Freedom of Expression** Theme: First Amendment Issues Listening One: *Interview with Newsweek Entertainment Editor* A radio interview Listening Two: *Interview with Former Chairman of MPAA Ratings Board* A radio interview	Hypothesize outcomes Recognize personal biases and assumptions Evaluate a ratings system Identify points of view in a text Defend a point of view Make informed judgments using information from interviews Develop arguments for or against an issue Define a problem and propose a solution	Identify main ideas Listen for details Interpret speaker's intent by analyzing tone and word usage Relate listening to personal experiences and values Listen for supporting ideas in an argument Synthesize information in two listenings Listen for word stress in speech Take notes on interview responses

Speaking Tasks	Pronunciation	Vocabulary	Grammar
Brainstorm words about privacy Make predictions Construct and perform a dialogue Practice correct stress patterns in extemporaneous responses Act out a scripted interview Use gambits to frame an argument Conduct a class debate Conduct short interviews and summarize findings	Stress on two-syllable words	Context clues Definitions Synonyms	Verb + gerund—two forms, two meanings
Make predictions Compare background experiences Use opening gambits to react to a text Express and defend opinions Pose and respond to questions using new vocabulary Retell a conversation Use gambits to stall and elucidate Develop and perform a public service announcement	Vowels /æ/-/ɑ/-/ə/ Tongue twisters	Context clues Synonyms Definitions Confusing pairs	Direct and indirect speech
Compare knowledge of and reactions to classical music Summarize information Use figurative language in extemporaneous responses Role-play an interview Use transitions to compare and contrast information Role-play a school board meeting Conduct an experiment	Joining final consonants	Context clues Synonyms Definitions Idiomatic expressions Vocabulary classification Figurative and literal usage	The passive voice and the passive causative
Make predictions Support an opinion with examples Use new vocabulary in a role play Use phrasal verbs in extemporaneous responses Express varying degrees of certainty with modals Use gambits to express doubts Conduct a debate Conduct short interviews and summarize findings	Word stress of phrasal verbs	Context clues Synonyms Word definitions Idiomatic expressions Phrasal verbs	Modals: degrees of certainty

Acknowledgments

The Second Edition of this book could not have been written without the support and assistance of many of my friends and colleagues.

I would like to thank Frances Boyd and Carol Numrich, the architects of the **NorthStar** series, for their extraordinary vision of combining innovative language learning with topics of high interest to students. Once again, I am grateful to Frances Boyd, my series editor, for her imaginative insights, her sense of humor, and her passionate dedication to the task. Frances motivated and inspired my writing with her creative and intelligent insights into the language learning process.

I also owe an enormous debt of gratitude to the following people at Pearson Longman. Paula Van Ells, my development editor, deserves credit for her clever, patient, and respectful editing. I appreciate her unflagging support, suggestions, hard work, and lighthearted approach. At Pearson Longman, I was also fortunate to have had an outstanding production team committed to editorial excellence and the highest standards of production quality: Kathleen Silloway, Senior Production Editor, and Linda Moser, Executive Managing Editor.

For making significant direct contributions throughout every step of the project, I owe an enormous debt of gratitude to Penny Laporte, Director of Development, and Debbie Sistino, Project Manager. I would also like to thank Aerin Csigay for his tremendous help with the art program, and Tiffany Torres, administrative assistant, for her work with the audioscripts and credits.

I am particularly grateful to three people who contributed generously of their time and materials to the book: David Alpern of *Newsweek on Air,* Kirby Wiggins of National Public Radio, and Dorothy Ferebee of *Fresh Air with Terry Gross.*

Between the first and second editions, I had the fortunate experience of traveling worldwide and working with teachers and students who were using the **NorthStar** series. My observations and their feedback provided much of the impetus for this revision. I appreciate their willingness to engage students in material that challenges their assumptions and allows them to think critically about themselves and the world.

Finally, as in the first edition, I owe heartfelt thanks to my mom, Bernice, my husband, Rich, and my children, Elyse and Alex, for providing me with constant love, support, and understanding.

Sherry Preiss

Reviewers

For the comments and insights they graciously offered to help shape the direction of the Second Edition of *Northstar*, the publisher would like to thank the following reviewers and institutions.

Lubie G. Alatriste, Lehman College; **A. Morgan Andaluz**, Leeward Community College; **Chris Antonellis**, Boston University CELOP; **Christine Baez**, Universidad de las Américas, Mexico City, Mexico; **Betty Baron**, Johnson County Community College; **Rudy Besikof**, University of California San Diego; **Mary Black**, Institute of North American Studies; **Dorothy Buroh**, University of California, San Diego; **Kay Caldwell**, Leeward Community College; **Margarita Canales**; Universidad Latinoamericana, Mexico City, Mexico; **Jose Carvalho**, University of Massachusetts Boston; **Philip R. Condorelli**, University of Massachusetts Boston; **Pamela Couch**, Boston University CELOP; **Barbara F. Dingee**, University of Massachusetts Boston; **Jeanne M. Dunnet**, Central Connecticut State University; **Samuela Eckstut-Didier**, Boston University CELOP; **Patricia Hedden**, Yonsei University; **Hostos Community College; GEOS Language Institute; Jennifer M. Gerrity**, University of Massachusetts Boston; **Lis Jenkinson**, Northern Virginia Community College; **Glenna Jennings**, University of California, San Diego; **Diana Jones**, Instituto Angloamericano, Mexico City, Mexico; **Matt Kaeiser**, Old Dominion University; **Regina Kandraska**, University of Massachusetts Boston; **King Fahd University of Petroleum & Minerals; Chris Ko**, Kyang Hee University; **Charalambos Kollias**, The Hellenic-American Union; **Barbara Kruchin**, Columbia University ALP; **Language Training Institute; Jacqueline LoConde**, Boston University CELOP; **Mary Lynch**, University of Massachusetts Boston; **Julia Paranionova**, Moscow State Pedagogical University; **Pasadena City College; Pontifical Xavier University; Natalya Morozova**, Moscow State Pedagogical University; **Mary Carole Ramiowski**, University of Seoul; **Jon Robinson**, University of Seoul; **Michael Sagliano**, Leeward Community College; **Janet Shanks**, Columbia University ALP; **Eric Tejeda**; PROULEX, Guadalajara, Mexico; **Truman College; United Arab Emirates University; University of Minnesota; Karen Whitlow**, Johnson County Community College

The Internet and Other Addictions

*"Hi. My name is Barry, and I check my E-mail
two to three hundred times a day."*

1 Focus on the Topic

A PREDICTING

Look at the cartoon, and read the caption. Barry introduces himself with his first name and his problem. What kind of problem could he have? What kind of group is this? Discuss your thoughts with a partner.

1

B   SHARING INFORMATION

In a small group, discuss your answers to the following questions.

1. Most people have heard that nicotine, the substance in tobacco, is addictive. What other substances or activities can people be addicted to or dependent on? Make a list of other addictions.

2. Do you know anyone who has been addicted to one of the items on your list? If so, describe that person and his or her addiction.

3. Anne Lamott, author of a book of essays called *Bird by Bird*, writes, "Getting all of one's addictions under control is a little like putting an octopus to bed." What does she mean? How do you feel about her analogy? Explain.

C   PREPARING TO LISTEN

BACKGROUND

Read the following article.

Bill, a student at the University of Maryland who doesn't want his last name used, said recently: "I'm online probably 4 or 5 hours a day, most days. So I guess that's over 30 hours a week. Am I an addict? I don't know, but I can't get through the day without checking my e-mail several times, downloading music, **surfing** the Net, or going into a **chat room**."

Bill, and students like him, are becoming increasingly common on college campuses all over the United States. Can **engaging in** a behavior such as computer use actually be considered an addiction? Should professors and students be **turning each other in** to campus police? For years, researchers have been trying to make sense of the biology and psychology of addiction, its causes, and its cures. "Addiction" used to mean abuse of substances such as drugs, alcohol, and nicotine. These days, though, the word *addiction* is also being applied to Internet use, gambling, sex, shopping, and even travel.

The results of two recent studies of college students by researcher Victor Brenner show cause for concern. Look at the data from these studies.

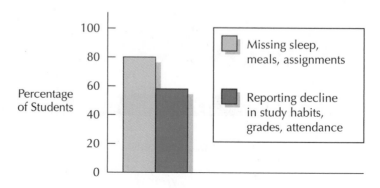

So, if students are **devoting** more time to **high-tech** play than to study, is this an addiction? Without defining it precisely, psychologists who have noticed the **compulsiveness** of Internet users suggest that some kind of **therapy** may be needed. In fact, some campus officials have responded by **putting together support groups** for students who **present with** a variety of addiction-like symptoms, including repetitive stress syndrome (severe wrist pain), excessive fatigue or tiredness, and back and eye strain.

Beyond college campuses, new issues are **coming out** as a result of increasing Internet use. One study of the general population, conducted by Dr. Kimberly Young of the University of Pittsburgh, showed that 8.1 million Americans are spending upwards of 40 hours a week on the Net. If this is so, they probably are not doing much else: not much socializing, going to movies, eating out, or supervising their children. Volunteering is decreasing; loneliness is increasing. **Fulfillment** becomes limited to interaction on a screen. What happens to community life?

Whether at college or at home, Americans and others around the world are increasingly dependent on the Internet for work and for fun. The medical community is alert to the dangers, both physical and psychological. Will "Internet addiction" soon be an entry in the *Physician's Desk Reference,* the chief diagnostic tool for doctors? You will have to check the latest news . . . on the Net!

*Read the statements, and write **A** (agree), **D** (disagree), or **?** (can't decide) in the blank. Compare your answers with those of a partner.*

_____ 1. A person who spends 40 hours a week online could be called an Internet addict.

_____ 2. It's as easy to get addicted to the Internet as it is to get addicted to nicotine.

_____ 3. Electronic communication (e-mail, chat rooms, online discussion groups) is cold and impersonal.

_____ 4. Internet addiction is not as serious as other addictions, such as gambling, nicotine, and drugs.

_____ 5. The Internet is fun, useful, and practical, and cannot be viewed as dangerous.

VOCABULARY FOR COMPREHENSION

Read the words or expressions below on the left. Then find the definition on the right that is similar in meaning to each word or expression. If necessary, read the background reading again for more clues about the meaning. Write the appropriate letter in the blank.

_____ **1.** surfing

_____ **2.** chat room

_____ **3.** engaging in

_____ **4.** turning each other in

_____ **5.** devoting

_____ **6.** high-tech

_____ **7.** compulsiveness

_____ **8.** therapy

_____ **9.** putting together

_____ **10.** support groups

_____ **11.** present with

_____ **12.** coming out

_____ **13.** fulfillment

a. treatment of problems by talking about them

b. technologically advanced

c. inability to control certain behavior

d. electronic discussion groups in which people exchange written messages

e. personal satisfaction

f. people who meet to help each other with a problem they all share

g. show signs of an illness by having a particular type of behavior or condition

h. spending or using time or effort

i. looking for information (on the Internet)

j. organizing

k. taking part in or participating in

l. identifying each other to the police or an authority

m. appearing

2 Focus on Listening

A LISTENING ONE: *Interview with an Internet Addiction Counselor*

You will hear a telephone interview from the radio news broadcast *Talk of the Nation: Science Friday*. It aired on National Public Radio in the United States. Ira Flatow, the host of the show, interviews psychologist Dr. Jonathan Kandell of the University of Maryland. Kandell counsels students who spend too much time online.

Work with a partner. Listen to the first 35 seconds of the interview. Write down three questions that you think Ira Flatow might ask Dr. Kandell, the counselor.

1. _____

2. _____

3. _____

LISTENING FOR MAIN IDEAS

Look at the chart below. Listen to the interview, and take notes on its main ideas by completing the prompts under Main Ideas. (You will use the Details column later.) When you have finished, compare your notes with those of a partner, and revise them if necessary.

MAIN IDEAS	DETAILS
Focus of interview *unusual or "other" addictions*	Examples of addictions *gambling, . . .*
Kandell's view of Internet addiction	Evidence for this view
Chief symptoms/warning signs of Internet addiction	Other symptoms/warning signs
Possible treatment	Reasons this treatment is helpful

LISTENING FOR DETAILS

 Look at the chart again. Read the information you wrote under Main Ideas, and then read the cues under Details. Fill in as many details to support the main ideas as you can. Then listen to the interview again to check your work. Compare your notes with your partner's, and revise if necessary.

REACTING TO THE LISTENING

 1 *Read the questions. Then listen to each excerpt from the interview. Answer the questions, and discuss your answers with a partner. Give reasons for your choices. Each question has more than one possible answer.*

Excerpt One

A *groupie* usually refers to someone, especially a young woman, who likes a musician, movie star, or sports star and follows this person around hoping to meet the star. Why does Ira Flatow, the host, use the word *groupie* to advise a certain group in the radio audience to listen? What does the word *groupie* imply in this context?

Excerpt Two

Kandell doesn't answer Flatow's question directly. What expressions show his hesitation? Why doesn't he answer Flatow directly?

Excerpt Three

How does Flatow feel about this topic at this point in the interview? How do you know? What words and tone of voice does he use to indicate his attitude?

2 *Discuss the following questions with the class. Give your opinions.*

1. Do you agree more with Kandell (that Internet addiction is possible) or with Flatow (that Internet overuse may not be an addiction)? Explain.

2. What's your own experience with people who use the Internet? Do you know people who overuse it? Do you overuse it? What are the warning signs? What cure or treatment would you recommend for Internet addicts?

3. How helpful can a support group like Kandell's—at the University of Maryland—be for Internet overusers? Explain. What other support groups do you know of? Would you ever join one? Why or why not?

B LISTENING TWO: *Time to Do Everything Except Think*

In this radio interview, David Alpern and Warren Levinson, hosts of *Newsweek on Air*, a popular radio broadcast in the United States, interview David Brooks, author, journalist, and commentator. Brooks comments on the new wired and wireless life of the twenty-first century—one in which people are using new devices (such as mobile phones, laptop computers, and handheld computers) to communicate.

1 *Listen to the excerpt from the interview. Take notes in the chart that follows. Fill in the main ideas on the left side of the chart, and support those ideas with as many details as possible on the right. Discuss your notes with a partner, and revise if necessary.*

MAIN IDEAS	DETAILS
Brooks's attitude toward communication and information in the twenty-first century *We are bombarded with so much information.*	Reasons for his attitude
Advantage of multitasking	Additional advantages of multitasking
General view of creativity and how it occurs	Specific ways to enhance creativity
Effect of technology on Brooks	Examples of effect on Brooks

2 *Read the following statements. According to Brooks's commentary, decide if they are true (**T**) or false (**F**), and write your answer in each blank. Then correct the false statements. Use your notes to help you. Discuss your answers in a small group. Give reasons for your decisions.*

_____ 1. You can really see that the new gadgets change who we are and how we act.

_____ 2. You can increase your effectiveness and even your intelligence by multitasking, that is, doing more than one thing at once.

_____ 3. Faster and easier access to information is a good thing that makes us more creative.

_____ 4. If you want to be successful in business, you should only read current business newspapers and magazines.

_____ 5. To be creatively productive, you should answer every e-mail that you get as soon as possible.

_____ 6. It's really hard *not* to check your cellular phone for messages all the time.

C   LINKING LISTENINGS ONE AND TWO

1 *David Brooks and Jonathan Kandell both have opinions about the effects of technology and the Internet on society. Read the statements below. Decide whether Brooks or Kandell would agree with them or not. Write **Agree** or **Disagree** in the space.*

Then decide if you would agree or disagree with the opinions, and put your answer in the column on the right.

Discuss your opinions in a small group.

STATEMENTS	KANDELL	BROOKS	YOU
1. Addiction to the Internet is as serious as addiction to drugs, alcohol, or tobacco.			
2. The widespread use of technology helps us get information but hurts our creativity and our off-line relationships.			
3. Talking with a therapist and/or other addicts is the best way to overcome technology addictions.			

2 *Look at the cartoon. Paraphrase the words in each thought bubble and write the paraphrase in the space below the cartoon. What is the message? Do you think it's funny? Why or why not? What would Dr. Kandell say about this recovery strategy? Does the idea behind the cartoon apply to other addictions?*

Frame 1: _____

_____

Frame 2: _____

_____

Frame 3: _____

_____

Frame 4: _____

_____

Now discuss your paraphrase with a partner.

3 Focus on Vocabulary

1 *Working with a partner, fill in the other forms of the words in the chart. An **X** indicates that there is no related form or that the form is not commonly used.*

Noun	Verb	Adjective
1. addict **2.** addiction	X	**1.** addicted **2.**
anxiety	X	anxious
1. compulsiveness **2.** compulsion	X	
		1. depressed **2.** depressive
enhancement		
fulfillment		**1.** **2.**
	isolate	
X		**1.** overwhelmed **2.** overwhelming
	X	problematic
	strategize	
support		**1.** **2.**
symptom	X	*symptomatic*
therapy	X	*therapeutic*

2 *Work in groups of three to fill in the blanks in the dialogue on page 11. Use the correct form of the words from the chart above. Not all words will be used. Then, in your groups, role-play the conversation with drama and enthusiasm. Add or change the lines if you like.*

Psychiatrists have been studying another unusual addiction: shopaholism, or "compulsive shopping disorder." According to recent research, 8 percent of all Americans may be shopaholics, and 90 percent of them are women. Like other people trying to overcome addictions, shopaholics attend support group meetings. Here is what they might say at their first meeting.

A: Hi. I'm Teresa. I became a (1) _____ shopper almost
(right Away)
overnight. My job had become just too stressful. So, to unwind after work,
I'd head off to the mall. I started buying small things I really didn't need, but
then I started spending more and more, and coming home later and later.
It was "shop 'til you drop." My spending spun out of control until I was
(2) _____ with debt.

B: Sounds familiar, Teresa. Hi, everyone. I'm Olivia. For me, work was not
(3) _____ at all. Rather, my personal life was a mess. The
guy I had been dating for 12 years suddenly left me for another woman.
So I ended up feeling nervous and unsettled; I started having sudden
(4) _____ attacks.

C: You mean headaches, rapid heartbeat, and sweaty palms?

B: Yeah, those were the (5) _____. But as soon as I pulled out my
credit card, my best friend, I felt better, kind of energized. I felt strangely
satisfied and (6) _____.

C: I feel the same way when I hold that little piece of plastic. Oh . . .
sorry . . . I forgot to introduce myself. I'm Maria. Whenever I feel sad or
(7) _____, charging a few hundred bucks on my card just
cheers me up. I've tried a bunch of different (8) _____ to try to
kick the habit, but so far I haven't found a way to do it. So, now here I am . . .
hoping you all will help.

A: Sure, we will. Ummm . . . have any of you gotten (9) _____ to
online shopping, catalogue shopping, home TV shopping, or something like that?

C: Nope, not me. Shopping at home is way too lonely and
(10) _____. I'd much rather be in a crowded shopping mall.

B: Yeah, me too, Maria. You know, this group is so helpful. We can really be
(11) _____ of each other by sharing our feelings openly like this.

A: Yes. I think so too. It's more (12) _____ than taking that new
medicine for shopaholism or seeing a private shrink. And the best part is that
we are here and not at the mall . . . at least for now.

3 *On a separate piece of paper, write a paragraph describing a person you know who has an addiction. Use at least eight words from the chart on page 10. Use as many different forms of the words as possible.*

4 *Match the underlined words in the sentences with a similar expression from the list on page 13. Write the corresponding letter in the blank. Then compare your answers with those of a partner.*

_____ 1. She was so thrilled at winning $2,000 playing "pachinko," a Japanese pinball-slot matching game, that she <u>turned into</u> a real pachinkoholic.

_____ 2. One of the students in Kandell's support group reported he <u>felt empty</u>, confused, and lonely after he went cold turkey and suddenly gave up talking to his friends in chat rooms every night.

_____ 3. When Dr. Kimberly Young's research on Internet addiction first came out, she was <u>bombarded with</u> requests for interviews. Reporters were shocked by her conclusions that Internet addiction was a serious illness.

_____ 4. Some psychologists believe that electronic forms of communication (e-mail, voice mail, mobile phone, pagers, chat rooms) are seriously <u>shaping our social interactions</u>.

_____ 5. In some parts of the United States, using a cell phone in the car is now illegal. Too many drivers are <u>multitasking</u>—eating, talking, working— while driving, which causes accidents.

_____ 6. Upon returning from a week or two of vacation, many employees are simply <u>overwhelmed</u> by the huge amount of e-mail that builds up. Some may receive nearly 400 messages a week.

_____ 7. After he gave up cigarettes, he <u>went through</u> withdrawal: hunger, discomfort, and other uncomfortable symptoms.

_____ 8. Many business people see technology as a positive way to <u>enhance</u> customer service through more immediate and consistent communication.

_____ 9. While <u>noodling around</u> one Friday afternoon, a team of product engineers came up with a new wristwatch that allows users to receive instant e-mail messages on their wrists.

_____ 10. Some parents should be blamed for <u>feeding</u> their children's addiction to television or computer games because they have no rules to limit use.

_____ 11. <u>Driven</u> to win the "top sales manager of the year" award, he turned into a total workaholic, putting in 18-hour days for months.

_____ 12. College administrators really don't know what's <u>going on</u> in many computer labs. They think students are doing research and studying, but in many cases the students are playing computer games and chatting with their friends online.

a. improve; enrich

b. doing different things at the same time

c. attacked by a lot of information, data, or questions

d. influencing our behavior in a particular way

e. upset, strongly affected

f. became (something different)

g. happening

h. experienced

i. playing with ideas creatively

j. increasing

k. was unhappy, sad, or lonely (because nothing seemed interesting or important)

l. trying extremely hard

5 *Work with a partner.*

Student A: Ask Student B questions 1 and 2.

Student B: Cover the left column. Answer Student A's questions using the key words in your column in any order. Answer as fully as possible. Then switch roles after question 2.

Example

A: Have you ever been addicted to a particular TV program?

B: (problematic, turn in, compulsive) Oh, sure! About five years ago, I felt totally **compulsive** about watching a soap opera called *General Hospital*. It was quite **problematic** because I used to arrange my university course schedule around the time of the show, so I'd be sure to watch it every day. For several hours each night, I went on the Internet to read about the show and its stars. My roommate threatened to **turn** me **in** to a counselor because she thought I had become addicted.

Student A

1. Can you describe a time in your life when you were really hooked on a hobby?

2. If your friend were a dataholic, what kind of advice would you give him or her?

Now switch roles.

3. If a close friend of yours insisted on bringing her laptop with her on her vacation, how would you convince her not to?

4. Can you describe a time when you were overly enthusiastic about a new product coming on the market?

Student B

1. shape, fulfill, driven

2. enhance, noodle around, bombarded

3. feel empty, overwhelmed, feed

4. come out (on the market), turn into, go through

4 Focus on Speaking

A PRONUNCIATION: Highlighting Important Words

> In general, one or two words in a sentence are most important to express the speaker's meaning and intention.
>
> We *highlight* the most important words by saying the words
>
> - on a high pitch, or
>
> - with strong stress: the stressed vowel is long and loud.
>
> Listen to these sentences:
>
> I've GOT to have a cigarette.
>
> I REALLY need to check my e-mail again.
>
> When you speak, make sure your voice is high enough when you highlight an important word. While many languages are two-toned, English is a three-toned language. Therefore, you may need to use higher pitch in English than you do in your own language.

1 *Listen to the sentences. Underline the words that are highlighted. Some sentences may have more than one highlighted word. Then practice saying the sentences with a partner.*

Patty

1. Patty was running up huge sums of money on her credit cards.

2. She spent thousands of dollars.

3. Nothing could stop her.

4. She was totally out of control.

Jim

5. Fifteen cups of coffee a day was the only thing that kept Jim going.

6. Totally overwhelmed by work, he drank from 5 in the morning to 11 at night.

7. Now, addicted to both coffee and the Internet, his life was a complete disaster.

8. He couldn't get to a therapist's office fast enough.

2 *Read the dialogue. Work with a partner, and underline the highlighted words. Then listen to the dialogue to check your answers. Correct any errors. Practice reading the dialogue with your partner, emphasizing the highlighted words.*

A: Workaholism isn't really an addiction. Some people have no choice but to work long hours.

B: Not only that. A lot of people are workaholics because they love what they do.

A: Agreed, but being driven to succeed at all costs may not be such a good thing.

B: Yeah, that makes me think of my father. He was so hooked on work, he used to drive talking on his cell phone and checking his e-mail at red lights.

A: You must be joking. That is multitasking at its best!

B: Well, not exactly. He just lost his driver's license after getting into his third accident and getting his fifth ticket.

B GRAMMAR: Wish Statements—Expressing Unreality

1 *Working with a partner, examine the dialogues, and discuss the questions that follow.*

Q: Is your son going to quit [sky diving]?

A: No, but <u>I wish he would</u>.

Q: Are your children addicted to video games?

A: Yes, unfortunately, but <u>I really wish they weren't</u> [addicted to video games]. They forget to do their schoolwork.

Q: Do you know how I can stop drinking so much coffee?

A: No, but <u>I wish I did</u> [know how to stop]. You might try to get more sleep.

Q: Did you start smoking when you were a teenager?

A: Yes, and <u>I wish I hadn't</u> [started smoking].

1. How are the first three underlined phrases similar? *more in present and future*

2. How is the last underlined phrase different from the first three? *more in past*

Wish Statements—Expressing Unreality

Use the verb **wish** when you want to express unreality—a desire for reality to be different or a regret that it was not different. The verb tenses and structures used in the clause after *wish* to express future, present, or past situations are outlined below.

Reality Question	Wish Situation
	Present and Future Wish
	Use *wish* + *would* or *could.*
Can you help me now?	**No, but I wish I could.**
Will he answer all his e-mails later?	**No, but he wishes he could.**
	Present Wish
	Use *wish* + past form of the verb.
Does she drink too much coffee?	**Yes, but she wishes she didn't** [drink so much coffee].
	Present Wish (verb *to be*)
	Use past form: *wish* + *were.*
Is he a compulsive gambler?	**Yes, but he wishes he weren't** [a compulsive gambler].
Is he giving up gambling?	**No, but he wishes he were** [giving up gambling].
	Past Wishes
	Use *wish* + *had* + past participle.
Has she been to the support group yet?	**No, but she wishes she had** [been there].
Did she feel overwhelmed when she first started learning English?	**Yes, and she wishes she hadn't** [felt overwhelmed].
Were you hooked on candy as a child?	**Yes, and I wish I hadn't been** [hooked on candy].

> **Past Wishes: *could***
>
> Use ***wish*** + ***could have*** + past participle.
>
> Could you make the meeting last night?   **No, but I wish I could have** [made the meeting].
>
> **GRAMMAR TIP:** The tense of the verb *wish* does not affect the tense of the verb in the clause following *wish*.
>
> In spoken, informal English we often use short answer phrases with *wish* statements (see phrases in exercise 1).

2 *Work with a partner.*

Student A: Ask Student B questions 1 through 6. Check Student B's answers with the correct answer in parentheses.

Student B: Cover the left column. Answer Student A's question using a short-answer wish statement. Then switch roles after question 6.

Student A

1. Will your friend install the new computer program for you tonight?
   (No, but I wish he would *or* could.)

2. Does your husband play poker every Friday night?
   (Yes, and I wish he didn't *or* wouldn't.)

3. Are you still buying lottery tickets every week?
   (Yes, but I wish I weren't.)

4. Could you finish your homework before midnight yesterday?
   (No, but I wish I could have.)

5. Did they know that the Internet could be addictive?
   (No, but they wish they had known.)

6. Was your mother addicted to caffeine when she was younger?
   (Yes, and she wishes she hadn't been.)

Student B

1. No, but I wish he _____.

2. Yes, and I wish he _____.

3. Yes, but I wish I _____.

4. No, but I wish I _____.

5. No, but they wish they _____.

6. Yes, and she wishes she _____.

Now switch roles.

7. Will she overeat at the holiday parties?
(Yes, but she wishes she wouldn't.)

7. Yes, but she wishes she _____.

8. Is your husband compulsive about cleanliness?
(Yes, and I wish he weren't.)

8. Yes, and I wish he _____.

9. Does she know how to use the new e-mail pager?
(No, but she wishes she did.)

9. No, but she wishes she _____.

10. Did he go through withdrawal when he stopped smoking?
(Yes, and he wishes he hadn't.)

10. Yes, and he wishes he _____.

11. Could you figure out how she got so addicted to gambling?
(No, but I wish I could have.)

11. No, but I wish I _____.

12. Were you able to find a program to help end your compulsive shopping?
(No, but I wish I had *or* could have.)

12. No, but I wish I _____.

C   STYLE: Expressions for Building on Others' Ideas

The following is a list of useful expressions that can be used in conversation to build and expand on each others' ideas.

- **To add to your idea, I think** students socialize differently online than they do when they are face-to-face.

- **Not only that, but I would also say that** people are thinking more creatively.

- **Your point makes me think of** another issue, which is the trend toward giving students access to the Internet in dorm rooms.

- **Another thing I'd like to bring up** is the fact that some addictions are more harmful than others.

- **You speak of** needing to stay connected; **then, can I also assume that** you carry your cell phone with you at all times?

Work with a partner.

Student A: Read each of the first four opinions aloud.

Student B: Cover the left column. Build upon, add to, expand on what your partner has said. Use the expressions listed on page 18. Support your opinion with a few other statements. Then switch roles after item 3.

Example

A: We live in an overcommunicated world that will become even more so in the future.

B: **Not only that, but I would also say that** this world will create a generation of dataholics.

Student A	Student B
1. Workaholism cannot really be an addiction. Working hard is good for you.	1.
2. Coffee and chocolate are just as addictive as alcohol.	2.
3. Our "plugged in" lives are destroying opportunities for creativity and innovation.	3.

Now switch roles.

4. Companies need to come up with strategies to help employees with information overload.	4.
5. Cigarette advertisements encourage teenage addiction to smoking.	5.
6. We have time to do everything these days, except think.	6.
7. Because students need the Internet to do research, preventing Internet addiction is virtually impossible.	7.

D SPEAKING TOPIC

Read the description of the situation and the roles for this simulation activity. In your discussions, refer back to the ideas and vocabulary from the unit, and to the language in the Grammar section (pages 15–18) and Style section (pages 18–19).

SITUATION AND ROLES

Every year, the National Psychological Association holds a conference to discuss professional issues. This year's theme is "Addiction." You are psychologists attending the conference. The afternoon sessions, or meetings, are made up of interactive discussions about addiction. During these special sessions, participants share and build on each other's ideas. Then they must summarize their discussions for the participants in the other sessions.

Session One: Addictive Personalities

Discussion Topic: Are some people more likely to develop an addiction than other people?

- Define an addictive personality.
- Identify different addictive personality types, and give examples from people you know.

Session Two: Recovery Methods

Discussion Topic: What are some of the different methods used around the world to help people recover from addiction?

- Identify different recovery strategies.
- Discuss the pros and cons of each method.

Session Three: Psychology of Online Communication

Discussion Topic: How is the Internet affecting our personal relationships?

- Identify the ways the Internet and e-mail may be affecting people's relationships.
- List the pros and cons of online communication.
- Make recommendations for the future use of online communication.

1. Break up into three groups, decide which session each group will role-play, and choose a leader and a note taker.

2. Conduct a highly interactive discussion session. Make sure the note taker writes down the main points. Use expressions like the following:
   - Not only that, but I would also say that _____.
   - Your point makes me think of _____.
   - Another thing I'd like to bring up is _____.
   - OK, and to add to that idea, I'd say _____.

3. Summarize your discussion for the whole class.

E   RESEARCH TOPICS

TELEPHONE RESEARCH

1. Make some telephone calls to find out if there is a support group for Internet addiction or other addictions in your area. Find out (1) how often it meets; (2) how a person can join; (3) what the process is to help the person recover from the addiction; (4) how it helps members who have recovered continue to resist their addiction in their everyday lives.

2. Report your findings to the class.

DESIGNING A SURVEY

1. Read the quiz on page 22. It is used to diagnose Internet addiction. Test yourself or a friend.

2. Work with a partner. Choose one of the "other addictions" such as compulsive shopping, workaholism, compulsive eating, compulsive gambling, exercise addiction, and so on. Using the Internet survey as a model, design your own survey to diagnose the addiction you chose. You may use the same scoring system as in the model.

3. Use your survey to interview a friend or a classmate. Share the results with the class.

HOOKED ON THE NET?
Let's Find Out

Take this quiz to see if your passion for the Net has become an all-consuming addiction. Check the appropriate boxes. Remember—be honest!

YES NO

☐ ☐ 1. Do you check your e-mail more than six times a day?

☐ ☐ 2. Do you lose track of the time because you are on the computer all night?

☐ ☐ 3. Do you dream about surfing the Net?

☐ ☐ 4. Have you ever missed class or called in sick to work because you were too busy online?

☐ ☐ 5. Do you introduce yourself by immediately giving out your e-mail address?

☐ ☐ 6. Do you neglect your pets because you are online and forget to feed and walk them?

☐ ☐ 7. Does your family constantly complain that you are spending too much time in front of the computer?

☐ ☐ 8. Have you forgotten to do your usual chores around the house?

☐ ☐ 9. Do you talk more to your friends around the world via e-mail than you do to your neighbors?

☐ ☐ 10. Do you feel uncomfortable at the thought of going on vacation without your computer?

SCORING

If you answered **YES** *to . . .*

0 to 4 questions: Don't worry! You can get a bit carried away, but it's just a fun hobby.

5 to 8 questions: You may be getting hooked. Try to cut down on the number of hours you're on the Net.

9 to 10 questions: Watch out! Stop cold turkey now, and run to the nearest support group.

For Unit 1 Internet activities, visit the NorthStar Companion Website at http://www.longman.com/northstar.

Celebration, Florida: Disney's Utopia

1 Focus on the Topic

A PREDICTING

Walt Disney, the creator of Mickey Mouse and founder of the Disney theme parks, also dreamed of creating the ideal American community, a utopian city where *real* people lived and worked. Disney said he would build a "special kind of community that more people will talk about and come to look at than any other area in the world."

Look at the photos above. Think about what life is like in this town. Work with a partner, and predict why so many people wanted to move there when it opened in 1996.

B   SHARING INFORMATION

In your opinion, what does an ideal community have to have? Look at the list of features, and choose the three features you feel are most important for you.

First, put a ★ (star) next to those features. Then choose the three features that are not really important to you. Put an X next to those. Finally, compare your answers with those of a partner. Explain the reasons for your choices.

To me, an ideal place to live has _____.

_____ 1. schools, shops, and offices within walking distance of my home

_____ 2. excellent educational and cultural facilities—good schools, libraries, museums, theaters, movies

_____ 3. historical homes, buildings, and overall historical significance

_____ 4. recreational facilities including golf courses, tennis courts, swimming pools, basketball courts, parks, and a fitness center

_____ 5. community activities such as volunteer programs

_____ 6. excellent health-care facilities

_____ 7. advanced telecommunication and information systems linking homes, schools, and hospitals

_____ 8. many kinds of housing—apartments, townhouses, and single-family homes

_____ 9. houses set back from the street, separated by wide lawns and fences

_____ 10. friendly neighbors

_____ 11. access to public transportation—trains, buses, taxis

_____ 12. a lively nightlife with bars, restaurants, pubs, and dance clubs

C   PREPARING TO LISTEN

BACKGROUND

The perfect place to live? The model community? The ideal society? For 3,000 years, humankind has been on a quest to explore, define, and create the perfect society, a world in which the problems of everyday life are solved and pure happiness is reached. The word *utopia* first appeared in 1516 in Thomas More's famous work called *Utopia*. The word comes from the Greek word *topos*, meaning "place." It is usually defined as a society of ordinary human beings who live in an ideal system in a fictional place.

Although utopian communities have been a part of history all around the world since biblical times, they have occupied a special place in the history of the United States since its founding.

Read the following time line of American utopian communities. Work with a partner. Summarize the principles behind each of the utopian movements. Then list the utopia below the theme(s) which drove its creation.

Utopian Place and Date	Background
Plymouth, Massachusetts, early seventeenth century	A group of Englishmen and women fled England because of religious persecution. The Pilgrims established a model society based on strict religious beliefs in the "New World."
New Harmony, Indiana, early nineteenth century	The visionary Robert Owen established a beautiful, well-planned, modern industrial town. His group focused on social and labor reforms. Men and women were treated equally. The typical work day was shortened from 12 hours to 10 hours, and children under 10 years of age were not allowed to work. Efforts to abolish a rigid social class structure included inexpensive housing, and free education and medical care. Owen established the first kindergarten and first free public library in the United States.
Brook Farm in West Roxbury, Massachusetts, late nineteenth century	Brook Farm was based on cooperative living. Each community member worked on the farm so that the community could be fully independent. Brook Farm's founder, George Ripley, was a Unitarian minister who had rejected the traditional church. Instead, he encouraged his group to find spirituality in nature. Brook Farmers included many famous American authors and educators. Brook Farm was famous for its outstanding school built on the progressive philosophy of "learning by doing."
Hippie Communes, rural United States, 1960–1975	"Flower children" and anti–Vietnam War protesters built small, intimate communities, called *communes*. Hippies wanted to escape the isolation of big cities or suburbs. Commune members grew their own food. They built low-tech, safe, and energy-efficient systems to maintain their self-sufficient communities.
New Urbanist Communities (Reston, Virginia; Seaside, Florida; Celebration, Florida), 1995–present	The New Urbanist movement is a reaction against the isolation and car-dominated culture of many suburbs. Planners designed towns which re-create small-town life in America in the 1930s, '40s, and '50s. Features aimed at promoting a sense of community are houses close together, with garages behind the houses; houses with graceful front porches; tree-lined streets and sidewalks; schools, shopping, and parks all within walking distance.

Religion	**Community**	**Environment**	**Education**
_____	_____	_____	_____
_____	_____	_____	_____
_____	_____	_____	_____
_____	_____	_____	_____

VOCABULARY FOR COMPREHENSION

Read the following fictional real estate Web page informing prospective residents about the real-life community of Celebration, Florida. Then read the list of expressions that follows. Working with a partner, write the number of the underlined word next to the related expression from the list.

Celebration

Go to: http://www.nvrehomes.com

- Maps
- Market Street
- Model Homes
- Selling a House?
- Homes for Sale
- For Sale by Owner
- Hotel
- School
- Golf
- Hospital
- Network
- Church
- Contact Us

Celebrate Life in Celebration: Turning Dreams into Reality

Celebration, Florida
Population: about 4,000

Looking for a place to call home?
Dreaming of lazy summer days and sipping iced tea on a graceful front porch?
COME HOME TO CELEBRATION—THE NEW TOWN WITH OLD-TOWN CHARM!

When you wish upon a star . . .
Once upon a time, long ago, Walt Disney had a vision of building a new community, a special community. Sadly though, these idealistic plans were **(1)** thwarted, and Disney died before his dream could be realized. Still, Disney's **(2)** laudable vision, which was the creation of a real utopian city, persisted. This vision **(3)** evolved over the decades, and finally in 1996—from the **(4)** boardrooms of the Disney company to the many acres of homes, businesses, schools, and parks—Celebration, Florida, was born.

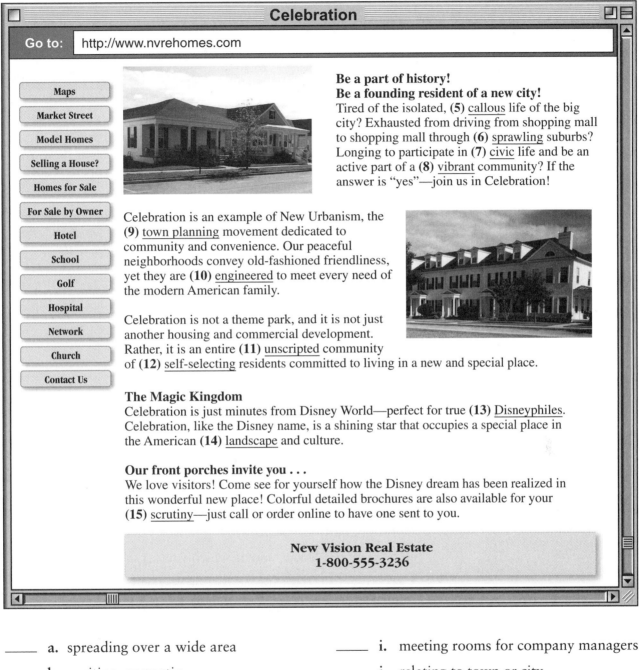

Celebration

Go to: http://www.nvrehomes.com

Maps
Market Street
Model Homes
Selling a House?
Homes for Sale
For Sale by Owner
Hotel
School
Golf
Hospital
Network
Church
Contact Us

Be a part of history!
Be a founding resident of a new city!
Tired of the isolated, **(5)** callous life of the big city? Exhausted from driving from shopping mall to shopping mall through **(6)** sprawling suburbs? Longing to participate in **(7)** civic life and be an active part of a **(8)** vibrant community? If the answer is "yes"—join us in Celebration!

Celebration is an example of New Urbanism, the **(9)** town planning movement dedicated to community and convenience. Our peaceful neighborhoods convey old-fashioned friendliness, yet they are **(10)** engineered to meet every need of the modern American family.

Celebration is not a theme park, and it is not just another housing and commercial development. Rather, it is an entire **(11)** unscripted community of **(12)** self-selecting residents committed to living in a new and special place.

The Magic Kingdom
Celebration is just minutes from Disney World—perfect for true **(13)** Disneyphiles. Celebration, like the Disney name, is a shining star that occupies a special place in the American **(14)** landscape and culture.

Our front porches invite you . . .
We love visitors! Come see for yourself how the Disney dream has been realized in this wonderful new place! Colorful detailed brochures are also available for your **(15)** scrutiny—just call or order online to have one sent to you.

New Vision Real Estate
1-800-555-3236

_____ **a.** spreading over a wide area

_____ **b.** exciting; energetic

_____ **c.** unkind and not caring; insensitive

_____ **d.** admirable

_____ **e.** frustrated; prevented from happening

_____ **f.** not perfectly planned before it is made

_____ **g.** created; designed

_____ **h.** view; the way things are situated

_____ **i.** meeting rooms for company managers

_____ **j.** relating to town or city

_____ **k.** choosing by oneself

_____ **l.** fans of Disney things

_____ **m.** thorough, detailed examination

_____ **n.** developed; grew

_____ **o.** the study of making cities more effective

2 Focus on Listening

A LISTENING ONE: *The Celebration Experiment*

You will hear an interview from the radio news broadcast *Marketplace*, aired on National Public Radio in the United States. David Brancaccio, the host of the show, interviews Andrew Ross, a professor of American Studies at New York University who lived in Celebration and wrote a book about his experience there.

 Despite high expectations, some of the residents of Celebration were disappointed with life in the new town. Working with a partner, brainstorm aspects of life which may have disappointed the early residents. List them here. Then listen to an excerpt of the interview to check your predictions.

1. *houses were poorly constructed* _____

2. _____

3. _____

4. _____

LISTENING FOR MAIN IDEAS

 Read the statements below. Then listen to the interview. Put a check (✓) next to the statements Professor Ross would agree with.

The town of Celebration, Florida, _____.

_____ **1.** was modeled after a Disney movie which was set in Seaside, Florida, another New Urbanist town

_____ **2.** is unusual because expensive homes there are right next to inexpensive homes

_____ **3.** is often visited by people interviewing residents and writing articles

_____ **4.** is a town where people settled to escape urban life

_____ **5.** was more interesting for its physical rather than social landscape

_____ **6.** can maintain its economic diversity even though affordable housing is less available

LISTENING FOR DETAILS

*Listen to the interview again. Then read the sentences, and write **T** (true) or **F** (false) in the blanks. Correct the false statements. Discuss your answers with a partner.*

    Seaside

__F__   **1.** The movie *The Truman Show* was shot in ~~Celebration~~, Florida.

_____   **2.** Seaside, Florida, is not a real town. It is a town built for a Disney movie.

_____   **3.** Celebration was designed so that residents would not need their cars to get around town.

_____   **4.** The interviewer criticizes Southern California communities because their garages face the street.

_____   **5.** According to Ross, Celebration residents felt comfortable speaking to the media about their community.

_____   **6.** Teachers, residents, and Disney officials often discussed whether or not the Celebration experiment was succeeding.

_____   **7.** Many residents had vacationed often at Disney resorts and expected the same kind of customer service in Celebration as they got at the theme parks.

_____   **8.** Disney officials chose a group of residents to live in Celebration to make sure the town would be successful.

_____   **9.** Most residents enjoyed the sense of community in Celebration.

_____ **10.** Andrew Ross may go back to live in Celebration.

REACTING TO THE LISTENING

 1 *Read the following questions. Then listen to each excerpt from the interview. Discuss your answers with a partner, then with the class. Begin your answers with one of the expressions indicated. Each question has more than one possible answer.*

Excerpt One

1. What is the interviewer's attitude toward the town of Seaside, the setting in *The Truman Show*? What words does he use to indicate this attitude?

   Perhaps he feels . . .

   He might feel . . .

Excerpt Two

2. Was Ross sympathetic to the people of Celebration? What strong words does he use to convey his attitude?

3. What words might he use if he didn't feel so strongly? Give synonyms that are more neutral in feeling.

   He could say . . .

   I'm not sure exactly, but he might use . . .

Excerpt Three

4. What is Ross's attitude toward the economic diversity of Celebration? How do you know? What words does he use to convey that attitude?

   Perhaps . . .

   I think he might . . .

Excerpt Four

5. What is the interviewer's attitude toward Ross's year in Celebration? What is Brancaccio's attitude toward Manhattan in comparison with Celebration? What in his tone of voice and choice of words reveals his attitude?

   I suppose . . .

   It could be . . .

2 *Read the following statements made by Celebration residents. Beginning with "sentence starter" **a** or **b,** complete the sentence with your opinion. Share your opinions with a partner.*

1. Being a part of a neighborhood—knowing my neighbors, spending time with them each day, sharing our daily lives—is really important.

   a. Yes, I think so too. For me . . .

   b. No, that's not for me. I don't really want to know my neighbors. What would be important to me is . . .

2. Having the media on our doorstep every day is nerve-wracking. I feel like I am living in a fishbowl. We really just want to be left alone and be able to get on with our lives. I don't think the media and the public need to scrutinize our every move.

   a. Well, if you ask me, if I lived in Celebration, I might feel . . .

   b. I understand that feeling. However, I think . . .

3. Disney deserves some credit. In developing Celebration, they really had laudable goals and a utopian vision. It would have been a lot easier for them to just build another subdivision, golf course, or theme park. I mean, really, they had dreams.

   a. Yes, I couldn't agree more. In spite of the frustrations that the residents experienced, . . .

   b. I take your point, but I see it differently. I think Disney just used Celebration to . . .

B LISTENING TWO: *Living in Celebration*

Douglas Frantz, a reporter for the *New York Times*, lived in Celebration for two years with his family, then wrote a book about the experience with his wife, Catherine Collins. In this excerpt, they discuss the town and the houses, as well as the rules for Celebration residents to follow.

Look at the chart below. Listen to the interview, and take notes on the details of the listening passage. Some have been done for you.

MAIN IDEAS	DETAILS
Design elements: small-town America	• houses close together • • front porches • tree lined st • access to town on foot • houses surround open areas •
Physical design: Social implications ("front-porch culture")	• •
Reality: "front-porch culture"	•
Collins's attitude toward rules	• • sometimes silly, sometimes not
Frantz's attitude toward rules	• some rules may go too far •

C   LINKING LISTENINGS ONE AND TWO

Work in small groups. Discuss the following topics.

1. Which of the three speakers in the interviews—Andrew Ross (Listening One), or Douglas Frantz or Catherine Collins (Listening Two)—is most positive about Celebration? Why? Which of the speakers is the most negative? Why?

2. Working in small groups of three or four, review Listening One and Listening Two. Use the audioscripts in the back of the book if necessary. Complete the chart on page 33. Read the list of six key features of the town. Rate each feature on a scale of **1** to **5,** with **5** being closest to your utopian ideal and **1** being furthest from your utopian ideal. Base your judgment on *your own* view of what utopia means, as well as on information about other utopias and Walt Disney's dream of Celebration. Write down the reasons for your decision.

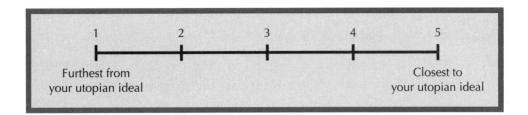

FEATURE OF CELEBRATION	RATING	REASON FOR THE RATING
Town-wide Internet service that connects residents to each other and all stores and services	3	*Being connected technologically is not that important. I can use the telephone to connect to others in the town.*
Environmentally friendly		
Expectation of civic involvement		
Mixed income		
Front porches		
Rules about your house: color of curtains, kind of flowers, etc.		

3 Focus on Vocabulary

An analogy shows relationships between two words and ideas. Look at the example analogy below. Read an analogy this way: "Laudable is to admirable as folks is to people."

Example

laudable : admirable :: folks : people

Relationship: *Laudable* and *admirable* are synonyms, and *folks* and *people* are also synonyms.

1 *Work with a partner. First figure out the relationship between the first two words on the left. Then choose the correct word or phrase to complete the similar relationship between the pair of words on the right.*

Read the analogies with your partner. Discuss the relationships. Then write an explanation under each one.

1. Walt Disney : Celebration :: Robert Owen : ___New Harmony___
   a. New Harmony
   b. Utopia
   c. Plymouth Rock

   Explanation: _Walt Disney envisioned Celebration in the same manner that_
   Robert Owen envisioned New Harmony.

2. callous : Manhattanites :: _____ : Disneyphiles
   a. burned out
   b. self-selecting
   c. idealistic

   Explanation: _____

   _____

3. scrutiny : performance anxiety :: _____ : burnout
   a. warm weather
   b. overwork
   c. smoking

   Explanation: _____

   _____

4. live by : rules :: _____ : principles
   a. scrutinize
   b. follow
   c. understand

   Explanation: _____

   _____

5. Disney planners of Celebration : nostalgia :: George Ripley of Brook Farm :

   _____
   a. happiness
   b. privacy
   c. sprituality

   Explanation: _____

   _____

6. "Front-porch culture" : small-town America :: _____ : Disney World
   a. Celebration
   b. Mickey Mouse
   c. theme park

   Explanation: _____

   _____

7. vibrant : energetic :: thwarted : _____
   a. prevented
   b. reduced
   c. slowed down

   Explanation: _____

   _____

8. envision : imagine :: engineer : _____
   a. create
   b. construct
   c. repair

   Explanation: _____

   _____

2 *Match each vocabulary item from the unit to its definition on the left. Write the letter on the line.*

_C_	**1.** tired; exhausted	**a.** access
_J_	**2.** manage on an income	**b.** assess
_E_	**3.** relating to a town or city	**c.** burned out
_O_	**4.** spreading over a wide area in an unattractive way	**d.** callous
_i_	**5.** follow; obey	**e.** civic
_F_	**6.** control or strongly influence	**f.** dictate
_H_	**7.** extremely hot	**g.** envision
_g_	**8.** imagine	**h.** hotter than hell
_K_	**9.** slightly sad feeling when remembering past happy events	**i.** live by
_N_	**10.** thorough and detailed examination	**j.** make ends meet
_A_	**11.** ability to enter	**k.** nostalgia
_M_	**12.** result	**l.** nurture
_P_	**13.** exciting; energetic	**m.** play out
_L_	**14.** develop; help to grow	**n.** scrutiny
_D_	**15.** unkind, not caring; insensitive	**o.** sprawl
_B_	**16.** judge; evaluate	**p.** vibrant

3 *Work with a partner. Student A will role-play a commentator discussing Celebration.*

Student A: Read the comments on page 37 to Student B.

Student B: Listen to the comments. Agree with the comment, and respond using one of the vocabulary words above. Then switch roles after comment 8.

If the response isn't correct, give a clue from the sentence. Clues are in italics. The answers are in parentheses.

Example

A: Celebration residents are *tired of* speaking to the media. (burned out)

B: Yeah, they are <u>burned out</u> on interviews.

Student A

1. Celebration residents *have trouble paying for everything* because the prices in downtown shops are so high. (make ends meet)

2. As part of Celebration, most residents feel it is their duty as *citizens* to be active in the *community*. (civic)

3. Some Florida developers want to put a shopping mall right outside Celebration, but the residents don't want Celebration to *spread out* like other suburbs. (sprawl)

4. The residents have to *follow* the boring *Pattern Book* rules—meaning all the houses look somewhat alike. (live by)

5. In fact, Disney *tells* the residents *exactly* what kind of curtains they can put in their front windows—no red allowed. (dictate)

6. People never sit out on their front porches anyway in the summer because it's *way too hot*. (hotter than hell)

7. Disney *dreamed of* a "state of the art" school system, but this dream has not been realized. (envision)

8. Urban geographers frequently visit Celebration to *judge* whether it has achieved racial and economic diversity. (assess)

Now switch roles.

9. Celebration *reminded me of the past*—lemonade stands, friendly neighbors, tree-lined streets, porch swings. (nostalgia)

10. It was tough for me to find someone to interview. The residents are tired of *being asked questions by* reporters. (scrutiny)

11. I found that the Celebration School is *completely wired* with technology. Technology is their pencil. (access)

12. I plan to report on the town next year to see how things in Celebration *are working*. (play out)

13. Celebration is a "*happening*" place—busy downtown, nature trails, lake activities, parks, snow festivals. (vibrant)

14. The Celebration School wants children to *love* learning for the sake of learning, not just to pass a test or get good grades. (nurture)

15. The real estate agents advertise Celebration as a warm, cozy town—not *cold* and *impersonal* like some big cities in the United States. (callous)

4 Focus on Speaking

A   PRONUNCIATION: Reduction of *as, has,* and *is*

Function words like articles, auxiliary verbs, conjunctions, prepositions, and pronouns are not usually stressed in speaking. Some function words have reduced pronunciations; they may lose sounds, and their vowels are usually pronounced /ə/.

The function words *as, has,* and *is* can all be pronounced the same, as /əz/, like the long plural ending in *watches*.

 Listen to how the underlined words sound in these sentences:

They <u>watch as</u> many Disney movies as I do.
My <u>watch has</u> been stolen.
My <u>watch is</u> a Disneyland souvenir.

The usual pronunciation of *as* is /əz/. Join *as* closely to the surrounding words.

• The first residents of Celebration came as pioneers.

Has is often reduced to /əz/ when it is used as a present perfect auxiliary. The "h" is dropped, and the vowel is reduced to /ə/. It is pronounced like an ending to the preceding word.

• Andrew Ross has written a book about Celebration. [say "Rosses"]

When *is* is not contracted, it is pronounced /əz/ or /ɪz/.

• The porch is red. [say "porches"]

---

 1 *Listen to the sentences. Each sentence has a word containing a reduced form with /əz/. Write the word(s) with their usual spelling in the blank after the sentence. Check your answers, and then practice reading the sentences with a partner.*

1. a. He's eating lunch /əz/ usual.   _____lunch as_____

  b. Lunch /əz/ ready.   _____is_____

  c. I ordered two lunch/əz/   _____es_____

  d. Lunch /əz/ been served.   _____has_____

2. a. The porch /əz/ need to be painted.   _is_

  b. The porch /əz/ in need of repair.   _is_

  c. The porch /əz/ been fixed.   _has_

  d. Please rebuild the porch /əz/ it was before.   _as_

3. a. The house /əz/ been put on the market.   _has_

  b. The house /əz/ way too pricey.   _is_

  c. They built that house /əz/ a model.   _as_

  d. The house/əz/ are very close to the street.   _es_

4. a. The garage/əz/ are hidden from view.   _es_

  b. The garage /əz/ behind the house.   _is_

  c. The design of the garage /əz/ finally been approved.   _has_

  d. They repainted the garage /əz/ fast as they could.   _as_

2 *Look at the first half of each sentence on the left, and match it to the end of a sentence on the right. Then compare your sentences with those of a partner. Practice reading the sentences, reducing the **as** to /əz/.*

_____ **1.** In New Harmony, Indiana, men and women were treated

_____ **2.** The New Urbanist movement began

_____ **3.** Plymouth, Massachusetts, was established

_____ **4.** Residents of Brook Farm regarded nature

_____ **5.** Members of hippie communes were known

a. as flower children.

b. as equal members of the town.

c. as a reaction against the car culture of suburban life.

d. as a model society based on strict religious beliefs.

e. as a source of spirituality.

B   GRAMMAR: Noun Clauses after Verbs or Expressions of Urgency

1 *In pairs, examine the sentences and discuss the questions that follow.*

- The Celebration "front-porch police" <u>insisted that</u> she remove her hot pink curtains from the front windows. Only white curtains are allowed.

- The new Celebration student was shocked when his teacher <u>didn't demand that he come to class</u> on time. Class schedules were flexible.

- The Celebration town planners strongly <u>recommended that the new Celebration school be built</u> right in the center of town.

1. How are the verbs *insist*, *demand*, and *recommend* similar in meaning?

2. How are the verbs in the examples—*remove*, *come*, and *be*—similar in form?

Noun Clauses after Verbs or Expressions of Urgency

Noun clauses after verbs of urgency are formed by using the base form of the verb in the noun clause.	• The Disney Company **suggested** that the famous architect, Robert Stern, **design** only six styles of homes.
Verbs of urgency include ***demand, insist, suggest, recommend, propose, request***, and ***urge***.	• The officials **demanded** that she remove the "For Sale" sign from her front lawn.
Expressions of urgency include ***it is essential, it is critical, it is vital, it is necessary, it is important, it is urgent, it is advisable***, and ***it is preferable***.	• **It is critical** that all new residents read the *Pattern Book* before moving to Celebration.
The verb in the main clause can be in any tense—present, past, or future.	• The Celebration Foundation **will suggest** that Jane Mansfield get the Celebration Good Neighbor Award.
For negative statements, use ***not*** plus the base form.	• The architects insisted that garages **not face** the street.
For passive voice, use ***be*** plus the past participle form of the verb.	• The new Celebration principal suggested that textbooks **be required** in all classes.
Using ***that*** after a verb is optional.	• The Celebration "Old-Timers" club recommended **[that]** all new residents attend the welcome event.

2 *Work with a partner.*

Student A: Ask Student B questions 1 through 5.

Student B: Cover the left column. Answer the questions using a noun clause after a verb of urgency and the cues provided. Add additional words where necessary. The first answer has been done for you. Then switch roles after question 5.

Student A	**Student B**
1. Does Seaside, Florida, have similar rules about the architecture of the homes?	1. Yes. The planners / insist / all houses / build / front porches *The planners insist all houses be built with front porches.*
2. What did Douglas Frantz say about the rules in Celebration?	2. recommend / future residents / live by / rules / not / move / Celebration
3. What might the residents tell the Disney Company at the meeting tonight?	3. insist / company / hire / new school principal
4. What advice would Andrew Ross give other journalists visiting Celebration?	4. essential / respect / residents / desire / avoid / media scrutiny
5. If you lived in Celebration, what changes would you suggest or demand?	5. (your idea)

Now switch roles.

6. What will the architects recommend at the next planning session?	6. recommend / less pricey / houses / build
7. After the census came out, what did the critics say about Celebration's population?	7. say / essential / Disney / achieve / racial / economic / diversity
8. What were the residents complaining about at the community meeting?	8. demand / mega supermarket / not / build / downtown
9. What did Walt Disney emphasize in his vision of Celebration?	9. critical / Celebration / free from / crime, grime, and traffic
10. If you lived in Celebration, what changes would you propose or recommend?	10. (your idea)

C   STYLE: Discussing Opinions

Here are some common expressions used to discuss opinions.

Asking for an Opinion

- What's your take on . . . ?
  (What do you think?)

- What's your view on . . . ?

- Would you agree . . . ?

Agreeing

- Yes, exactly. There's no doubt in
  my mind that . . .

- We are exactly on the same page.

- I couldn't agree with you more.

Expressing an Opinion

- My take is . . .

- As far as I'm concerned . . .

- Well, if you ask me . . .

Disagreeing politely

- Yes, but don't you think that . . .

- Perhaps, but I can't help thinking
  that . . .

- I take your point, but I see it
  differently. I think . . .

Work in groups of three.

Student A: You are the discussion leader. Use the information about a controversial issue to pose a discussion topic to the group. Use the expressions for asking for an opinion.

Students B and C: Express your opinions. Agree or disagree with each other. Use as many of the expressions in the boxes as possible.

Then change roles so that Student B becomes the discussion leader for the next issue. Continue to alternate roles.

Example

Controversial Issue: Front Porches and Privacy
The planners of Celebration designed houses with front porches, and the Residents Association encourages people to use them as a social space—to meet and greet neighbors, and so on. The planners also built the homes close together. Some residents feel uncomfortable using their porches.

Student A (Summarizes the issue, poses discussion topic): Houses in Celebration are right next to each other. The Residents Association encourages all residents to sit out on their front porches every night. <u>I wonder if you would agree</u> that this kind of physical closeness would limit the residents' privacy.

Student B (Voices an opinion): <u>Well, if you ask me,</u> I wouldn't want to live so close to my neighbors. It would drive me crazy. I would feel a loss of privacy. What do other people think?

Student C (Agrees or disagrees with the opinion): <u>Yes, but don't you think</u> it would help you feel secure to know your neighbors were right next door? It wouldn't bother me at all.

Controversial Issues in Celebration

1. **Role of Disney**
   The Disney Company owns and manages the town. There is a Residents Association that helps manage the town and organize events. But the Association has no real power to make decisions.

2. **Housing**
   Housing in Celebration is pricey. There are very few apartments and low- to middle-income houses. Employees who work for Disney in the nearby theme parks in Orlando cannot afford to live there. The town lacks diversity.

3. **Media Scrutiny**
   Celebration is unique and important to Disney's reputation, so reporters, journalists, and filmmakers flock there to study this twenty-first century utopia.

4. **Downtown Celebration**
   There are no stores serving the residents' everyday needs. For example, there is no hardware store, pharmacy, video store, gas station, or florist. Restaurants and upscale specialty boutiques do attract tourists, generate income, and enhance the overall uniqueness of the town, but they also add to traffic congestion.

D | SPEAKING TOPIC

You are going to have a Celebration town meeting to discuss the Pattern Book *rules with Disney representatives. You will need to prepare for the meeting and know how to conduct it.*

PREPARING FOR THE MEETING

1. Divide into two groups:

   Group One: Residents of Celebration
   Group Two: Disney representatives who administer Celebration

2. Read the agenda for the town meeting. You are going to discuss the New Business this evening.

Celebration Residents Association

AGENDA OCTOBER 2

7:00–7:15	Call to order, Todd Owens, Residents Association Director
7:15–7:30	Introduction of new residents in September
7:30–7:45	Announcements of October activities
	October 9 Lights and Lemonade Party Great Lawn Lakeside Park
	October 22 Fall Festival Market Street

7:45–8:00	Old Business
	1. Election of Todd Owens, Residents Association Director, for two-year term
	2. Requests for architectural changes
	  • RC 045 Request for privacy fence not approved
	  • RC 461 Request for front yard trees approved
	3. Downtown shopping discussed. Task Force to research options.

8:00–9:00	New Business: **Pattern Book** Rules
	  • House color rules
	  • Shade and shutter color rules
	  • Vehicle parking rules
	  • Ban on "For Sale" signs
	  • Rules on changes to porches and facades

Now read the positions below. Group One will take certain positions, and Group Two will respond. Then conduct the discussion.

Positions on New Business

Group One: RESIDENTS

You believe the *Pattern Book* rules are too restrictive and undemocratic. They also give the town a "creepy," unreal feeling since the rules make many of the houses look alike. (There are hundreds of yellow houses, and each one has white curtains in front!)

Some of the rules you oppose are:

- Houses must be painted only the specific color listed in the *Pattern Book*.

- Front shades and shutters must all be the same color.

- Non-running cars or recreational vehicles may not be parked in front of the house.

- "For Sale" signs are not allowed.

- Porches may not be removed. Facades may not be changed.

Group Two: DISNEY REPRESENTATIVES

You believe it's essential the town maintain the rules in order to preserve the quality of life in Celebration. The rules:

- preserve the look of "yesteryear" and the small-town feeling.

- guarantee that everyone's neighborhood is kept clean and appealing.

- are part of the residents' basic commitment to living in Celebration. Everyone knows them ahead of time; if they don't like them, they don't have to live in Celebration.

CONDUCTING THE DISCUSSION

1. One member of the residents group moderates the discussion. The moderator:
   - opens the discussion by introducing the participants and explaining the purpose
   - conducts the discussion by eliciting comments and questions from the participants
   - encourages the participants to negotiate
   - closes the meeting by summarizing the main recommendations and conclusions

2. During the meeting, all participants should use the expressions for discussing opinions on page 42 whenever appropriate.

E RESEARCH TOPICS

WATCH A MOVIE

Several movies portray life in a perfect town, including The Truman Show, Pleasantville, *and* A Man for All Seasons. *With your class or at home, watch one of the movies. Meet in a small group to discuss the following questions. Then, in pairs, tape-record a two-minute radio movie review, and play your review for the class. You can take turns giving your opinions. Use the questions below as a guide.*

   a. What is the movie about? Summarize it in a few sentences.

   b. Describe the utopian community portrayed. Provide details.

   c. Were the people in the community affected by their environment? In what ways?

   d. Would you recommend this movie? Why or why not?

BE A JOURNALIST

Journalists from radio, television, and newspapers often visit Celebration to ask the residents how they feel about living in this unique community. Choose a resident from your community or a nearby community to interview. Find out how this person feels about issues related to the town or neighborhood: what he or she likes and dislikes, and what changes the resident would like to see.

Review the issues presented in the Background on pages 24–25 and Linking Listenings One and Two on pages 32–33. Review the expressions for discussing opinions (Style) and noun clauses after verbs or expressions of urgency (Grammar).

   1. Working with a partner, brainstorm at least six questions to use in your interview. Share your questions with another pair, and add to your list. Two have been provided for you.

   a. What do you like most/least about your town?

   b. Tell me about your neighbors and the level of interaction you have with them.

   2. While you interview, try to take notes as the interviewees answer the question. Elicit as many details and examples as possible.

   3. Present a summary of your findings to the class. Show photographs of the community if possible.

   4. Discuss your experience as a journalist.

For Unit 2 Internet activities, visit the NorthStar Companion Website at http://www.longman.com/northstar.

The Bold and the Bashful

1 Focus on the Topic

A PREDICTING

Look at the drawing above and the title of the unit. How would you describe the people in the drawing? Which of the people do you most identify with? Why? The man on the far right is bashful, or shy. How do you think it feels to be shy?

B SHARING INFORMATION

1 *Are you shy? Take the quiz. Add up the points to find out!*

HOW SHY ARE YOU?

For each statement below, rate yourself on this scale. Circle your answer.

1 Never	**2** Almost Never	**3** Sometimes	**4** Often	**5** Always

1. I'm tense and nervous when I'm with people I don't know well.	1	2	3	4	5
2. It's difficult for me to ask other people for information.	1	2	3	4	5
3. I'm often uncomfortable at parties and other social gatherings.	1	2	3	4	5
4. When I'm in a group of people, I have trouble thinking of the right things to say.	1	2	3	4	5
5. It takes me a long time to overcome my shyness in new situations.	1	2	3	4	5
6. It's hard for me to act in a natural way when I'm meeting new people.	1	2	3	4	5
7. I'm nervous when I'm speaking to someone in authority.	1	2	3	4	5
8. I find it hard to talk to strangers.	1	2	3	4	5

TOTAL SCORE:

WHAT YOUR SCORE MEANS: **30–40** = very shy

21–29 = somewhat shy

below 21 = probably not shy, although you may feel shy in some situations

2 *Discuss the results of the shyness quiz in a small group.*

1. Who had the highest score in your group? Who had the lowest score? Did your own results seem right to you?

2. When you speak English, do you feel shy or bold? In what situations do you feel shy? Describe those situations.

C PREPARING TO LISTEN

BACKGROUND

1 *Work with a partner. Try to guess the results of a study of shyness among Americans by a Stanford University psychologist. Indicate your answers by writing the percentage next to the corresponding description. Then check the results on page 241.*

Of the Americans surveyed, _____.

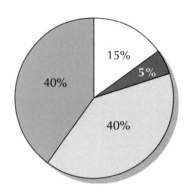

1. ____%____ tend to be shy in most situations

2. ____%____ used to be shy as children, but are not shy as adults

3. ____%____ are shy in certain situations

4. ____%____ have never experienced shyness

2 *Discuss your answers to the following questions with a partner.*

1. Do these results surprise you? Why?

2. Why do people who live in the United States have the reputation for being "optimistic" and "outgoing"? Do you agree with this widely held view? Why?

3. In your opinion, is shyness a positive or negative quality? Explain.

3 *Working with a partner, read the factors below that psychologists believe make people shy. Decide how important each factor may be in causing shyness. Write **V** (very important), **S** (somewhat important), or **N** (not very important) next to each factor. Then discuss the reasons for your choices.*

_____ 1. heredity

_____ 2. cultural values

_____ 3. birth order (oldest, middle, or youngest)

__V__ (4.) life experiences (moving, changing schools, divorce in family)

_____ 5. gender

__V__ 6. competition

_____ 7. use of electronic communication (e-mail, voice mail, chat rooms)

_____ 8. parents' behavior

_____ 9. lack of social skills

_____ 10. physical attractiveness

_____ 11. use of computer and video games

VOCABULARY FOR COMPREHENSION

1 *Read the following sentences. Try to determine the meaning of the underlined words from the context of the sentences. Then write a definition or similar expression under the sentence.*

1. In English class, some students tend to speak out a lot. Others are somewhat <u>reticent</u>.

   _____

2. A public-speaking <u>phobia</u>, called glossophobia, prevented the businessman from delivering formal presentations at work.

   _____

3. If people cannot explain their ideas well, others may assume those ideas have no <u>merit</u>.

   _____

4. One of Professor Philip Zimbardo's studies indicated that Israelis were not shy and introverted. On the contrary, they were outgoing and <u>extroverted</u>.

   _____

5. Some shy people are successfully shy and comfortable with their personality. However, for others, shyness has <u>adverse</u> consequences.

   _____

6. Some psychologists describe shyness as a <u>syndrome</u>, with patterns of physical and emotional symptoms.

   _____

7. <u>Chronic</u> shyness that persists from childhood to adulthood can have negative consequences such as low self-esteem and loneliness.

   _____

8. My friend and I regard each other as <u>kindred souls</u>. We are both painfully shy.

   _____

9. People often make terrible <u>misattributions</u> about those who are shy. They assume shy people are cold and unfriendly instead of merely bashful.

_____

10. Of the Indian students surveyed, 82 percent reported that shyness was a problem or <u>handicap</u> that made them unhappy and unfulfilled.

_____

11. Many employees thought the company president was <u>aloof</u> and unfriendly. But in truth, she was just very shy.

_____

12. It was not her intention to be rude or <u>condescending</u> toward her staff. She behaved this way in order to cover up her extreme shyness.

_____

2 *Now match the words on the left with a definition or similar expression on the right. Write the appropriate letter in the blank space. Then compare your answers with those of another student.*

_F_	**1.** reticent	**a.** condition
_C_	**2.** phobia	**b.** distant
_J_	**3.** merit	**c.** very strong fear
_H_	**4.** extroverted	**d.** negative
_D_	**5.** adverse	**e.** disadvantage
_A_	**6.** syndrome	**f.** unwilling to talk
_L_	**7.** chronic	**g.** false assumptions
_I_	**8.** kindred souls	**h.** very sociable
_G_	**9.** misattributions	**i.** people having similar traits
_E_	**10.** handicap	**j.** value
_B_	**11.** aloof	**k.** treating others as inferior
_K_	**12.** condescending	**l.** continual (in a medical sense)

2 Focus on Listening

A   LISTENING ONE: *Americans Are Getting Shyer*

You will hear an interview from the radio news program *Morning Edition,* aired on National Public Radio in the United States. The interviewee, Dr. Philip Zimbardo, comments that many of the shy people he spoke to say, "Shyness is undesirable, [it] has adverse consequences."

 Work with a partner. Predict some of the problems that you think shy people may have as a result of their shyness (for example: staying in a dead-end job, avoiding social situations). Discuss your predictions with your partner. Then listen to this excerpt of the interview to check your predictions.

LISTENING FOR MAIN IDEAS

 Read the following topics. Then listen to Part One of the interview, and take notes as you listen. Do the same for Part Two. Compare your notes with those of another student.

Part One

1. Results of Dr. Zimbardo's new study

_____

_____

2. Reasons Americans are becoming shyer, according to Dr. Zimbardo

Cultural factors: _____

_____

Social factors: _____

_____

Part Two

3. Professor Zimbardo's descriptions of *situational* and *dispositional* shyness

Situational: _____

_____

Dispositional: _____

_____

4. Dr. Zimbardo's advice to shy people to help them cope at parties or in conversations

_____

_____

5. Problem that shyness presents to attractive people

_____

_____

LISTENING FOR DETAILS

Read the sentences. Then listen to the interview again. As you listen, circle the letter of the answer that completes each sentence correctly. Compare your answers with those of another student.

Part One

1. According to the interviewer, Alex Chadwick, these days Americans are having difficulty _____.
   a. meeting people
   b. dressing appropriately
   c. asking questions

2. Philip Zimbardo _____.
   a. teaches in a shyness clinic
   b. runs in Palo Alto
   c. manages a shyness clinic

3. Zimbardo's latest research focused on shy _____.
   a. adults
   b. children
   c. children and adults

4. The researchers discovered that over the past ten years, the number of Americans who label themselves as shy has increased by _____.
   a. 48 percent
   b. 18 percent
   c. 20 percent

5. One thing that Zimbardo does *not* say about shy people is that they are
_____ .
a. competitive
b. reticent
c. self-conscious

6. The electronic revolution means that many people's jobs are being replaced by computers. Philip Zimbardo *doesn't* mention _____ as being replaced by computers.
a. gas station owners
b. bank tellers
c. telephone operators

Part Two

7. In Dr. Zimbardo's survey, _____ of people said shyness was undesirable.
a. 70 percent
b. 79 percent
c. 75 percent

8. One example of situational, or momentary, shyness *not* mentioned by Philip Zimbardo is _____ .
a. going on a blind date
b. playing the piano in public
c. speaking in public

9. Quasimodo is the hunchback in Victor Hugo's novel *The Hunchback of Notre Dame*. Zimbardo compares shyness to Quasimodo's hump because
_____ .
a. everyone notices it
b. you always carry it with you
c. it's chronic

10. Zimbardo feels that shy people should be aware that nearly _____ of the population is shy.
a. 15 percent
b. 50 percent
c. 40 percent

11. According to Dr. Zimbardo, when you are too shy, people may assume you are also _____ .
a. unintelligent
b. motivated
c. unattractive

12. Philip Zimbardo tells Alex Chadwick that he is not shy because he is the oldest child in a _____ .
a. small Italian family
b. large Italian family
c. large Greek family

REACTING TO THE LISTENING

 1 *Read the following questions. Then listen to each excerpt from the interview. Discuss your answers with a partner, then with the class.*

Excerpt One

1. What do you think the interviewer, Alex Chadwick, means by the phrase "Friends, take heart"? Why does he use the word *friends* to address the anonymous radio audience?

2. What is Chadwick's attitude toward the topic of shyness?

Excerpt Two

3. Zimbardo clearly believes that his research is important and interesting. How does he show this attitude in the excerpt?

Excerpt Three

4. How does Zimbardo feel when Chadwick asks him whether he is shy? What can you hear in his voice?

2 *In a small group, discuss your answers to the following questions.*

1. At his clinic at Stanford University, Zimbardo works to help people overcome shyness. Do you think shyness is a problem that needs to be overcome? Explain.

2. Zimbardo thinks that computers and video games are making some people shyer. Does this make sense to you? Explain.

3. Go back to the causes of shyness you identified in the Preparing to Listen section. Do you still agree with what you said? Explain.

B LISTENING TWO: *The Pollyanna Syndrome*

In Listening Two, a Public Radio International commentator, Julie Danis, describes a "Pollyanna." A Pollyanna refers to a certain personality type: an annoyingly optimistic person who refuses to accept that anything bad can happen. The name comes from the heroine of a 1913 novel, *Pollyanna,* who had an overly optimistic outlook on life.

In the commentary, Danis gives examples of ways that one co-worker was able to "make lemonade out of lemons." What might this phrase mean? Have you ever known any Pollyannas? If so, describe them.

1 *Read the items below. Then listen to Julie Danis's commentary. Listen again, and match Danis's unlucky event with Pollyanna's "bright side" view.*

Danis

___C___ **1.** went to the eye doctor but did not get a diagnosis for the problem of blurred vision

___E___ **2.** stop-and-go commute

___A___ **3.** computer crashes and 1-800-HELP line is very busy

___B___ **4.** snowed in with no hope of flying

___D___ **5.** toothache and no dental insurance for the root canal

Pollyanna

a. time to purge, or clean out, the computer files

b. time to catch up on movies

c. a chance to skip the mascara and rest eyes every two hours

d. no solution

e. a chance to listen to language tapes while doing relaxation exercises

2 *In the commentary, Danis refers to several common idioms. However, she uses these idioms in a slightly unusual way. All the idioms have generally the same meaning: "making lemonade out of lemons," or finding the positive in a negative situation. Work with another student. Use the common idioms to talk about a time when you had to find the positive in a negative situation.*

Danis's Use

1. "[The Pollyannas] find the silver lining inside the darkest cloud."

2. "[They are always] driving others to distraction with their 'find the bright side' philosophy."

3. "You can't cry over something that can't cry over you."

Common Use of Idiom

1. Every cloud has a silver lining.

2. Look on the bright side.

3. Don't cry over spilt* milk.

Example

<u>Don't cry over spilt milk</u>. Once the damage is done, it's done. I remember one time when _____.

C   LINKING LISTENINGS ONE AND TWO

1 *Look at the following questions. Choose one to which you can answer yes. Then describe the experience in detail to a small group.*

Have you ever _____?

1. had an experience that started badly but turned out great

---

* ***spilt:*** spilled.

2. been forced to overcome shyness in order to perform a task such as delivering a presentation, performing in public, or hosting a party

3. suffered from a phobia, such as fear of flying, fear of spiders, or fear of heights

4. helped a friend or family member overcome a phobia

2 *Work with another student. Improvise a dialogue between a negative, pessimistic person and a Pollyanna who always looks on the bright side of things. Use the following situation. Then present the dialogue to your class.*

Situation

Student A: You are a Pollyanna who has learned that your co-workers are annoyed by your overly enthusiastic attitude about everything. They feel you see the world unrealistically, through "rose-colored glasses."

Student B: You are a pessimistic co-worker. Give advice to Pollyanna to persuade her to give up her sunny temperament.

3 *Work with a partner. Look at the cartoon, and discuss the answers to the questions below.*

Drawing by M. Twohy, © 1996 The New Yorker Magazine, Inc.

1. What does "low self-esteem" mean?

2. The man apologizes to his diary. Why does this illustrate low self-esteem? What do people typically write in a diary? What advice would you give to the man to boost his self-esteem?

3 Focus on Vocabulary

1 *Read the following letters to a newspaper, and fill in the blanks with the correct form of the appropriate expression from the list below. Compare your answers with those of a partner.*

break the ice	in the first place	take things as	widespread
draw out	mark (v.)	think of	wind up
fill the void	outlook	virtually	

Each week the *Star Daily* summarizes responses to a question we pose to our readers. Here are some of our favorite responses to the question:

BIRTH ORDER: DOES IT MATTER?

Dear *Star Daily*:

I'm the youngest of five children. I know that

_____Virtually_____ all later-born children
1. (almost)

are reserved, but not necessarily aloof. I have a

positive _____outlook_____ on life and
2. (point of view)

take thing as they come.
3. (accept experiences as)

Nancy Kakowski
Springfield, Missouri

Dear *Star Daily*:

I realize that acceptance of this birth

order theory is becoming more

_____widespread_____, but I just can't buy it.
4. (common)

in the first place I think personality
5. (First of all)

traits are determined by genetics. Second, theories

like birth order are actually harmful in that they

may _____mark_____ people unfairly,
6. (label)

leading to misattributions about people's

personalities.

Martha Johnson
New York City, New York

Dear *Star Daily*:

I'm the firstborn in my family. My siblings

complain that I'm arrogant, but I don't

_____think of_____ myself that way. At
7. (consider)

social gatherings, I _____wind up_____
8. (end up)

being the life of the party. I see my role as

_____drowning out_____ my more introverted
9. (encouraging)

friends.

Mark Baldino
Portland, Oregon

Dear *Star Daily*:

I'm an independent, only child. So I spent a great

deal of time alone. To _fill the void_
10. (overcome loneliness)

I had to learn many new skills. For example, I

learned how to lose my awkwardness and self-

consciousness. Now, I'm usually the one to

_____break the Ice_____
11. (get people socializing and enjoying themselves)

at social occasions.

Patty LaFond
Austin, Texas

2 *Work with a partner. Discuss birth order theory.*

Student A: Read each statement aloud, and ask the related questions.

Student B: Cover the left column. Answer the questions. Speak at length using the new vocabulary in any order. Then switch roles after question 2.

Student A	**Student B**
1. Philip Zimbardo says, "I'm a firstborn from a big Sicilian family, so my job was making all the other kids feel comfortable."	wind up break the ice mark think of oneself as
How do you think being "firstborn" affected Zimbardo? Does this apply to the firstborn in families you know?	*Being the oldest, Zimbardo **wound up** always **breaking the ice** at family gatherings. He was **marked** as the gregarious one. My brother is the firstborn in my family, and he also **thinks of himself** as the leader of the group.*
2. According to Frank Sulloway, author of *Born to Rebel: Birth Order, Family Dynamics, and Creative Lives,* later-born children are more adventurous and receptive to innovation.	draw out outlook in the first place virtually
Why do you think later-born children have this temperament? How does this apply to your family?	

Now switch roles.

3. It is said that only children are selfish, arrogant, and self-absorbed.	in the first place widespread wind up think of oneself as
Why do you think only children may be like this? Can you apply this idea to a family you know?	
4. Some psychologists say that the middle children have the worst reputation. They are either very strange or troublemakers. They go out of their way to be different and get people to pay attention to them.	outlook fill the void wind up widespread
Why do you think middle children turn out this way? Do you know any real-life examples of middle children like this?	

3 Work with a partner. Look at the words listed below that can be used to talk about personality and temperament. Write each word in the most appropriate category on the chart. Some words may fit in more than one category. For help, use information from the unit and a dictionary.

E assertive	E life of the party	reserved	I standoffish
bashful	P negative	reticent	talk a blue streak
I bold	I open	I self-conscious	timid
P gloomy	E outgoing	shrinking violet *very shy*	upbeat
E gregarious	I petrified	E sociable	wallflower
I inhibited	O Pollyanna	E social butterfly	I whiny
killjoy	O positive		

Introvert*	Extrovert*	Pessimist*	Optimist*

4 Work with a partner. Describe yourself to your partner using the words from the chart you completed in Exercise 3. Overall, what kind of person are you—an introvert, extrovert, pessimist, or optimist?

---

* *Introvert* and *extrovert* refer to behavior, whereas *pessimist* and *optimist* refer to attitude.

5 *Work in small groups. Read the questions below. Discuss the answers, and defend your opinions. Use words from the box on page 60 to help you express yourself. Play devil's advocate if possible. (If you "play devil's advocate," you pretend to disagree with something so that there will be a discussion.)*

WHO WOULD YOU RATHER HAVE?

1. Who would you rather have for your doctor?

Someone who is _____.

a. highly experienced, but also reticent and standoffish

OR

b. a recent graduate, but also outgoing and positive

2. Who would you rather have for your teacher?

Someone who is _____.

a. talkative, gregarious, but also at times gloomy

OR

b. reserved, confident, but also at times a bit self-conscious

3. Who would you rather have as your spouse?

Someone who is _____.

a. sensitive, kind, but also reticent and introverted

OR

b. the life of the party, gregarious, but also at times arrogant and cranky

4. Who would you rather have as your guide on a tour of a foreign country?

Someone who is _____.

a. extremely knowledgeable, detail-oriented, but a killjoy

OR

b. sociable, assertive, but inexperienced and a bit disorganized

4 Focus on Speaking

A PRONUNCIATION: Grouping Words Together

When you speak, break sentences into shorter phrases or thought groups. Thought groups help the listener understand speech in the same way that punctuation marks help readers understand writing. Pronounce the words in a thought group together.

- I'm the firstborn from a large family.

Join thought groups together smoothly. Hold the end of one thought group briefly before you start the next group. There is often a small change in the pitch of your voice between thought groups.

- I'm the firstborn from a large family.

There are no fixed rules for the length of thought groups. Many thought groups are also grammatical groupings, like prepositional phrases, article + noun, or short clauses. As you become more fluent, you will be able to use longer thought groups.

 1 *Listen to the sentences. Underline the thought groups. Then work with a partner to compare your groupings, and practice reading the sentences. If you and your partner have different groupings, discuss these differences.*

1. We discovered that about 40 percent of all Americans label themselves as currently shy.

2. Over the past ten years, that figure has increased to about 48 percent.

3. Do you find these days that it's more difficult meeting people?

4. Two out of every five people you meet think of themselves as shy.

5. There are just many things in a culture, our culture, which lead lots of people to be shy.

6. Children don't see . . . don't have the opportunity to see their parents and relatives relating in a natural, easy, friendly way.

7. When you're at a party, or just in a conversation with someone anywhere and you recognize that they're shy, what do you do to draw them out or try to make them more comfortable?

8. Admitting your shyness is really an important first step because if you don't, people make misattributions.

2 *Listen to the sentences, and circle the letter of the one you hear. Then, working in pairs, choose sentence **a** or **b** to read to your partner. Your partner will tell you which one you have chosen. Then switch roles.*

1. **a.** "Philip," said the doctor, "doesn't suffer from shyness."
   b. Philip said, "The doctor doesn't suffer from shyness."

2. **a.** My sister, who lives in California, is a Pollyanna.
   b. My sister who lives in California is a Pollyanna.

3. **a.** Suzanne's manager told me she's gotten over her shyness.
   b. Suzanne's manager told me, "She's gotten over her shyness."

4. **a.** Zimbardo interviewed the students, who had admitted they were shy.
   b. Zimbardo interviewed the students who had admitted they were shy.

5. **a.** Everything he said was based on research.
   b. "Everything," he said, "was based on research."

6. **a.** The therapy, which the clinic provides, gets people to be more outgoing.
   b. The therapy which the clinic provides gets people to be more outgoing.

B   GRAMMAR: Adjective Clauses—Identifying and Nonidentifying

1 *Working with a partner, examine the following sentences, and discuss the questions that follow.*

- Our research, <u>which we've been conducting since 1972</u>, focuses on adults <u>who are shy</u>.

- We are losing the social lubrication <u>that's essential for people to feel comfortable in the presence of others</u>.

- I am more like a Zorba the Greek–type person <u>whose job in the world it is to make people feel comfortable</u>.

- Misattributions, <u>most of which are totally false</u>, are often applied to shy, attractive people.

   1. What is the purpose of the underlined clauses?

   2. Compare the five underlined clauses. How are they similar? How are they different?

Adjective Clauses

Adjective clauses are used to add variety, sophistication, and interest to sentences. They are useful in combining sentences to provide more detail and information. There are two kinds of adjective clauses: identifying and nonidentifying.

Identifying Adjective Clauses	Examples
An **identifying adjective clause:**	
• has a subject and a verb	• We are losing the social lubrication **that's essential for people to feel comfortable in the presence of others.**
• modifies specific nouns and pronouns	
• can be introduced by *who, whom, which, that, whose, where,* and *when*	• Consider the division between those **who always see the bright side** and those **who'd rather wallow in their misery.**
• is not set off by commas	
• is essential to the meaning of the sentence	

Nonidentifying Adjective Clauses	Examples
A **nonidentifying adjective clause:**	
• has a subject and a verb	• Our research, **which we've been conducting since 1972,** focuses on adults.
• is used with the relative pronouns *who, whom, which,* and *whose.* It is also used with *where* and *when,* and cannot be used with *that*	
• must describe a specific person or thing	• Dr. Lynn Henderson, **who is co-director of the Shyness Clinic,** says nearly everyone experiences shyness.
• is set off by commas	
• is not essential to the meaning of the sentence and may be omitted	

Quantifying Expressions	Examples
Nonidentifying adjective clauses often contain **expressions of quantity** such as *many of, most of, some of, none of, two of, several of, half of, all of, each of, both of,* and *a number of.* Use the following structure: quantifier + preposition + relative pronoun (only *who, whom, where, when,* or *which*).	• Misattributions, **most of which are totally false,** are often applied to shy, attractive people. • The participants, **all of whom were adults,** met with the therapist twice a week to talk about their problems with shyness.

2 *Read the following paragraph. Underline all the adjective clauses. Circle the pronouns. Draw an arrow from each clause to the noun it modifies. Label the clause I (identifying) or N (nonidentifying).*

The Palo Alto Shyness Clinic was founded by Philip Zimbardo, who is a

N

professor at Stanford University, in Palo Alto, California. The clinic provides

group and individual therapy for people who are trying to overcome loneliness

and shyness. The clinic, which is currently directed by psychologist Dr. Lynn

Henderson, uses a specialized treatment model called the Social Fitness Model

that trains people in social skills in much the same way that people get trained in

physical fitness. Dr. Henderson, who invented the Social Fitness Model, believes

that problems of shyness, most of which can be overcome, must be explored in a

supportive, positive environment.

3 *Work with another student.*

Student A: Ask Student B questions 1 through 4.

Student B: Cover the left column. Answer the questions. Use a variety of adjective clauses in your answers. Then switch roles after question 4.

Student A	Student B
1. Who is Philip Zimbardo?	**1.** Oh. *He's the one who runs the Shyness Clinic.*
2. What is Stanford University?	**2.** Hmm. I think (that) . . .
3. What's an extrovert?	**3.** As far as I can remember . . .
4. What's situational shyness?	**4.** I'm not sure I remember, but I think . . .

Now switch roles.

5. What's an introvert?	**5.** Well . . .
6. What's a Pollyanna?	**6.** Oh . . .
7. Who is Quasimodo?	**7.** I guess he . . .

C | STYLE: Starting a Conversation and Keeping It Going

At the end of the interview with Alex Chadwick, Dr. Zimbardo says, "I'm a firstborn from a big Sicilian family, so my job was making all the other kids feel comfortable, and so I . . . I am more like a Zorba the Greek–type person whose job in the world it is to make people feel comfortable, you know, at life's party."

Zimbardo admits that "making people comfortable at life's party" is a social skill that comes naturally to him. However, for many people, feeling comfortable and relaxed in social situations is a challenge. Philip Zimbardo and other psychologists suggest that there are social skills that introverted people can learn in order to help them cope with feelings of shyness in social situations.

An important first step is learning how to start and maintain a conversation.

Breaking the Ice	Examples
Introduce yourself.	"Hi, how are you?"
	"Hello, I'm Philip Zimbardo."
Comment on something shared:	
• weather	"Nice weather, don't you think?"
• shared situation	"Have you ever been here before?"
• noncontroversial news	"What a game last night, huh?"

Maintaining a Conversation	Examples
Ask open-ended and follow-up questions.	"What brings you to Palo Alto?" "What kind of work do you do?"
Volunteer information.	"I run a shyness clinic here in the city."
Listen actively and look interested.	"Really?" "You're kidding!" (Use eye contact.) (Smile or nod your head occasionally.)
Change the topic if the conversation is dying, or excuse yourself.	"On another topic, did you see …?" "Excuse me. I'd like to get a drink."

ROLE PLAY

Work in pairs. Follow the directions below for starting and maintaining a conversation, using the chart above as a guide.

Procedure

1. Choose a role play from the list of situations that follows.

2. Student A starts the conversation. Students A and B keep the conversation going for at least three to four minutes. Do not let it die.

3. Change roles. Choose another role play.

Situations

1. You are in a long checkout line at the supermarket. Start a conversation with the person behind you.

2. You are on an airplane. Start a conversation with the person next to you.

3. You are on a treadmill at a health club. Start a conversation with the person on the next treadmill.

4. You are at a cocktail party and feeling very self-conscious. Start a conversation with a person who also looks shy. Admit your uneasiness. As Philip Zimbardo advises, look for a kindred soul.

D   SPEAKING TOPICS

Surprisingly enough, despite great success and public attention, many celebrities consider themselves shy. One well-known singer-songwriter, Suzanne Vega, speaks openly about her shyness. The following song, which appeared in the movie *Pretty in Pink,* expresses Vega's feelings and perspective on her shy temperament.

 1 *Listen to the song. Then listen again, and fill in the missing words. Compare your answers with those of a partner.*

> *Left of Center*
> If you want me
> You can find me
> Left of center
> Off of the _____
>
> In the _____
> In the fringes*
> In the corner
> Out of the _____
>
> When they ask me
> "What are you looking at?"
> I always _____
> "Nothing much" (not much)
> I think they know that
> I'm looking at them
> I think they think
> I must be _____
>
> But I'm only
> In the outskirts
> And in the _____
> On the edge
> And off the _____
> And if you want me
> You can find me
> Left of center
> Wondering about you

---

* more common: **on** the fringes.

I think that somehow
Somewhere inside of us
We must be _____
If not the same
So I continue
To be wanting you
Left of center
Against the _____

If you want me
You can find me
Left of center
Off of the strip
In the outskirts
In the fringes
In the corner
Out of the grip

When they ask me
"What are you looking at?"
I always answer
"Nothing much" (not much)
I think they know that
I'm looking at them
I think they think
I must be out of touch

But I'm only
In the outskirts
And in the fringes
On the edge
And off the avenue
And if you want me
You can find me
Left of center
Wondering about you
Wondering about you

2 *Read the lines from the song. Then circle the letter of the expression that best explains the line(s).*

1. "If you want me / You can find me / Left of center / Off of the strip"

   In this line and in the title of the song, "left of center" refers to a _____.
   a. physical location
   b. psychological state of mind
   c. temporary emotional feeling

2. "In the outskirts / In the fringes / In the corner / Out of the grip"

   The singer implies that she is _____.
   a. withdrawn and shy
   b. lost and lonely
   c. excluded and angry

3. "When they ask me / 'What are you looking at?' / I always answer / 'Nothing much' (not much) / I think they know that / I'm looking at them. / I think they think / I must be out of touch"

   These lines imply that the singer feels other people regard her as _____.
   a. emotionally unstable
   b. unaware
   c. unconnected to the group

4. "I think that somehow / Somewhere inside of us / We must be similar / If not the same"

   These lines suggest that the singer feels _____.
   a. other people are shy like herself, but hide it well
   b. all shy people are the same
   c. like she wants to meet someone who is not shy

5. "So I continue / To be wanting you / Left of center / Against the grain"

   "Against the grain" implies that the singer's love is _____.
   a. a secret
   b. forever and endless
   c. different and unusual

3 *Discuss these questions with a partner.*

1. Did you like the song? Why or why not?

2. What is the main point of the song?

3. Do you think the song is a good song to illustrate shyness? Why or why not?

4. Have you ever felt like the character in the song? Explain.

4 *Work in pairs. Do the role plays below.*

ROLE PLAY 1

Student A: You are a radio reporter. You are going to interview Suzanne Vega about her shyness. Look at your outline of information below. Form questions using the information in items 1–4 below. Take notes.

Student B: You are Suzanne Vega. Read the information on page 241. Listen to the reporter's questions, and answer them in your own words.

Interview with Suzanne Vega, singer-songwriter

Student A

Date: _____   Time: _____

Start: Hello, my name is _____, and I work for radio station _____. Thanks so much for stopping by the station to talk with us, Suzanne. It's great to have you on the show. You know, you've often mentioned in your interviews that you see yourself as a shy person. Could I ask you a few questions about that?

1. how people describe you

2. your experience performing in front of 100,000 people

3. your earliest memory of being shy

4. the way you cope with being famous

End: Thanks, Suzanne, for speaking with me today.

ROLE PLAY 2

Student B: You are a radio reporter. You are going to interview Dr. Cardoza about shyness. Dr. Cardoza is a psychologist who specializes in counseling the "successfully shy" person. Look at your outline of information below. Form questions using the information in items 1–3 below. Take notes.

Student A: You are Dr. Cardoza. Read the information on page 241. Listen to the reporter's questions, and answer them in your own words.

Interview with Dr. Cardoza, psychologist

Student B

Date: _____   Time: _____

Start: Hello, my name is _____, and I work for radio station _____. Thanks so much for stopping by the station to talk with us, Dr. Cardoza. It's a pleasure to have you on the show. As you know, this week we are talking about shyness, so I'd like to explore a few issues with you.

1. definition of a successfully shy person

2. advantages to being shy

3. ways to help people learn how to be successfully shy

End: Dr. Cardoza, it's been a pleasure to have you on our show. Thanks!

E   RESEARCH TOPICS

PREPARATION

Work with a partner. Philip Zimbardo and other psychologists refer to shyness as a social phobia. There are many other things that people can be afraid of. Look at the list of phobias, or fears. Choose one to research and present.

acrophobia: fear of heights
agoraphobia: fear of leaving the house
ailurophobia: fear of cats
arachnophobia: fear of spiders
aviophobia: fear of flying

claustrophobia: fear of closed spaces
glossophobia: fear of public speaking
testophobia: fear of taking tests
technophobia: fear of VCRs, computers, etc.
triskadekaphobia: fear of the number 13

RESEARCH ACTIVITY

Go to the library or log on to the Internet to find out more information about one or two of these phobias. Organize your research in three parts:

1. Definition and statistics, particularly from different countries

2. Examples from research and personal experience

3. Treatment options

PRESENTATION

Organize your presentation as outlined above, and present your research to the class.

For Unit 3 Internet activities, visit the NorthStar Companion Website at http://www.longman.com/northstar.

The Tipping Point

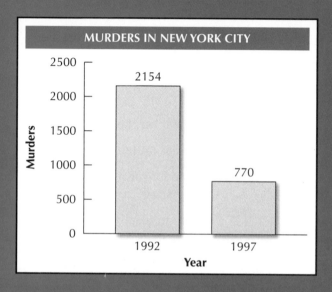

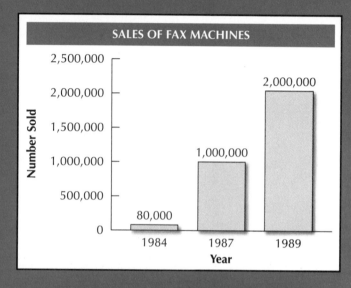

1 Focus on the Topic

A PREDICTING

Look at the graphs above. Working in a small group, analyze the results, and answer the questions.

1. What do the two graphs have in common?

2. For each graph, discuss several factors that may have contributed to the sudden changes illustrated.

3. Look at the title. What do you think this unit will be about?

B SHARING INFORMATION

The graphs on page 73 show a dramatic decrease in the murder rate in New York City, and a dramatic increase in sales of fax machines in the United States. Why do you think certain trends develop so suddenly?

1 *Work with a partner. Interview your partner to find out what factors influence his or her behavior or ideas. There can be more than one factor. Record the letter(s) of your partner's answers on the blank lines, and then have your partner interview you.*

What influenced you to _____?   Factors

_____ 1. see the last movie or TV show you saw

a. word of mouth (everyone is talking about it!)

_____ 2. read the last book you read

b. someone you respect told you

_____ 3. go to your last vacation spot

_____ 4. check out the last Web site you visited

c. saw it on the Internet

d. saw it on television

_____ 5. go to the last restaurant you ate at

e. read about it in a newspaper or magazine

_____ 6. perform some charitable act (volunteer, donate money, etc.)

f. other (specify)

_____ 7. buy the last piece of clothing or shoes you bought

_____ 8. (do something else you did) _____

2 *Working with your partner, review your answers to the exercise above. What patterns do you notice? What people or things influence your behavior and thinking the most?*

C PREPARING TO LISTEN

How can we make something happen? How do advertisers get us to buy products or go see a movie? Why do people suddenly stop doing something the way they have always done it, and do it in a different way?

Read the following background information about a challenge confronting a famous university. Then, working in a small group, do the activity that follows.

BACKGROUND

A university health center has tried to encourage students to get a tetanus shot immediately. A tetanus shot is an inoculation given to help prevent tetanus, a serious and sometimes deadly disease. Tetanus causes muscle pain, stiffness, high blood pressure, pneumonia, and other nervous system complications. A person can get tetanus simply by stepping on a rusty or dirty nail, getting scratched or bitten by an animal, or even pricked by a splinter or thorn.

The health center has already tried to have students get shots by:

- distributing a seven-page booklet explaining the dangers of tetanus and the importance of inoculation

- offering free tetanus shots at the campus health center

- illustrating the dangers with color photographs of tetanus convulsions, wounds, and other graphic depictions

These attempts have all failed. So now the center is sponsoring a contest, and asking the students to encourage other students in to get the shots.

IN THE NEWS: YOUR HEALTH CENTER TODAY

TETANUS SHOT CONTEST LAUNCHED TODAY

Want to win a terrific prize? How about free pizza for an entire semester for you and your friends?

Enter the University Health Center tetanus shot contest!

Q: What's the contest?

A: Come up with the <u>best</u> idea to get students into the health center for a tentanus shot.

Q: Why is the Health Center sponsoring this contest?

A: We MUST have all students inoculated by March 15.

Q: How does the contest work?

A: Get together with a group of friends, and come up with an idea for the spring tetanus shot campaign. Submit your idea on a card with your names (up to six people) and student residence. Put the card in the Health Center mailbox by midnight, January 15.

Q: What do the winners get?

A: Three large pizzas delivered to your residence every Monday during the spring semester.

IMAGINE A SOLUTION FOR PREVENTION!
ENTER THE CONTEST NOW!!!

1 *Work in small groups. Imagine you are a group of university students interested in winning the contest. Present your ideas to the class.*

2 *When you have finished, turn to page 242 to read about how the problem was actually solved at Yale University in 1964. Does this story make you think of anything you've noticed or experienced?*

Then, in your small group, discuss why the Yale University solution was successful. List your ideas here:

_____

_____

VOCABULARY FOR COMPREHENSION

1 *Work with a partner. Read the following sentences, and try to guess the meaning of the underlined words. Write a synonym or definition on the lines.*

1. Because tetanus was becoming an <u>epidemic</u> at some universities, Yale wanted to urge students to get tetanus shots.

_____

2. The <u>transmission</u> of ideas often occurs in the same way as the passing of germs from one person to another. Every day, people spread the message.

_____

3. Fashion designers told other fashion designers about Hush Puppies shoes. Cool kids told other cool kids about the shoes. Before long, everyone was wearing Hush Puppies. The trend started in a <u>word-of-mouth</u> way.

_____

4. <u>Mavens</u> like to know about everything. They are also obsessed with telling people what they know. A fashion maven, who is a famous designer, helped to spread the Hush Puppies shoes epidemic.

_____

5. In the late 1960s, educational television producers wanted to <u>generate</u> interest and enthusiasm for reading and writing among preschool children.

_____

6. To figure out how to make preschool TV shows "sticky," or memorable, among preschoolers, the producers <u>got a hold</u> of the top psychologists in the country, who began conducting experiments on children's television viewing habits.

_____

7. <u>Consumed by</u> trying to find the "stickiness factor," psychologists and TV executives carefully recorded specific moments when kids paid attention to shows and when they stopped watching.

_____

8. <u>Relentless</u> in their search, the researchers finally figured it out. From their many studies, they found that kids always paid attention when real adults and children were shown on the TV screen at the same time as the puppets.

_____

9. The children's show producers also discovered that they could <u>win</u> kids <u>over</u> to certain programs by making scenes not only flashy and exciting, but comprehensible.

_____

10. In his book *The Tipping Point,* Malcolm Gladwell <u>profiled</u> the high-tech firm Gore Associates. Gore Associates adheres to the "Rule of 150"—a belief that a group made up of fewer than 150 people operates more effectively than a larger group.

_____

11. According to Wilbert "Bill" Gore, the CEO of Gore Associates, the <u>root</u> of many companies' problems is that employees work in groups with more than 150 people.

_____

12. Gore's "sticky and infectious" philosophy <u>goes a long way toward</u> ensuring the company's profitable performance.

_____

13. Some people believe that the "Rule of 150" <u>holds</u> for religious groups, schools, and communities, not only companies. They think that it is more efficient to manage a group with fewer than 150 members.

_____

2 Work with another student to match the words and expressions in the left column with the definition or synonym in the right column. Write the appropriate letter in the blank. Compare your answers with those of other students.

_____ 1. epidemic

_____ 2. transmission

_____ 3. word-of-mouth

_____ 4. mavens

_____ 5. generate

_____ 6. got a hold of

_____ 7. consumed by

_____ 8. relentless

_____ 9. win [someone] over

_____ 10. profiled

_____ 11. root

_____ 12. goes a long way toward

_____ 13. holds

a. is true

b. contacted; communicated with

c. related to people telling people

d. large number of cases of an infectious disease occurring at the same time

e. totally involved in

f. very determined

g. cause; source

h. persuade someone to do something

i. passing of something from one person, place, or thing to another

j. people who know a lot and talk a lot about a particular subject

k. produce or create

l. succeeds in

m. described

2 Focus on Listening

A   LISTENING ONE: *The Tipping Point*

In his book *The Tipping Point: How Little Things Can Make a Big Difference*, Malcolm Gladwell explores why changes in behavior or ideas happen unexpectedly and suddenly. Why did the New York City crime rate drop so dramatically? Why did fax machines become popular so quickly in the United States?

In the interview, Gladwell describes a type of person called a **connector.** He says that connectors play a huge role in spreading ideas. What kind of person is a connector? Working with a partner, complete this sentence with as many descriptions as possible. Then listen to the excerpt to check your predictions.

Connectors are people who _____.

- *make a lot of telephone calls*   • _____

- _____   • _____

LISTENING FOR MAIN IDEAS

Gladwell identifies three kinds of people who spread ideas: mavens, connectors, and salesmen. Listen to the interview. Then complete the sentences. Compare your answers with those of a partner.

1. Connectors are people who _____

_____

2. Mavens are people who _____

_____

3. Salesmen* are people who _____

_____

LISTENING FOR DETAILS

*Listen to the interview again. Read the sentences, and write **T** (true) or **F** (false) in the blanks. Correct the false statements. Then discuss your answers with a partner.*

_____ 1. Word-of-mouth epidemics are transmitted by a huge number of exceptional people.

_____ 2. Gladwell gives a "names test" to people to find out how many people you know with the same last name.

_____ 3. By using his "names test," Gladwell concluded that out of 350 people, most people know more than 130 people.

_____ 4. People who score well on Gladwell's names test are considered "connectors," because they know a lot of people and can spread ideas quickly.

_____ 5. Gladwell can't start a word-of-mouth epidemic because his circle of friends is too small.

_____ 6. Connectors can spread ideas and news quickly to a lot of people in a very short time.

_____ 7. Ariel, a friend of Gladwell's, is a professional restaurant critic.

_____ 8. Most restaurants in lower Manhattan are filled with customers who are friends of Gladwell and Ariel.

_____ 9. There are only about two dozen restaurant mavens in Manhattan.

_____ 10. Gladwell describes mavens as the "Ariels of the world."

---

* The more commonly accepted term is *salespeople*.

_____ **11.** A word-of-mouth epidemic is most successful if a maven works with a connector to spread the epidemic.

_____ **12.** According to Gladwell, Tom Gau, one of the best salesmen in the United States, is successful because he can easily persuade you to do or believe in something.

REACTING TO THE LISTENING

 1 *Work in a small group. Listen to the excerpts, and answer the questions. Then discuss your answers with the group.*

Excerpt One

1. How would you characterize the interviewer's style? Why? Do you think the style is effective? Why or why not? How would you change it?

Excerpt Two

2. Why is the interviewer, Lydon, "afraid" that he is a connector? How does Gladwell react to Lydon's remark? Why?

Excerpt Three

3. What is Gladwell's attitude toward the fact that the restaurant market is an "epidemic market"? How do you know?

4. How does he feel about the power of his friend Ariel? How do you know?

Excerpt Four

5. How does Lydon feel about the fact that he is not a salesman? How do you know? What is Gladwell's attitude toward Lydon's admission?

2 *In a small group, discuss your answers to the following questions.*

1. Are you a maven, a connector, or a salesman? Explain. Which of your classmates, friends, co-workers, or family members fits one of these descriptions? How?

2. Gladwell's friend Ariel knows all about restaurants in lower Manhattan and recommends her favorite restaurants to all her friends, who then obediently follow her recommendations. Do you know someone who resembles Ariel? Describe this person.

3. Think of some widespread trends today in health behavior, criminal behavior, fashion, consumer products, environmental awareness, and so on. Do you think Gladwell's "tipping point" explains their popularity? How?

B LISTENING TWO: *Tipping Points in Fighting Crime*

You are going to listen to another interview with Malcolm Gladwell discussing the dramatic decline in crime in New York City.

 1 *Read the incomplete sentences. Then listen to the excerpt. Circle the letter of the correct phrase to complete the sentence. Then compare your answers with those of another student.*

1. Todd Mundt, the host and interviewer, believes that the reason crime fell so dramatically in New York is _____.
   a. well known and documented
   b. unknown
   c. being researched now

2. Gladwell believes that crime fell because of _____.
   a. community action
   b. behavior of certain influential people
   c. sudden small changes

3. According to George Kelling's "broken windows" theory, _____.
   a. criminals are definitely affected by the environment
   b. criminals may be affected by the environment
   c. criminals are not affected by the environment

4. According to Kelling, a broken window in a car probably means that the car is parked in an area which is _____.
   a. poor
   b. dangerous
   c. unsupervised

5. Traditional conservative thinking blames high crime rates on _____.
   a. an ineffective police force
   b. the criminals themselves
   c. the environment

6. Kelling believes crime can be reduced by _____.
   a. encouraging criminals to be more sensitive to the environment
   b. teaching moral and socially responsible behavior to all citizens
   c. making small environmental changes

7. In the early 1980s, the subway system in New York City was _____.
   a. disorganized and messy
   b. confusing and chaotic
   c. dirty and dangerous

8. Former New York City Police Chief William Bratton tried many ways to improve the subways. He tried everything except removing _____.
   a. graffiti
   b. turnstiles
   c. garbage

9. The police helped reduce subway crime by _____.
   a. encouraging people not to litter or throw garbage on the ground
   b. washing off the graffiti
   c. arresting anyone who entered the subway without paying

2 *Work in small groups. Explain the broken window theory in your own words. Do you think it is an effective or ineffective approach to reducing crime? Why or why not? Can you think of any other societal problems that might be solved by this approach?*

C   LINKING LISTENINGS ONE AND TWO

ROLE PLAY

Work in groups of three to prepare this role play.

Your Role: Neighborhood "clean up" advisory committee.

Situation: Several blocks in your city are struggling with troubling neighborhood problems such as:

- roadside litter (cans, bottles, newspapers, household garbage)
- broken-down cars on the side of the road
- stray animals
- small, teenage gangs hanging out on street corners
- small burglaries and robberies in homes and cars on weekend nights

You have been asked by the city's mayor to combine two of Gladwell's ideas when considering your recommendations:

- Power of Context (Listening Two—small but significant changes in the environment can create large change)
- Law of the Few (Listening One—mavens, connectors, salesmen)

In your groups, fill in the chart with specific recommendations for ways in which mavens, connectors, salesmen, and context (environment) can help improve the quality of life in these troubled neighborhoods. Use the information from Listenings One and Two as well as your own creativity, imagination, and personal experience. Then present your ideas to the class. Use visual aids such as posters and overhead transparencies.

MAVENS	CONNECTORS	SALESMEN	CONTEXT (ENVIRONMENT)
Get a well-known and locally respected sociologist or professor of urban planning to make public service announcements on the importance of keeping neighborhoods beautiful.	Get some of the long-time residents and active community members to take on roles in organizing a campaign.		

3 Focus on Vocabulary

1 *Some words and phrases can have both literal and metaphorical meanings. Look at the example. Then complete the activity below.*

Example

The murderer pulled the <u>trigger</u> of the gun and killed the security guard. (Here, *trigger* is used literally: The "trigger" is the part of the gun that you press with your finger to fire it.)

"Maybe we can go into those little <u>triggers</u>, because I find this really interesting because we're talking about such a big change that takes place, uh, being <u>triggered</u> by very small things, uh, what do you think some of those were?" (Here, *trigger* is used metaphorically: "Triggers" are things that cause or inspire change.)

Work in a small group. Look at the list of metaphors, and place the expressions into their appropriate categories in the chart below.

viral marketing	float an idea	a ripple effect
a social epidemic	swim against the tide	infected
be immune to an idea	a flood of ideas	the tide is turning
make a splash	wave	Band-Aid solution
contagious idea		

METAPHORS RELATED TO ILLNESS	METAPHORS RELATED TO WATER OR WEATHER

2 *Look at the underlined words. Try to determine their metaphorical meaning from the context. Then, working with a partner, complete the following sentences to show you understand the meaning of the underlined words. Discuss your sentences with those of another pair.*

1. Many companies now rely on viral marketing to get customers to buy or use their products.

   A <u>viral marketing strategy</u> they might use is *to get trendy people to wear the company name on clothing products.*

2. An epidemic occurs when many cases of a disease occur at the same time.

   Although epidemics are usually not desirable, an example of a positive <u>social epidemic</u> is _____

3. The cold virus is incredibly contagious, easily passed from person to person.

   An example of a highly <u>contagious idea</u> is _____

   _____

4. If you infect people with a disease such as a cold, you give them that illness.

   A "salesman's" enthusiasm for an idea <u>infects</u> others simply by _____

   _____

5. People who are immune to a particular illness cannot be affected by it.

   In the same way, those who are <u>immune to new ideas</u> or trends _____

   _____

6. A wave is a ridge of water that rises and curls in the ocean.

   We may experience a <u>crime wave</u> when _____

   _____

7. When the 250-pound Olympic wrestler jumped into the swimming pool, he made an enormous splash and got everyone nearby totally wet.

   The first Polaroid customers who brought their instant picture taking cameras to parties also <u>made a splash</u>. In a few short months, Polaroid _____

   _____

8. After three days of rain, the river flowed over its banks and flooded the town.

   After Sony game developers asked customers for ideas for new video games, the Sony Web site was <u>flooded</u> with _____

9. Ocean beach lifeguards face the difficult challenge of swimming against the tide when they dive in to help someone.

   When it comes to fashions, some people like to <u>swim against the tide</u> by ____

   _____

10. The tide must be turning because the waves were reaching the top of the beach, but now they are only reaching the rocks.

    In the late 1990s stock in Internet companies, "dot-coms," was considered very valuable. Suddenly, however, the <u>tide turned</u> and _____

    _____

11. In order to find out if a boat will float, it must be tested in the water.

    Most people will mention a new idea to a select group of people at first to watch their reaction. The New York City mayor <u>floated</u> his crime-fighting <u>ideas</u> with his advisors because _____

    _____

12. If you drop a stone into calm water, you will notice a ripple effect—low waves on the surface that spread out in circles.

    In business, a <u>ripple effect</u> occurs when _____

    _____

13. A Band-Aid is a piece of thin material that you use to cover cuts and other small wounds. Using a Band-Aid is an inexpensive, fast, and convenient treatment.

    International terrorism is a big problem that cannot be solved by a <u>Band-Aid</u> <u>solution</u> such as _____

3 *Read this imaginary interview between David McIntosh, senior manager at the Center for Business Innovation, and author Seth Godin, who, like Malcolm Gladwell, researches the spread of ideas. First, complete each sentence with the best form of the word or phrase from the list. Then, with a partner, role-play the interview. Read aloud with drama, interest, and expression.*

come around	ideavirus	~~spread~~
contagious	immune	transmit
epidemic	infected	trigger
get a hold of	ripple effect	viral marketing
went a long way	sneezers	went through the roof

Ideaviruses: A Conversation with Seth Godin

A (MacIntosh): Seth, in your book, *Unleashing the Ideavirus,* you argue that an idea (**1**) _____ *spreads* _____ like a bad cold. Is that right?

B (Godin): Yes, exactly. Ideas can spread rapidly or become

(**2**) _____ just like a virus.

A: So, if a company wants to spread, or (**3**) _____, an idea, it should imitate a virus?

B: That's right.

A: And in your book, you introduced a special term, (**4**) "_____,"
now often used in business circles. The term refers to a very powerful form of person-to-person communication. If this type of marketing succeeds, it's possible we can witness a very big change in attitude, preference, or habits.

B: Exactly! To persuade people, or to get them to (**5**) _____
to a new idea, you have to make a big impact. You need a "virusworthy" idea, something everyone wants to talk about. And if the right people

(**6**) _____ the idea, it will spread incredibly fast.

A: Oh, I see. And in that case, we'll witness a word-of-mouth

(**7**) _____. Interesting. Now Seth, can you give me an example of this thing you call, ummm, a virusworthy idea?

B: Sure, think about Hotmail.* Every piece of Hotmail has the Hotmail name on it. You can't miss it. Nobody is (8) _____ to the Hotmail ideavirus.

A: And in your book, you give a special name to people who spread ideaviruses: (9) "_____." Is that correct?

B: Yes. For example, Oprah Winfrey, the well-known actress and talk show host, is one. Ms. Winfrey used to recommend books on her show, and those books would suddenly become hot bestsellers. Each viewer told his or her friend or neighbor. The friend or neighbor told another friend and then another. The group of readers just got bigger and bigger, like a stone thrown in a pond; the recommendations created a (10) _____.

A: I see. Basically, her recommendation is a (11) _____ for millions of Americans to run out and buy her recommended book. Hmmm. Another question: In your talk, you also mention Post-It Notes, those sticky little pieces of notepaper that everyone seems to use. How did people become (12) _____ with the Post-It Note virus?

B: It's a great story. The secretary at the 3M Company liked the Post-It Notes. So she sent them to the secretaries in other big companies. In about two months, sales exploded. They (13) _____!

A: So the Post-It Note trend is an example of the classic (14) _____. The secretary "sneezed" by sending those very first packages to other secretaries.

B: Yeah, those packages (15) _____ toward making Post-It Notes one of the best-selling office products of the twentieth century.

A: Thanks, Seth, for talking with me.

B: My pleasure.

---

* Hotmail is a provider of free, Web-based e-mail. The company is owned by the Microsoft Corporation.

4 Focus on Speaking

A PRONUNCIATION: Stress Changing Suffixes

One group of letters in a word has primary stress. The vowel in that group or part is long and loud. When you add certain suffixes to base words, a different part of the word may be stressed:

define + tion ⟶ definition

proverb + ial ⟶ proverbial

Stress usually falls on the part of the word just before these suffixes:

-tion / sion	connection
-ial / -cial / -tial	financial
-ity	publicity
-ic / -ical	realistic

1 Listen to the words, and repeat them. Make the stressed vowel long and loud. Put a stress mark (ˊ) over the stressed syllable.

1. sensitivity   criminality   responsibility   popularity

2. energetic   fantastic   realistic   apologetic

3. transmission   organization   decision   documentation

4. financial   artificial   commercial   influential

5. logical   musical   critical   theoretical

2 Listen to the words, and repeat them. Make the stressed vowel long and loud. Put a stress mark (ˊ) over the stressed syllable. Check your stress marks with a partner.

1. **a.** able   **b.** possible   **c.** public

2. **a.** invite   **b.** inoculate   **c.** complicate

3. **a.** president   **b.** benefit   **c.** office

4. **a.** category   **b.** chaos   **c.** symbol

3 *Work with a partner. Add the suffix to the words below, and put a stress mark over the stressed syllable in the new word. Take turns reading the new words. Listen to each other to make sure you stress the correct syllable and pronounce it with a long, loud vowel.*

	-ity		-ial / -cial / -tial
1. a. able	*ability´*	**3. a.** president	_____
b. possible	_____	**b.** benefit	_____
c. public	_____	**c.** office	_____

	-tion / -sion		-ic / -ical
2. a. invite	_____	**4. a.** category	_____
b. inoculate	_____	**b.** chaos	_____
c. complicate	_____	**c.** symbol	_____

B   GRAMMAR: Adverb Clauses of Result

1 *Examine the pairs of sentences below. Then, with a partner, discuss the questions that follow.*

1. a. Tom Gau is an extraordinary salesman.

b. Tom Gau is <u>such an extraordinary salesman that</u> people from all over the world want to learn his secrets of persuasion.

2. a. George Kelling's "broken window theory" led to effective solutions.

b. The solutions were <u>so effective that</u> the crime rate in New York City dropped dramatically in the early 1990s.

3. a. Criminals are sensitive to subtle environmental changes.

b. New York City criminals were <u>so sensitive to subtle environmental changes that</u> they stopped committing subway crimes when the graffiti was removed.

1. What is the difference between **a** and **b** in each pair?

2. Why is *such* used in **1b** and *so* used in **2b** and **3b**?

Adverb Clauses of Result

Adverb clauses of result with *such . . . that* and *so . . . that* present the result of a situation that is stated in the first clause.

Adverb clauses of result are introduced by:

such + noun or noun phrase + ***that*** + clause of result	• The subways were **such a mess that people hated to ride them.**
so + adjective + ***that*** + clause of result	• The shoe brand became **so popular that sales went through the roof in only a few short months.**
so + adverb + ***that*** + clause of result	• The flu spread **so quickly that 50 percent of Manhattanites were sick on Christmas Day.**

So is also used before *many, few, much,* and *little.*

so + ***much/little*** + uncountable noun + ***that***	• Rachel Carson's book, *Silent Spring,* brought **so much attention to the dangers of pollution that the modern environmental protection movement was born.**
so + ***many/few*** + count noun + ***that***	• Carson exposed **so many environmental dangers that the government began to scrutinize the chemical industry.**

NOTES:

1. In spoken English, *that* is often omitted.

2. Placing **such** or **so** at the beginning of the sentence results in an inverted word order. This structure is emphatic.

   • **So** sensitive **were** New York City criminals to the subway environment that they stopped committing crimes after the graffiti was removed.

   • **Such** enormous impact **did** Carson's book **have** that President John F. Kennedy ordered a special advisory committee to examine the issues the book raised.

2 *Read the following story. Fill in the blanks with* **so, such,** *or* **that.** *Compare your answers with those of a partner.*

In April 1775, a young boy working at a livery stable* in Boston, Massachusetts, overheard a British army officer say, "Tomorrow is the day. Tomorrow we will attack the colonists." The boy was (**1**) _____ frightened and excited upon hearing about the imminent battle (**2**) _____ he immediately ran to report the news to a silversmith** named Paul Revere.

Revere was (**3**) _____ a popular and well-known citizen (**4**) _____ he had already heard from several others the very same news. Revere became (**5**) _____ convinced of the truth of these rumors, (**6**) _____ he immediately jumped on his horse and under the cover of darkness began his legendary "midnight ride" to Lexington. In just two hours, he covered 13 miles, shouting "The British are coming!" The sensational news spread (**7**) _____ quickly (**8**) _____ the colonial American army had enough time to organize and meet the British enemy with fierce resistance.

That same night, another colonial American revolutionary named William Dawes had heard the same forecast that "the British were coming." Like Revere, Dawes jumped on his horse and carried the message in another area near Boston. Unfortunately, though, Dawes's ride was ineffective. (**9**) _____ few men from his area showed up the next day to fight (**10**) _____ most people thought Dawes had ridden through a pro-British community. But he hadn't.

Why was Revere's ride successful and Dawes's a failure? Revere was a "connector," and Dawes wasn't. In fact, Revere was (**11**) _____ an intensely

---

* **livery stable:** a place where people paid to have their horses cared for, or a place where horses could be rented.
** **silversmith:** someone who makes things out of silver.

social "connector" (**12**) _____ when he died, thousands of Bostonians attended his funeral. Knowing everyone, belonging to every club around, enormously popular, Revere had built (**13**) _____ a wide circle of friends (**14**) _____ he knew exactly how to spread that piece of critical news as far as possible. Revere's tale, his word-of-mouth epidemic, is a legend told in every history textbook in America. And William Dawes? He was (**15**) _____ anonymous (**16**) _____ almost no one remembers his ride from that night.

3 *Work with a partner.*

Student A: Cover the right column. Ask the question.

*Student B: Cover the left column. Answer the question using the cue and the information provided in parentheses. Use **so that** or **such that** in your answer. You may rephrase the information in your own words. Then switch roles after Question 4.*

Student A	**Student B**
1. How popular were Hush Puppies in the fall of 1995?	**1.** (popular shoes) They were _____ the famous designers Calvin Klein and Donna Karan asked their models to wear them in their fashion shows.
2. Did Rachel Carson's book, *Silent Spring,* really educate people about the dangerous chemical called DDT?	**2.** (few) Clearly it did. Before her book came out, _____ Americans understood DDT _____ no one worried about it.
3. Is the Internet a powerful tool to make ideas tip?	**3.** (powerful tool) Absolutely. The Internet is _____ connectors can use the Internet to spread infectious ideas with a single e-mail.
4. How anonymous was William Dawes in Boston right before the start of the Revolutionary War?	**4.** (anonymous) William Dawes was _____ no one listened to his warnings of the British invasion.

Now switch roles.

5. How influential was Kelling's "broken window" theory?

5. (influential theory) Well, it was _____ the mayor based his crime strategy completely on Kelling's ideas.

6. Is yawning contagious?

6. (contagious) Believe it or not, it is _____ if you start to yawn, it is likely that the person next to you will yawn, and soon everyone in the room will be yawning.

7. Was the first Yale University tetanus shot campaign a success?

7. (a failure) Unfortunately, the first one wasn't. It was _____ only 20 out of 2,000 students got inoculated.

8. How strongly does the CEO of Gore Associates feel about the "Rule of 150"?

8. (strongly) Obviously he feels _____ about it _____ each Gore-tex factory has only 150 parking spaces. When cars begin to park on the grass, the company builds a new factory. Gore has 15 factories all within a 12-mile area.

C STYLE: Making a Point with Metaphors

Malcolm Gladwell values metaphors for their ability to demonstrate comparisons in a powerful and imaginative way. He uses many metaphors to communicate his concept of the "tipping point." Politicians, journalists, public speakers, advertisers, and poets use metaphors frequently because they can be such an effective communication tool.

1 *Underline the metaphors, or expressions that imply a comparison between two things:*

- "There is a small number of exceptional people who play a huge role in the transmission of epidemic ideas."

- "Crime is such a fundamentally contagious thing."

2 *Work in pairs.*

Student A: Read items 1 and 2 on the next page silently. Then put the statements in your own words, using words or expressions that can be used metaphorically from the left column in the box below.

Student B: Listen to Student A's statements. After each item, restate the information that Student A gave you, using the introductory expressions from the right column in the box below. You may also add any words and expressions that can be used metaphorically. Switch roles after item 2.

Example

Student A reads silently: Yale University students were asked to get tetanus shots but rarely did so. University officials asked for and received *many* ideas for getting students to come to the Health Center for shots. In the end, the university distributed a map and appointment times, which *finally brought crowds of* students in for shots.

Student A says: Yale University students were asked to get tetanus shots but rarely did so. University officials asked people how to get students to come to the Health Center for shots, and then they were *flooded* with ideas. In the end, the university distributed a map and appointment times, which *turned the tide* on this problem.

Student B responds: *In other words,* just a little bit of the right information *triggered* a great response!

Words and Expressions That Can Be Used Metaphorically	Clarifying Introductory Expressions
contagious	In other words . . .
epidemic	So, . . .
float an idea	What you're saying, then, is . . .
flood	To put it another way . . .
go through the roof	
immune	
infected	
make a splash	
open the floodgates	
ripple effect	
trigger	
turn the tide	
wave	

1. Cleaning up litter and graffiti were small things that caused a big change in New York City's crime rate.

2. At a fashion show in 1994, two famous designers drew a lot of attention when they wore Hush Puppies shoes. Immediately, sales of the shoes increased. Kids everywhere were suddenly wearing Hush Puppies.

Now switch roles.

3. Before *Sesame Street* appeared on television, the creators tested the idea out on a lot of kids. Educational experts strongly opposed the show because they mistrusted television's ability to be educational. In the end, *Sesame Street*'s proven success created a lot of interest in children's educational television.

4. Rachel Carson's interest in the environment was sparked when she began investigating chemical pesticides. Prior to the 1962 publication of her book *Silent Spring,* most people felt protected from any harmful environmental dangers. The book was criticized by the chemical industry, which didn't believe Carson's accusations against it.

D   SPEAKING TOPIC

In order for an epidemic to "tip," there are two critical factors:

- the messenger
- the message

The messengers—"mavens, connectors, and salesmen"—help spread ideas. But the content of the message is important too. The message can only be successful if it has the quality of "stickiness"—meaning that it sticks in our minds, or that we can remember it. If the message is sticky, it can create change.

Public service announcements (PSAs) are short messages broadcast on television and radio. Their purpose is not to advertise a product. Instead, they inform the public of important health and safety issues. Generally, in the United States, non-profit organizations produce public service announcements, and television and radio stations are required to broadcast them.

 1 *Listen to the PSA about improving your community. Work with a partner, and answer these questions.*

- What is the message of the PSA? Is it memorable? Why?
- Could it help change attitudes and behaviors? Why?
- How would you improve the PSA to make it a "stickier" message?

2 *Listen again. Fill in the outline below that gives the general structure of the PSA.*

PSA Campaign: *"Save Something"* _____

Number of speakers: _____

Speakers: _____

Sound effects: _____

Opening line (used to get the listener's attention): _____

Problem: _____

Suggestions to solve the problem: _____

3 *Working in small groups, write and present a PSA.*

1. Decide on an issue of public concern such as water quality or water use, air quality, teenage smoking, Internet addiction, safe driving, saving endangered species, clean environment, and so on.

2. Use the outline of the "Save Something" PSA as your guide in writing a PSA about your chosen issue.

3. Make sure your PSA is "sticky," so it can tip an important issue. Choose sound effects, and record it.

4. Present your PSA to the class. Play the tape. Have the other students in the class answer these questions: What is the message? Is it sticky? Why or why not?

E   RESEARCH TOPICS

1. Can you start or stop a trend? Work in a small group. Decide on a trend you would like to start or stop.

   For example:
   • You want your university to be car-free and have all students ride bikes on campus or take the campus shuttle bus.
   • You want your office to start recycling paper to cut down on paper use and cost.
   • You want people in your community to start running groups and run each weekend.
   • You want to stop cell phone use on commuter trains and in restaurants.

   To get more ideas, you may also conduct research on the Internet, in your community, or in your school to find out what things people would like to see changed in their environment.

You would like your trend to "tip," or happen, as soon as possible. Prepare a strategy using all three components of Gladwell's model:
- Law of the Few: mavens, connectors, and salesmen
- Power of Context: small environmental changes can trigger larger changes
- The Stickiness Factor: memorable messages help make an idea "sticky," or successful

Present to the class your strategy that illustrates how your group intends to get your trend to tip. Use visual and sound aids. Be creative!

2. Contact a company in your area. Find out which of its products has been extremely successful recently. Interview a manager from the company to find out what helped make the product suddenly successful. Was it powerful connectors? Contextual changes? Sticky advertising? Present your findings to the class.

 For Unit 4 Internet activities, visit the NorthStar Companion Website at http://www.longman.com/northstar.

Feng Shui: Ancient Wisdom Travels West

"A million two does seem a bit heavy for a one-bedroom at first, but this unit has the best feng-shui in the building."

1 Focus on the Topic

A PREDICTING

Look at the cartoon. A New York City real estate agent admits that $1,200,000 is a very high price for a one-bedroom apartment. However, she suggests that good *feng shui* increases the value a great deal. If you have never heard of feng shui (pronounced fung shway), can you guess what it might be? How might good feng shui increase the value of an apartment?

B SHARING INFORMATION

Working in a small group, read the following quotes that discuss the relationship between people and place (our homes, communities, environment). Paraphrase each quote, and comment on it. What does it mean? How do you feel about it? How does the environment in which you live, study, or work affect you?

"As places around us change—both the communities that shelter us and the larger regions that support them—we all undergo changes inside. This means that whatever we experience in a place is both a serious environmental issue and a deeply personal one."

—Tony Hiss, *The Experience of Place*

"The basic principle that links our places and states is simple: A good or bad environment promotes good or bad memories, which inspire a good or bad mood, which inclines us toward good or bad behavior. The mere presence of sunlight increases our willingness to help strangers and tip waiters, and people working in a room slowly permeated by the odor of burnt dust lose their appetites, even though they don't notice the smell. On some level, states and places are internal and external versions of each other."

—Winifred Gallagher, *The Power of Place*

C PREPARING TO LISTEN

BACKGROUND

1 *Divide into groups of five. Each person should choose one section of the background information. Read your section, taking brief notes on a separate piece of paper. Then close your books, and use your notes to summarize your paragraph for the group.*

Introduction
More and more Western architects, real estate developers, and interior designers are using the principles of feng shui in their life and work. Previously, Westerners dismissed feng shui as mere superstition. Now, however, feng shui is becoming more accepted in the United States and many other countries in Eastern and Western Europe, and Central and South America.

The Meaning of Feng Shui

Feng shui, meaning "wind" and "water" in Chinese, is an ancient form of geomancy, or the art of arranging the physical surroundings to create harmony and good luck. An art and a science, feng shui is concerned with creating both physical and psychological comfort. Practitioners believe that the arrangement of the elements in our environment can affect many aspects of our lives such as health, happiness, and fortune.

The Theory of Feng Shui

The theory behind feng shui is that there is an invisible life force or energy, called *ch'i* ("chee"), that flows through all things—rooms, buildings, people, hills, rivers, power lines. If ch'i flows smoothly and freely, then things go well for people. If ch'i is blocked, then the people in that space may feel discomfort or unhappiness. Sharp corners, narrow openings, poor lighting, and clutter are some of the many factors that can create blocked or unfavorable ch'i. Relying on tools and knowledge that are centuries old, trained feng shui experts give advice on the design and placement of objects in certain ways that promote the flow of ch'i. They consider the shape, size, and location of objects as well as materials, colors, and numbers.

The Origin of Feng Shui

Feng shui grew out of the practical experience of farmers in southern China over 3,000 years ago. Those who built their huts facing north were battered by the wind and dust from the Gobi Desert in Mongolia. In contrast, those who built their huts facing south enjoyed the warmth of the sun and protection from the wind. As a result, south became the favored direction. Over the years, south came to be associated with fame, fortune, summer, the color red, and the number nine.

The Spread of Feng Shui

Today the work of feng shui masters is in great demand among Chinese populations in Taiwan, Singapore, Hong Kong, Malaysia, and the Philippines. It is estimated that nearly 85 percent of Hong Kong residents apply feng shui principles when choosing an apartment or business. Now the ancient art of feng shui has migrated to the West. In the United States, for example, dozens of books on feng shui are published each year. In New York City, several major buildings have recently been constructed with the advice of a feng shui master. The influence and popularity of feng shui is no doubt the result of an increasing number of Asian immigrants, as well as the result of an ongoing fascination with ancient Eastern practices.

2 *Working with a partner, decide if each aspect of the environment listed on the chart creates favorable or unfavorable feng shui. Check (✓) your choice, and discuss the reason for your decision.*

ASPECTS OF THE ENVIRONMENT	FAVORABLE FENG SHUI	UNFAVORABLE FENG SHUI	REASON
clutter (things piled up in a messy way)			
an aquarium			
plants and flowers			
the colors red and purple			
mirrors			
a desk facing a view			
living near a cemetery			
living on a quiet dead-end street			
an odd number of dining room chairs			
pictures of bats on the walls			

3 *Discuss the environmental aspects with your partner. Which ones seem like good common sense? Which ones seem like superstitions?*

VOCABULARY FOR COMPREHENSION

Read the following sentences. Circle the letter of the word or expression that has the same meaning as the underlined words. Then compare your answers with those of another student.

1. Donald Trump, a well-known New York real estate developer, always consults an expert feng shui practitioner. To begin, the expert determines if the building is <u>aligned</u> in relation to the environment and to the principles of feng shui.

   a. parallel to other buildings   **b.** positioned properly

2. The feng shui expert did not get to the point right away. He <u>made digressions</u>. Finally, he returned to the topic.

   a. talked about another topic   **b.** took a long time

3. Some modern Chinese <u>frown upon</u> feng shui, claiming that it is superstitious and unscientific.

   a. disapprove of   **b.** get angry about

4. Many feng shui books are filled with <u>anecdotes</u> about people whose lives were changed after implementing feng shui principles.

   a. personal stories   **b.** folktales

5. Reputed to be a <u>hard-bitten</u> manager—conservative, focused on the bottom line—she reluctantly agreed to attend a lecture on feng shui.

   a. overly negative   **b.** tough, experienced

6. Feng shui practitioners instruct people not to sit with their backs to the door because they can be <u>caught off guard</u>, and most people don't like to be surprised.

   a. startled   **b.** hurt

7. For centuries, people have explored the reasons for the success of feng shui. Expert practitioners offer explanations that are both scientific and <u>transcendent</u>.

   a. within the limits of   **b.** beyond the limits of ordinary
       ordinary experience   experience

8. The feng shui expert told his client that the ch'i was not <u>circulating</u> properly because the staircase was too close to the door. The staircase was blocking movement.

   a. flowing freely   **b.** blowing

9. According to feng shui, fish in an aquarium symbolize <u>abundance</u>, as in the saying, "There are always more fish in the sea."

   a. a large quantity   **b.** food

10. Although feng shui is gaining acceptance in the West, there are still many architects and designers who view the practice <u>skeptically</u>.

   a. with doubt   **b.** with sarcasm

11. A well-known feng shui expert was recently <u>quoted</u> in a major newspaper. She recommends that all schools paint the wall behind the teacher's desk in bright colors. According to feng shui, bright colors will capture students' attention.

   a. repeated precisely   **b.** mentioned often

12. On entering a room, a geomancer, or feng shui master, can <u>sense</u> immediately if the ch'i is circulating properly.

   a. analyze and study   **b.** feel and know

2 Focus on Listening

A   LISTENING ONE: *Interview with a Feng Shui Expert*

Sedge Thomson, the radio host of *West Coast Live* from San Francisco, interviews Kirsten Lagatree, author of the book *Feng Shui: Arranging Your Home to Change Your Life*. At the end of the interview, Thomson asks Lagatree how favorable feng shui makes you feel.

 Working with another student, predict how favorable feng shui might make a person feel. Write your predictions on the lines below. Then listen to an excerpt from the interview to check your answers.

1. _____

2. _____

3. _____

4. _____

5. _____

6. _____

LISTENING FOR MAIN IDEAS

 Listen to the interview, and then complete the chart on page 105 by writing a brief explanation of the main idea. Share your answers with a partner.

MAIN IDEA	EXPLANATION OF THE MAIN IDEA
Part One **1.** definition of feng shui	*System of arranging things around you to create harmony and balance and to make you feel better.*
2. popularity of feng shui in other countries	
3. Donald Trump's attitude toward feng shui	
4. basic design of Lagatree's home office	
Part Two **5.** role of mirrors	
6. Lagatree's overall attitude toward feng shui	
7. who can sense good feng shui	

LISTENING FOR DETAILS

 Read the following questions. Then listen to the interview again, and write short answers. Compare your answers with those of a partner. Complete the questions with as much detail as possible.

Part One

1. Lagatree doesn't think feng shui is a way to keep out evil spirits. Why not?

   _____

2. Thomson says that feng shui is very important in Asia. What three examples does he give to support this statement?

   _____

3. What two countries make up part of Lagatree's background? How?

_____

4. Why do some Chinese people living in San Francisco ask to have one-way street signs removed?

_____

5. Why didn't Lagatree put her desk facing the window?

_____

6. How does she feel about the impact of feng shui on the design of her home office?

_____

Part Two

7. What two reasons does Lagatree give for not putting mirrors in the bedroom?

_____

8. What three reasons does she give for putting mirrors in other rooms?

_____

9. As a journalist, how did Lagatree feel about feng shui at first?

_____

10. When Lagatree's skeptical friends asked her if she believed in feng shui, how did she respond?

_____

11. You don't have to be a feng shui expert to know if a place has good feng shui. Why not?

_____

REACTING TO THE LISTENING

🎧 **1** *In the interview, Kirsten Lagatree's and Sedge Thomson's opinions and attitudes about feng shui are not readily apparent just from their words; attitudes are also shown in their tones. Listen to the excerpts, paying attention to the speakers' tones and choices of words. Then work in pairs, and discuss the answers.*

Excerpt One

1. Thomson probably feels that feng shui is _____.

2. Lagatree may feel that Thomson's question is _____.

Excerpt Two

3. Lagatree mentions Donald Trump to emphasize that _____.

4. Thomson's quick response, "a famous feng shui expert, as we all know," implies that he thinks Donald Trump is _____.

Excerpt Three

5. Lagatree told her friends, "Don't quote me." She probably said this because _____.

2 *Work in a small group, and discuss the answers to these questions.*

1. What is the most interesting thing you have learned so far about feng shui?

2. Would you be interested in applying feng shui principles to make changes in your home? If so, what changes would you like to make? If not, why are you skeptical?

3. Does feng shui remind you of any practices from other cultures? Which ones?

4. What do you suppose leads Westerners to adopt Eastern practices, such as yoga, feng shui, and so on? Does a traditional Eastern practice change when it becomes Westernized? In what ways?

B **LISTENING TWO: *Feng Shui in the Newsroom***

First, look at the bagua chart on page 108. It is an octagonal grid used in feng shui to determine which parts of the house or room relate to various areas of one's life. The feng shui master places the bagua over the floorplan of the room or house to see how to arrange the areas to promote the flow of "good ch'i." The bagua chart is used like a compass. Unlike Western compasses, in this Chinese compass, south is placed on the top, the most important direction. The components of the bagua include: five basic elements (fire, earth, water, metal, and wood), colors of nature, numbers, animals, and areas of life (health, wealth, relationships, wisdom, business, and so on).

Lagatree visits a radio newsroom to record this interview. She suggests changes in the newsroom based on feng shui principles.

 Listen to the interview with host Steve Scher. Then listen again, and fill in the missing information on the bagua chart. Also, draw arrows from the desks (both Steve Scher's and the news writers') and the aquarium to where Lagatree suggests placing them.

Bagua Chart

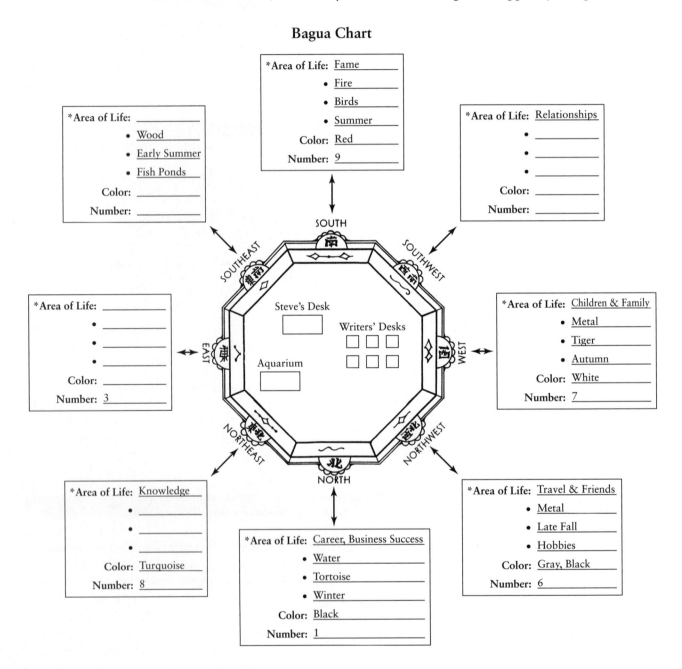

*Area of Life: Fame
- Fire
- Birds
- Summer

Color: Red

Number: 9

*Area of Life: _____
- Wood
- Early Summer
- Fish Ponds

Color: _____

Number: _____

*Area of Life: Relationships
- _____
- _____
- _____

Color: _____

Number: _____

*Area of Life: _____
- _____
- _____
- _____

Color: _____

Number: 3

*Area of Life: Children & Family
- Metal
- Tiger
- Autumn

Color: White

Number: 7

*Area of Life: Knowledge
- _____
- _____
- _____

Color: Turquoise

Number: 8

*Area of Life: Career, Business Success
- Water
- Tortoise
- Winter

Color: Black

Number: 1

*Area of Life: Travel & Friends
- Metal
- Late Fall
- Hobbies

Color: Gray, Black

Number: 6

SOUTH
SOUTHEAST
SOUTHWEST
EAST
WEST
NORTHEAST
NORTHWEST
NORTH

Steve's Desk

Writers' Desks

Aquarium

C   LINKING LISTENINGS ONE AND TWO

Follow the steps below to apply the feng shui principles you studied in the listenings.

Step 1: Choose a space (a room in your house, your office, your classroom) to redesign according to feng shui principles. Draw the space on a sheet of paper. Include as many details as possible.

Step 2: Review the principles of feng shui you have learned so far in this unit. Use the bagua chart on page 108. Working with a partner, discuss your drawing, and brainstorm changes that you'd like to make according to feng shui principles. Draw the new plan on another piece of paper.

Step 3: Implement the changes in your "real life." Draw the new space, and present the results to the class. Describe the space before and after. Describe any other life changes that may have occurred.

3 Focus on Vocabulary

1 *Work with a partner. Take the role of Kirsten Lagatree (the author) or Donald Trump (the famous New York City real estate developer). Complete the imaginary interview with the appropriate forms of the words from the box below. Then read the interview aloud, with drama, interest, and expression.*

align	hard-bitten	make a move	scare the heck out of
can't hurt	huge	peppy	sharp
clean	in the midst of	quote	talk [someone] into
get into	keep out	rise or fall	work around

LAGATREE: Mr. Trump, ever since I heard you _____ feng shui, as
                                           1. (became interested in)

           a journalist, I've been dying to meet you. I often _____

                                                     2. (repeat)

           you when I do interviews or speak on book tours.

TRUMP: Kirsten, the pleasure is mine. I've read your handbook on feng shui

           and have always thought you were a _____,

                                         3. (quick, smart)

           intelligent writer.

LAGATREE: Why, thank you, Mr. Trump. Now, I understand that you absolutely

           do not _____ in business without consulting your
                     4. (take action)

           feng shui master, Mr. Tin Sun. Is that true?

TRUMP: Absolutely. I am currently _____ complicated
        5. (involved in)

        negotiations involving some highly valued property on the Hudson

        River in New York City. However, Master Sun has informed me that

        the windows and doors are not _____ properly and
        6. (positioned)

        the views are not that great. I thought about selling the property, but

        Master Sun _____ me _____ keeping
        7. (convinced)

        it. He said it is very valuable and, by applying feng shui principles,

        we can easily _____ the problems. Fortunately, the
        8. (compensate for)

        overall design of the building is _____ .
        9. (simple)

LAGATREE: How did such a _____ businessman like yourself get
           10. (tough, experienced)

           into feng shui?

TRUMP: I've been doing business in Asia for years and am well aware of the

        fact that feng shui is _____ there. In Hong Kong, you
        11. (very popular)

        know, business deals _____ on feng shui.
        12. (succeed or fail)

LAGATREE: Have you used feng shui in your home as well?

TRUMP: Yes, Kirsten, I have. Master Sun started working on my house

        five years ago. I must admit that when he first came over, he

        _____ me. He connected many of my personal and
        13. (frightened)

        physical problems to the poor circulation of ch'i in my house. After

        many adjustments and a great deal of money, I was finally able to

        _____ the unfavorable ch'i.
        14. (prevent from entering)

LAGATREE: I'm sure. I know there are many skeptics out there. However, I do

           believe that if you live in a house with good feng shui, you feel

           _____ and more energetic.
           15. (livelier)

TRUMP: Of course. Anyway, I always tell those hard-bitten businessmen who

        tease me, "Try feng shui. It _____ ."
        16. (can do no harm)

2 *Work with a partner.*

Student A: Cover the right column. Ask questions 1 through 5.

Student B: Cover the left column. Answer each question, using the key word or expression in parentheses. Then switch roles after question 5.

Student A	**Student B**
1. After learning about feng shui, how would you talk a skeptic into using it?	1. I guess . . . (couldn't hurt)
	*I guess I'd say that it's been around for thousands of years, so it must work. At the very least, it **couldn't hurt.***
2. Do you really believe that feng shui can affect people's moods and feelings?	2. Hmmm . . . (sharp, peppy)
3. What other Eastern practices would you be interested in getting into?	3. Perhaps . . . (get into)
4. What is your favorite way of keeping out unfavorable ch'i?	4. Let me see . . . I think . . . (keep out)
5. Why do you think feng shui has become so popular recently?	5. I imagine it . . . (huge) . . .

Now switch roles.

Student A	**Student B**
6. Do you prefer simple, clean designs or more complicated, cluttered arrangements?	6. Actually, I think . . . (clean)
7. What kind of ch'i did you sense when you first walked into your current home?	7. I'm not sure I remember, but . . . (sense)
8. Can you describe a place you know with good feng shui?	8. Sure, I felt like I was . . . (in the midst of) good feng shui when I . . .
9. If your classroom had poor lighting and immovable desks that faced the wall, what would you do to create good feng shui?	9. Wow. That's a tough one. I guess . . . (work around) . . .

4 Focus on Speaking

A   PRONUNCIATION: Reductions with the Auxiliary *have*

 Listen to the following statements. Then read the explanation.

- And I was going to put my desk facing out the window, and . . . uh . . . but I would have had my back to the door . . .
- I've got a better floor plan than I would have figured out for myself.

> In spoken English, the auxiliary **have** is reduced when used with ***could, might, must, should,*** and ***would*** in the unreal conditional tense as well as in modal perfect forms. It is pronounced /əv/, like the preposition *of,* and joins to the preceding word. The main verb is stressed.

 Listen to these modal perfects:

- could have done, would have done, should have done, might have done, must have done
- couldn't have done, wouldn't have done, shouldn't have done, mustn't have done

 1 *Read and listen to the story told by a feng shui master. As you listen, fill in the verbs in the blanks. Listen again, and put a stress mark (◜) over the stressed word in the verb phrase. Make a line through the* **h** *of* ***have,*** *and join it to the preceding word. Use (◡) to join the words. With a partner, practice pronouncing the sentences using the reduced form.*

KUNG FU MASTER MEETS FENG SHUI DISASTER

Listen to my tale of a true tragedy that occurred in Hong Kong several years ago. Most people say Bruce Lee, the famous kung fu actor,
(1) ___shouldn't have bought___ the house in the valley. The wind in the valley can destroy the ch'i. People didn't understand why he chose that particular area, since the wealthy actor (2) _____ anywhere in Hong Kong. Rumor has it, though, that in order to change his feng shui, he put a mirror on a tree in the backyard. This (3) _____ if there hadn't been an accident. The tree was destroyed in a storm, and he never replaced the tree or the mirror. If he had, most people say that he (4) _____ . It is said

that the unfavorable feng shui (5) _____ his death. Replacing the tree and the mirror immediately (6) _____ his life.

2 *Work with a partner.*

Student A: Cover the right column. Make the statement, or ask Student B the question.

*Student B: Cover the left column. Respond to your partner using **would've, should've, could've, might've, must've,** or their negative forms. Use the appropriate forms of the words. Then switch roles after question 6.*

Student A

1. Kirsten Lagatree's interview was too long.

2. How do you think Lagatree felt when her friends questioned her interest in feng shui?

3. Thomson jumped when Lagatree entered the room.

4. I heard Thomson recently got married.

5. Do you think Lagatree consulted feng shui experts to help her write her book?

6. Do you think Thomson read Lagatree's book before interviewing her?

Now switch roles.

7. So, your sister lost 35 pounds last year on a diet of only brown rice, corn, oats, wheat, and barley. What diet was that?

8. Guess what: I tried acupuncture to help my leg heal, and it really worked.

9. What martial art were those people practicing on the grass in Central Park?

10. Did your doctor really get a license to practice acupuncture?

11. Did your sister really hire a feng shui master to decorate her house?

Student B

1. Uh-huh, I think so too. She should/not/digress.

   Uh huh. I think so too. She shouldn't have digressed.

2. Hmmm . . . I'm not sure, but she must/be/embarrassed.

3. Hmmm . . . I know. His desk could/be/facing/the wrong direction.

4. Uh-huh . . . right after he learned about feng shui. He must/move/his bed/to the southwest corner.

5. Absolutely! She must _____. Her book is filled with interesting anecdotes.

6. Let's see . . . No, he could _____. He knew nothing about feng shui.

7. I'm not really sure . . . it could/be/a macrobiotic diet. It's nicknamed "feng shui for the body."

8. Sure. I told you it would work. You should/try it earlier.

9. I have no clue. I didn't see them, but it might/be tai chi. Tai chi practitioners believe it helps to circulate ch'i throughout the body.

10. Well, I don't really know. He might _____. I heard he had spent two years in China studying acupuncture.

11. Uh-huh! She must _____. There are wind chimes, mirrors, and aquariums everywhere.

B   GRAMMAR: Spoken Discourse Connectors

1 *Working with a partner, examine this excerpt from Listening One, and discuss the questions that follow.*

Before Sedge Thomson invited Kirsten Lagatree to be interviewed on *West Coast Live*, he asked his researcher, Robin Tennenbaum, about her qualifications.

THOMSON: Is Kirsten Lagatree a feng shui master?

TENNENBAUM: Well, Sedge, she doesn't claim to be a feng shui master. I mean, she hasn't studied in China or anything. <u>But</u>, she has done a great deal of research, especially on the spread of feng shui in the United States. <u>On top of that</u>, she's written a well-respected book on the subject, which has led to a number of positive book reviews and successful radio interviews. <u>As a result</u>, she's become known as somewhat of an expert on feng shui.

1. What purpose does each of the underlined phrases serve? Name all three.

2. What other words could substitute for them?

Spoken Discourse Connectors

Discourse connectors are words and expressions that can connect ideas in speaking and writing. They join ideas both within sentences and between sentences. In written English, we use formal connectors—***In contrast, moreover, furthermore, consequently, therefore***—to express the meaning of contrast, addition, and result. In spoken English, we use more informal connectors to express the same meaning.

Contrast (unexpected result)	Addition	Result
but	plus	so
however	in addition	as a result
on the other hand	on top of that	

2 *Fill in the blanks in the story with the appropriate discourse connectors from the box above. There may be more than one correct answer. Then read the story aloud with drama, interest, and expression.*

A feng shui master told this story:

One client told me that her business was doing very poorly and she needed to take some action. (**1**) _____, she was eager to revive her social life as well. (**2**) _____, she hired me and I spent several hours assessing her home. At first glance, I sensed that the ch'i was flowing smoothly throughout the house. (3) _____, a few minutes later, I did notice an old armchair in her living room blocking the front door. I asked her where she had bought it. She told me it was from the set of a movie about a dangerous killer. (4) _____, she mentioned that she had only had the chair for about four months, and that this was the time when her business and social life began to fail. It was clear to me that the chair had negative energy, which was related to her bad luck. (5) _____, we moved the chair outside immediately. As soon as we did, the telephone rang. It was a friend asking her on a date. (6) _____, one month later, her business took off. (7) _____, she now understands the importance of bringing objects with only positive ch'i into the house.

3 *Working with a partner, take turns reading the following statements aloud. Select a discourse connector for the meaning given, and make additional statements.*

1. Feng shui is an Eastern practice. [contrast]

   But, it's becoming very popular in the West. In particular, Western corporations are using feng shui in business.

2. Some people say feng shui is just a superstition. [addition]

3. Placing a plant in a corner can help positive ch'i circulate. [result]

4. Many real estate developers in Western countries are consulting feng shui experts. [result]

5. In Hong Kong, feng shui is taken quite seriously. [contrast]

6. To create positive ch'i, you can put an aquarium in the southeast corner of the room. [addition]

C   STYLE: Emphasizing a Point

When speaking informally to a skeptical listener, English speakers may use an emphatic speaking style. In Listening One, for example, Kirsten Lagatree knows that Sedge Thomson and many listeners may be skeptical of feng shui. As a result, she emphasizes her point by using certain expressions such as *boy* and *would no more do [this] than [that]*, and by using emphatic intonation.

1 *Listen to the examples, and read the examples below as you listen. Then look at the explanation and examples in the box below before you do the second exercise.*

- "Well, <u>I wouldn't say</u> to keep out evil spirits. <u>But I would say</u> it's a system of arranging all the objects around you at home or at work."

- "He <u>would no more</u> start working on a building project without a feng shui master <u>than he would</u> without, you know, if it was L.A., without a seismologist."

- "The new Regency Hotel in Singapore just opened with two beautiful fountains in the lobby. <u>Talk about</u> great feng shui! The hotel is booked solid for the next two months!"

- "Now, based on just simple things I've done, and also lots and lots of people I talked to for the book, <u>I'd have to say</u> it works . . . and at the very least it couldn't hurt."

- "We can't see it, but <u>boy</u> is it there doing things."

Expression	Explanation	Example
Boy . . .	used as an exclamation followed by an inversion, auxiliary then main verb	*Boy,* did Bruce Lee have bad luck!
I wouldn't say . . . , but I would say . . .	used to clarify the meaning	*I wouldn't say* feng shui is huge in the United States, *but I would say* it's becoming popular.
. . . would no more . . . than . . .	followed by something obviously unreasonable	I *would no more* hire a feng shui expert to design my house *than* I would hire a palm reader to predict my future.
Talk about . . .	followed by an explanation	*Talk about* a perfect location! The house was surrounded by lovely streams and beautiful gardens.
I'd have to say . . .	used to emphasize a strong point	Well, since I moved my desk to the northeast corner, *I'd have to say* my writing has improved.

2 *Work with a partner.*

Student A: Ask the question or make the comment.

Student B: Cover the left column. Respond emphatically or skeptically. Use an expression from the box on page 116 and appropriate intonation. Add further comments. Then switch roles after question 5.

Student A

1. You really hired a feng shui expert to boost profits? Did it work?

2. How about hiring a professional "Clutter Consultant" to clean the clutter out of your house? A trained professional will clear the "stuck energy" in your house and bring you instant luck.

3. Listen to this! You won't believe it! A Chinese American millionaire paid a feng shui expert $50,000 to advise him on the alignment of his building.

4. I think feng shui practitioners are nothing more than superstitious fortune tellers with a compass.

5. Don't you think that feng shui is really more than just putting up mirrors or hanging wind chimes?

Now switch roles.

6. My friend Michael had robberies in his apartment. Then he used a feng shui expert, who advised him to set up an aquarium. He's had no robberies since.

7. Another friend added flowers, wind chimes, crystals, and mirrors in his house. Two days later, he got the biggest promotion of his life.

8. Would you buy a house near a cemetery?

9. What do you think of other Eastern practices like tai chi, macrobiotic diets, and so on?

10. Feng shui is just a passing fad in the West now. It'll fade in a few years.

Student B

1. Boy, _did it!_ Profits are up 100 percent.

2. Are you kidding! I would no more hire a professional "Clutter Consultant" than I would _____ (add something unreasonable).

3. Talk about _____ (add an explanation)!

4. Well, I wouldn't say _____, but I would say _____.

5. Absolutely! I'd have to say _____.

6. That's amazing! Talk about _____, (add an explanation), but I don't think feng shui had anything to do with it.

7. Boy, _____ (use an inversion).

8. No, I would no more _____ than _____.

9. Well, I'd have to say _____.

10. I wouldn't say _____, but I would say _____.

D SPEAKING TOPIC

Read this fictional article and do the activity that follows.

President Back from Hong Kong Plans to Implement Feng Shui in White House
First Lady Outraged!!

Once again, there is trouble in the White House. The President is frustrated by his low approval ratings, rumors of scandals, and high staff turnover. As a result, he is choosing a radical approach: FENG SHUI. Back from a three-week Asian tour, the President has decided that redesigning the White House according to the principles of feng shui is just the thing he needs to rid the country of its recent problems, improve his relationships with his staff, and make his family life more harmonious. However, it is rumored that the First Lady is outraged by this suggestion and will do everything in her power to fight the changes.

What inspired him? After visiting many buildings in Hong Kong, the President became convinced that feng shui could be the key to creating peace and harmony at home and throughout the nation. His idea was to redesign both the public display and private living areas according to feng shui principles. Right away, he observed that the circulation of ch'i in the Lincoln Bedroom and the Oval Office could be vastly improved. On a philosophical level, he sees the United States as a country full of multicultural influences and would like

the White House to be a showplace celebrating this very multiculturalism.

In contrast, the First Lady envisions the White House as the symbol of American history, taste, and tradition. She wants to continue the work started by Jacqueline Kennedy, who filled the nation's first home with antiques and crafts representing different periods in American history. To the First Lady, feng shui has nothing to do with traditional American interior decorating. Moreover, she does not see any relationship between moving a desk or hanging a few crystals and solving the country's domestic problems.

1. Divide into two groups:

   • the President and his advisers

   • the First Lady and her advisers

2. Using the information in the news article, outline the arguments for each side.

3. Conduct the meeting in which both groups present their opinions. Use discourse connectors presented on page 114 and the emphatic style expressions presented on page 116.

4. Decide how the president will handle the feng shui incident.

5. Express your own opinion on the matter. Write a summary for the White House Press Secretary, who will then make a formal public announcement.

E   RESEARCH TOPICS

EXPLORING OTHER ANCIENT TRADITIONS THAT HAVE TRAVELED WEST

Besides feng shui, other traditional Eastern practices have become popular in the West. Examples are tai chi, yoga, reiki, shiatsu massage, karate, and tae kwon do.

1. Conduct an interview. Try to find someone who practices one of these arts. Look for either a professional or an amateur. Ask friends or neighbors, or look in the telephone book or business directory.

2. Work with a partner. Brainstorm a list of questions that you would like to ask the practitioner. For example:
   • How did you get into this practice?
   • How and why did this art become popular in the West?
   • How is it practiced differently here?

3. Conduct the interview, and take notes.

4. Report your findings to the class.

WEB RESEARCH

In the past few years, the popularity of feng shui has skyrocketed all over the world. Many people are studying feng shui and applying its principles in order to improve their lives. However, some people think these principles are being exploited for commercial reasons. For example, a cosmetics company recently launched a new line of makeup called "feng shui makeup." Company representatives claim that this new makeup contains the right "feng shui" balance of colors and texture to guide the user through a smooth or rocky passage as her face ages.

You can find many of these kinds of products on the Internet. Do research on the Web to find the most unusual applications of feng shui. What is your opinion of them? Take notes, and report your findings and opinions to the class.

For Unit 5 Internet activities, visit the NorthStar Companion Website at http://www.longman.com/northstar.

Spiritual Renewal

1 Focus on the Topic

A PREDICTING

1. Look at the photograph of the monastery. What do you know about monasteries? Why do you think someone would choose to live in a monastery?

2. The number of visitors to monasteries and other spiritual retreat centers has increased dramatically over the past few years. Why do you think this is happening? Why do you think someone would choose to visit a monastery?

B   SHARING INFORMATION

Work in a small group. Read the following quotations about spiritual renewal. Paraphrase them, and then choose your favorite one. Explain your reasons.

1. A fourth-century European monk explains the power of "common property" as a form of spiritual renewal in a monastic community:

   "No single man is sufficient to receive all spiritual gifts, but according to the proportion of the faith that is in each man the supply of the Spirit is given; consequently, in the common monastic life, the private gift of each man becomes the common property of his fellows."

   —St. Basil

2. A twentieth-century American baseball team manager explains the idea of "heart" to renew the spirit of his players:

   "I tell guys, 'I'm not here to challenge you, I'm here to change you.' Challenge is a mind thing. Change is from the heart. If you can get in your heart, you can change. My mission is to change their hearts to the commitment it takes to win a world championship."

   —Jerry Manuel, manager of the
   Chicago White Sox major
   league baseball team

3. A modern American doctor explains the spiritual practice of "quietude," intentionally remaining quiet, as a health-giving habit:

   "We have learned scientifically by carrying out the practices [of meditation, or prayer] for 10 to 20 minutes once or twice a day that the health, the mental health, the quietude, the ability to deal with stress that the monks have can be captured by us within our busy lives."

   —Herbert Benson, MD, author of the book
   Timeless Healing: The Power and Biology of Belief

4. A famous contemporary American monk focuses on "solitude," intentionally spending time alone, as spiritual renewal for anyone:

   "The aspect of solitude is important in every person's life; it's like a conversation or music. You've got to have space in between the notes, or it doesn't mean anything. The solitude is space between the notes."

   —Thomas Merton in his book
   Thoughts in Solitude

C   PREPARING TO LISTEN

BACKGROUND

There are many forms of spiritual renewal in modern life. Many people practice small daily rituals such as intentionally remaining quiet or spending time alone; a growing number of people choose to retreat from society for a few days, often by visiting a spiritual community; and a few people withdraw from mainstream society to live in a monastery. What do you know about modern monastic life?

*Read the paragraph. Then read the list of statements. Write **F** (fact) or **M** (myth) before each statement. There are three of each. Then compare your answers with those of a classmate. Read the explanations on page 242.*

A monastery is a place occupied by a community of persons, called *monks* (males) or *nuns* (females), who follow strict religious vows, or promises. Monasteries transcend cultural, national, and religious boundaries: There are Buddhist, Indian, Christian, hermit, and wandering monks. All monasteries throughout the world share a similar commitment: brotherly or sisterly love, harmony, prayer, and communal work.

Modern Monastic Life: Fact or Myth?

_____ 1. Most monks and nuns are quiet, introverted people.

_____ 2. Monks and nuns never retire and generally work until they die.

_____ 3. Monks and nuns have made few contributions to the outside world, since they devote themselves to an inner, spiritual world.

_____ 4. Monks and nuns are chosen from birth to become monks and nuns by the family or the community.

_____ 5. It is not necessary for monks and nuns to be vegetarians, shave their heads, or wear special robes called "habits."

_____ 6. Although most monks and nuns follow strict daily schedules, most monasteries are open to outside visitors.

VOCABULARY FOR COMPREHENSION

Spiritual retreats have become increasingly popular. The following diary passages tell of one man's journey from Los Angeles, California, to Mt. Athos, Greece. The account appeared on the Web in a travel newsletter about Athos, the oldest surviving group of monastic communities in the world.

Read the text, and notice the underlined words. Then match them to the definitions in the list on page 125.

Mt. Athos, Greece

Monday, 27 March, early morning—Ouranoupolis

A dream come true. While waiting for the ferry, I look out across the sea toward the sacred, thousand-year-old holy mountain, Mt. Athos, which rises more than 6,500 feet straight out of the water. Attracted by its beauty, no doubt, **(1)** <u>prophets</u> came in the first century to practice their ancient **(2)** <u>ascetic</u> traditions of self-denial, such as **(3)** <u>fasting</u>. The mist, the white haze, the feathery silhouette all give the mountain a **(4)** <u>divine</u> presence as it rises high into the clouds. I check my pocket for the zillionth* time to make sure I have my four-day permit allowing me to visit the 20 monasteries on the mountain. To preserve the beauty of the monastic mountain, the Greek government **(5)** <u>enacted</u> a law limiting the male-only tourist visits to four days.

Monday, 27 March, noon—Daphni

By noon, my ferry has arrived at Daphni, the primary port on the Holy Mountain. I am stunned by the confusion and commotion. It is a **(6)** <u>vibrant</u> and vital port. The noise is **(7)** <u>pervasive</u>—roaring trucks, police sirens, shouting tourists with cell phones held tight to their ears, barking dogs, blaring radios. I ask myself, "Is this really an escape from my **(8)** <u>hectic</u> life in Los Angeles? Will I really be able to **(9)** <u>replenish</u> my soul?"

Monday 27 March, late afternoon—Karyes

Finally, I get to Karyes, a charming, peaceful village at the tip of Mt. Athos. I take

The Monastery of Gregoriou

a deep breath. A sense of satisfaction and **(10)** <u>well-being</u> fills my heart. I hike the 20 minutes to Monastery Koutloumousiou through thick trees and bushes. A bearded, unsmiling monk wearing black robes greets me. Speaking little, the guest master brings me to a cavelike room for the offering traditionally given to visitors: chewy candies and strong black Greek coffee.

The guest master then explains that all the monks are fasting at this time of the year, meaning they **(11)** <u>refrain from</u> eating and drinking most of the day. Therefore, the evening meal will be later than usual. The monks need a lot of **(12)** <u>discipline</u> to keep the fast. Besides the fast, they need a strong **(13)** <u>will</u> to endure the many hours of prayer. On top of all that, they have few hours of sleep each night. Wow!! This makes me realize that the monk's life is not for me.

Tuesday, 28 March, very early morning—Karyes

I wake up at 2:30 A.M. to attend the daily prayer service. Praying and singing together **(14)** <u>fosters</u> a spirit of community and brotherhood in the monastery.

After the service, I take a walk and think about my first 24 hours on Athos. I feel sincere **(15)** <u>gratitude</u> to my hosts for their hospitality. I am in awe of their displays of **(16)** <u>humility</u> and generosity to each other and to the hundreds of visitors searching for a few days of silence and solitude. Athos is a mystical place.

*zillionth: fictional number, meaning an incredibly high number.

_____ **a.** living without any physical pleasures or comforts, especially for religious reasons

_____ **b.** made a new official rule

_____ **c.** widespread

_____ **d.** controlled behavior according to rules or orders

_____ **e.** not being too proud

_____ **f.** determination

_____ **g.** eating little or no food for a special reason

_____ **h.** develops

_____ **i.** full of energy and life

_____ **j.** thankfulness

_____ **k.** not do something you want to do

_____ **l.** a feeling of being happy or satisfied

_____ **m.** very busy; full of activity

_____ **n.** coming from God or a god

_____ **o.** holy men

_____ **p.** renew and refill

2 Focus on Listening

A   LISTENING ONE: *The Religious Tradition of Fasting*

You will hear a report from the radio news broadcast *All Things Considered*, aired on National Public Radio in the United States. Duncan Moon discusses the ideas of four professors of religion on the subject of religious fasting.

Working with a partner, predict the reasons that inspire people of many religions to fast. List your ideas. Then listen to an excerpt from the interview to check your predictions.

1. _____

2. _____

3. _____

4. _____

LISTENING FOR MAIN IDEAS

 Read the lists of religions and the reasons for fasting. Then listen to the interview. Match each religion on the left with the essential reason for fasting associated with that religion.

Religion(s)

_____ **1.** Eastern religions

_____ **2.** all religions

_____ **3.** Episcopalian

_____ **4.** Mormon

_____ **5.** Muslim

Reason for fasting

a. spiritual renewal

b. spiritual discipline

c. asceticism

d. anti-competitiveness

e. anti-materialism

LISTENING FOR DETAILS

Read the following questions. Then listen to the interview, and write short answers. Compare your answers with those of a partner.

1. According to Judaism, Christianity, and Islam, who were the first religious leaders to fast?

_____

2. According to Diana Eck, professor of comparative religion at Harvard Divinity School, what does a fast symbolize?

_____

3. What does Barbara Patterson, professor of religion at Emory University, think about the stress that might be created by fasting?

_____

4. How often do Mormons fast?

_____

5. What do Mormons do with the money they save by fasting?

_____

6. When do Muslims fast, and for how long?

_____

7. According to Ahbar Ahmed, the Islamic studies professor, why is fasting so important now?

_____

8. In addition, according to Ahmed, why is fasting so difficult these days?

_____

REACTING TO THE LISTENING

In Listening One, Duncan Moon does not interview the speakers directly in a question-and-answer format. Instead, he introduces the speaker's ideas in a short, simple, introductory statement. He then uses the speaker's actual quotations to support and explain the introductory statement.

 1 *Listen to each excerpt. Look at Moon's statement in the left column. In the middle column, write down the phrases used by that speaker to explain the statement. In the third column, write down your understanding of the statement and explanation.*

Excerpt One

Moon's statement	Eck's words	My own words
"[fasting breaks] an attachment to <u>material things</u>"	*earthly things, consumption, materialism*	*Fasting is a way to get away from the most common kind of consumption— eating.*

Excerpt Two

Moon's statement	Patterson's words	My own words
"[fasting is] a spiritual gym"		

Excerpt Three

Moon's statement	Ahmed's words	My own words
"[fasting is] vital to spiritual well-being"		

2 *What do you think is the purpose of Moon's introductory statements? Explain.*

3 *Discuss the following questions in a small group.*

1. Why do you think fasting is a spiritual practice in so many religious traditions?

2. Have you ever fasted? If so, describe your experience.

3. As you heard in the report, many people fast to become more disciplined. How else can this kind of discipline be achieved?

B   LISTENING TWO: *Describing Monastic Life*

William Claassen, a journalist and author, recently wrote a book describing monastic life in 11 countries. To research his book, he visited monastic communities around the world. In Listening Two he discusses his experiences in Thailand, Greece, and Spain.

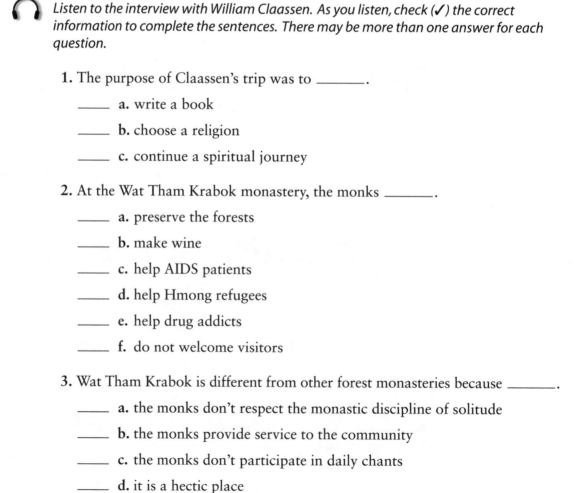

Listen to the interview with William Claassen. As you listen, check (✓) the correct information to complete the sentences. There may be more than one answer for each question.

1. The purpose of Claassen's trip was to _____.

    _____ **a.** write a book

    _____ **b.** choose a religion

    _____ **c.** continue a spiritual journey

2. At the Wat Tham Krabok monastery, the monks _____.

    _____ **a.** preserve the forests

    _____ **b.** make wine

    _____ **c.** help AIDS patients

    _____ **d.** help Hmong refugees

    _____ **e.** help drug addicts

    _____ **f.** do not welcome visitors

3. Wat Tham Krabok is different from other forest monasteries because _____.

    _____ **a.** the monks don't respect the monastic discipline of solitude

    _____ **b.** the monks provide service to the community

    _____ **c.** the monks don't participate in daily chants

    _____ **d.** it is a hectic place

4. On Mt. Athos, Claassen learned a term, the "two-legged wolf," which refers to people who _____.

_____ **a.** visit monasteries only for fun and interest

_____ **b.** are not primarily spiritually motivated

_____ **c.** visit Mt. Athos for a week to ten days

_____ **d.** prefer the beaches of Thailand to the monasteries on Mt. Athos

5. In Spain, at the Monasterio de Santo Domingo, the monks _____.

_____ **a.** won international acclaim for their music

_____ **b.** produced an album of their Gregorian chants

_____ **c.** started recording their music in the early 1990s

_____ **d.** record music to draw more visitors to their monastery

_____ **e.** record music to make money

_____ **f.** use the profits from the albums to support the work of the monastery

C LINKING LISTENINGS ONE AND TWO

As you heard in Listenings One and Two, the desire for spiritual renewal is pervasive. However, the approach to achieving this renewal varies widely.

1 *Look at the list of the different spiritual practices. Do any of them appeal to you? Which ones? Rank them in order of personal preference, and discuss the reasons for your choices. Compare your choices in small groups, and discuss them.*

_____ fasting

_____ meditating

_____ chanting

_____ taking daily walks

_____ doing daily breathing exercises

_____ doing weekly community service

_____ visiting a monastery for a few days

_____ attending religious services regularly

_____ (your own idea) _____

_____ (your own idea) _____

2 *Working with a new partner or in a small group, brainstorm reasons why people seek a more spiritual life or spiritual renewal. List your ideas below. Then compare your lists with those of another group, and discuss them.*

_____   _____

_____   _____

_____   _____

3 Focus on Vocabulary

Some say Thomas Merton was the greatest living monk in the twentieth century. An outgoing American teenager who gradually withdrew from the "real" world, Merton converted to Catholicism and ultimately joined the Trappist order of monks, an order based on the strict practices of silence and solitude.

1 *Work in pairs. Read the following biographical sketch of Thomas Merton. Match each underlined word in the passage to its synonym or definition on page 131.*

The Talkative Trappist

Thomas Merton was born in 1915 in France and died in 1968 in Thailand. He was one of the most famous Roman Catholics of the twentieth century. Losing his mother to cancer when he was six years old, young Thomas experienced an unconventional childhood as the son of a restless painter. His father, who moved around often, periodically shipped Merton off to stay with relatives and friends in England, France, or America. Merton enjoyed this **(1)** <u>hectic</u>, gypsy sort of life and developed an amazing capacity for observation and understanding of others and the world around him. Merton graduated from Columbia University and began graduate studies there. Although he immersed himself in his academic studies, spiritually, Merton felt restless and confused. He then began another phase of his **(2)** <u>quest</u>—to deepen his knowledge of himself and the world.

In his autobiography, Merton **(3)** <u>traces</u> his conversion to Catholicism <u>back</u> to a single day in Manhattan. While sitting in the back of a church, he mysteriously felt so drawn to God that he instantly committed himself to the Catholic faith. As a practical expression of his newly found faith, Merton **(4)** <u>took on</u> volunteer work in Harlem, a poverty-stricken neighborhood near the University. This experience not only gave him a spiritual sense of **(5)** <u>well-being</u> but also **(6)** <u>fostered</u> a concern for racial and economic equality in an America filled with injustices and inequalities.

In 1941, still not feeling completely spiritually complete, Merton left New York and chose to become a Trappist monk. Some of his close friends and family were baffled by what they perceived as his sudden (**7**) <u>notion</u> that he should be a monk. What drove Merton to this unusual decision? Why would this vibrant, brilliant young man choose to (**8**) <u>pull back</u> from daily life and commit himself to the monastic life of ascetism—fasting, silence, and prayer?

In the early days at Our Lady of Gethsemani monastery in Kentucky, Merton suffered through the loneliness and rigors of the monastic life. It took great will for this active, outgoing young man to (**9**) <u>refrain from</u> smoking, drinking, speaking, and living the life he previously had enjoyed. Worried about his somber mood, the older monks worked hard to (**10**) <u>draw him out</u>. (**11**) <u>Over time</u>, they discovered Merton's great gift: He had an amazing ability to comment on spirituality, contemplation, nature, art, relationships, and God.

In 1948, his autobiography, *The Seven Storey Mountain,* was published. It (**12**) <u>caught on</u> quickly and sold more than one million copies its first year. For the next 20 years, while living as one of the silent Trappist monks at Gethsemani, Merton "talked" through the more than 100 books, articles, and essays he wrote and had published. He donated all his (**13**) <u>royalties</u> from his books to Gethsemani. Religion was not the only topic Merton treated in his writings; he wrote prolifically for the general public on the civil rights movement (1960s), nonviolence, peace, and the nuclear arms race. Legislators in Congress even quoted from his work when attempting to (**14**) <u>enact</u> civil rights legislation in the 1960s. Merton died from an electrical accident in 1968, just months after a momentous meeting with the Dalai Lama, a meeting which brought about a deeper understanding between Christians and Buddhists throughout the world.

_____ **a.** make a rule or law

_____ **b.** became popular

_____ **c.** finds the origins of something

_____ **d.** idea

_____ **e.** started

_____ **f.** search

_____ **g.** feeling of being happy or satisfied

_____ **h.** very busy; full of activity

_____ **i.** money paid to a writer

_____ **j.** not do something you want to do

_____ **k.** make someone willing to talk

_____ **l.** developed

_____ **m.** eventually

_____ **n.** withdraw

2 *Work with a partner.*

Student A: Cover the right column. Ask Student B questions 1 through 4.

Student B: Cover the left column. Answer the questions using any of the key words and one expression for hesitation. Explain your ideas in detail. Use the information about Thomas Merton from the previous exercise. Then switch roles after question 4.

Expressions for Hesitation

- Hmm, let's see now …

- Hmm, I'm not exactly sure, but maybe …

- Well, let me think for a minute …

- Well, that's a good question …

Student A

1. Can you understand why a young, modern American with a good life would choose to go into a monastery?

2. Why do you think the title of the passage is "The Talkative Trappist"?

3. How do you think Merton's early volunteer work in Harlem influenced his writing?

4. What impressed you most about Merton's life?

Now switch roles.

5. Why is Merton's work so popular with the general public?

6. How do you think the other monks at Gethsemani felt about Merton's writing career?

7. What part of Merton's life would you like to find out more about?

8. What impressed you most about Merton's life?

Student B

1. hectic, quest, well-being

   *Hmm, let's see now, he had lived a very **hectic** life, but in his **quest,** he found that he needed solitude to achieve spiritual **well-being.***

2. refrain, draw out, over time

3. trace back, take on, foster

4. (Use any of the words from items 1–3 above, and one of the hesitating expressions from the box above.)

5. notion, enact, foster

6. over time, catch on, royalties

7. pull back, draw out, take on

8. (Use any of the words from items 5–7 above, and one of the hesitating expressions from the box above.)

4 Focus on Speaking

A PRONUNCIATION: Vowel Alternation

The stressed vowel in some pairs of related words shifts, or alternates. The alternation is the result of a historical sound change in English, the Great Vowel Shift. The Great Vowel Shift affected only one of the words in the pairs.

🎧 *Listen to the difference between the underlined vowels in these pairs of words.*

divine–divinity   grateful–gratitude   heal–health
/ay/   /ɪ/   /ey/   /æ/   /iy/   /ɛ/

🎧 **1** *Listen to the pairs of words, and repeat them.*

1. /ay/ divine   /ɪ/ divinity
   a. rite   ritual
   b. decide   decision
   c. write   written

2. /ey/ grateful   /æ/ gratitude
   a. explain   explanatory
   b. Spain   Spanish
   c. nation   national

3. /iy/ compete   /ɛ/ competitiveness
   a. keep   kept
   b. steal   stealth
   c. please   pleasure

2 *Work with a partner. Say the pairs of words. Circle only the pairs that alternate. Say the circled pairs again. Write **1** if they alternate like* divine–divinity; *write **2** if the alternation is like* grateful–gratitude; *and **3** if the alternation is like* heal–health.

_____ 1. deal–dealt

_____ 2. race–racial

_____ 3. line–linear

_____ 4. pervade–pervasive

_____ 5. life–live

_____ 6. nature–natural

_____ 7. advise–advisor

_____ 8. sleep–slept

_____ 9. divide–division

_____ 10. danger–dangerous

_____ 11. sane–sanity

_____ 12. faith–faithful

B   GRAMMAR: Count and Non-Count Nouns and Their Quantifiers

1 *Working with a partner, examine the statements below, and discuss the questions that follow.*

- <u>Very few</u> spiritual **journeys** can compare to visiting the monasteries on Mt. Athos.

- With 20 monasteries and a limit of 4 days, it took Claassen <u>quite a bit of</u> **effort** to see more than 6 monasteries on one trip.

- Some monks are concerned about the growing <u>number of</u> **pilgrimages** to Mt. Athos these days.

- It takes a <u>great deal of</u> **discipline** to fast for a month.

1. Categorize the boldfaced nouns into count and non-count nouns.

2. What do the underlined expressions of quantity tell us?

Count and Non-Count Nouns

All nouns in English can be divided into two groups: count nouns and non-count nouns. **Count nouns** are those that can be counted and made plural (*monasteries, monks*). In contrast, **non-count nouns** can be considered as a mass and cannot be made plural (*music, air*). Non-count nouns may refer to categories made up of different things (*money, furniture*), phenomena that occur in nature (*darkness, weather*), or abstractions (*violence, greed, honesty*).

Certain expressions of quantity, called **quantifiers,** state the amount of the noun. Some quantifiers are used with count nouns, and others are used with non-count nouns.

Quantifiers before Count Nouns	Quantifiers before Non-Count Nouns
a lot of	a lot of
many/a great many	a great deal of
quite a few	quite a bit of
a bunch of	a large amount of
a (large) number of	
certain	
not many	not much

Quantifiers before Count Nouns

very few (just a few/only a few)

a few/few

fewer

Quantifiers before Non-Count Nouns

very little (just a little/only a little)

a little/little

less

GRAMMAR TIP: Notice the change in meaning when the indefinite article *a* is placed before *few* and *little*.

Few/Little

- negative meaning
- similar to *not much* and *not many*

A few/A little

- positive meaning
- similar to *some* (when talking about a small quantity)

Compare:

- *Few* people can fast more than three days in a row.
- *A few* people from our group decided to return to the monastery for another visit.

2 *Working with a partner, decide if the nouns listed are count or non-count nouns, or both. Label them **C** (count) or **NC** (non-count) or **C/NC** (both). Seven of them are commonly used as either count or non-count nouns.*

_____ 1. consumption

_____ 2. discipline

_____ 3. effort

_____ 4. faith

_____ 5. fast

_____ 6. gratitude

_____ 7. humility

_____ 8. impact

_____ 9. journey

_____ 10. monastery

_____ 11. notion

_____ 12. pilgrimage

_____ 13. quest

_____ 14. soul

_____ 15. spirituality

_____ 16. stress

_____ 17. will

_____ 18. work

3 *Read the following sentences. Indicate if each underlined word is being used as a count (**C**) or a non-count (**NC**) noun. The words or phrases in parentheses give you a hint. Refer to the chart on pages 134–135, and add a quantifier when appropriate. Use a variety of quantifiers. Put an **X** in the blank if a quantifier is not appropriate.*

1a. _NC_ Obeying the rigorous routine and monastic rules requires

_____quite a bit of_____ discipline (controlled behavior) on the part

of the monks.

b. _C_ _____Certain_____ disciplines (areas of knowledge or training)

such as yoga, meditation, or fasting develop spirituality.

2a. _____ Addicts being treated at the Wat Tham Krabok monastery must have

_____ will (determination) to endure and succeed.

b. _____ Although the attorney works for the monastery, she doesn't write

_____ wills (legal document to distribute

someone's money and property) for the monks. Most monks have

no material possessions to leave to anyone.

3a. _____ Dr. Ahbar Ahmed put _____ stress (emphasis) on

the importance of fasting to replenish the soul.

b. _____ According to Ahmed, fasting helps people pull back from their daily

lives and thus have _____ stresses (worries).

4a. _____ Monasteries sometimes produce _____ works

(something produced by a writer, artist, or musician) of art which are

commercially successful.

b. _____ The Spanish monks are notorious for doing _____

spiritual work (activity) since they made it big in the music business.

5a. _____ The nuns live in a dangerous, noisy, impoverished area of the city. So

the sisters must put _____ effort (physical or

mental energy) into maintaining their contemplative life.

b. _____ The area benefits from the nuns' food, blanket, and clothing

distributions, in addition to _____ city-sponsored

efforts (attempts) to improve the neighborhood.

6a. _____ Wat Tham Krabok helps drug addicts from _____ different <u>faiths</u> (religions).

b. _____ Optimistic and determined, the Thai monks always have

_____ <u>faith</u> (conviction, belief) in their treatment.

7a. _____ The monks believe that regular and disciplined meditation replenishes

the _____ <u>soul</u> (inner character)

b. _____ Many Buddhist monks perform good deeds so that their

_____ <u>souls</u> (spirits) will return to a better life

after death.

Tibetan Buddhist nun Tenzin Palmo has frequently been interviewed as someone who has demonstrated exceptional spiritual genius. Her spiritual journey is the subject of two recent books.

4 _Work with a partner. Fill in the blanks with_ **few, little, a few,** _or_ **a little.** _Then role-play the imaginary interview. Listen carefully, look at each other as much as possible, and say your lines like you mean them._

Student A: You are the interviewer.

Student B: You are Tenzin Palmo.

INTERVIEWER: Ani-la,[*] I've come a long way to see you. Thank you for taking

(**1**) _____ time to talk to me. I am very grateful.

TENZIN PALMO: Thank you. It's a real pleasure to meet you. Tea?

INTERVIEWER: Yes, please. OK. Let's get started. You were the young English girl named Diane Perry, growing up in London's East End?

TENZIN PALMO: Yes, and I was your typical British teenager in the 1950s— rebellious, unfocused, and definitely having (**2**) _____ or no interest in spirituality or religion.

INTERVIEWER: Then what happened?

TENZIN PALMO: Well, when I was 21, and a student at London University, I started to develop (**3**) _____ interest in Eastern

---

[*] _Ani-la,_ a special term that indicates full status as a Tibetan nun.

religions. I had become curious at University about Buddhism in particular, so I went to India on a spiritual quest. It was there I met my guru, my true mentor, Khamtrul Rinpoche. He spoke (4) _____ words in English and had had (5) _____ contact with Westerners.

INTERVIEWER: And then, is it true that within a month you broke up with your boyfriend, a man you had been engaged to for only (6) _____ weeks?

TENZIN PALMO: Uh-huh . . . sad but true. My experience in India transformed me. I shaved my head, put on nun's robes and entered a monastery. I was the only woman among 100 male monks.

INTERVIEWER: Other people had (7) _____ faith that you could endure monastic life longer than a week, but you proved them wrong and stayed there for eight years, right?

TENZIN PALMO: Yes, until I went on my solitary retreat.

INTERVIEWER: Would you describe that retreat?

TENZIN PALMO: Sure. I lived alone as a hermit on a 13,000-foot (3,962-meter) mountain for 13 years. I ate very (8) _____ food, mainly lentils and turnips. I slept upright on a small, wooden meditation box. I survived illness, wolves, freezing storms, even (9) _____ very dangerous avalanches.

INTERVIEWER: (10) _____ people, if any, could have survived not just the physical dangers, but the long periods of solitude. How did you do it?

TENZIN PALMO: I have (**11**) _____ fear of death. The solitude awarded me a sense of infinite time and space.

INTERVIEWER: You have since built a convent school in northern India dedicated to girls, future nuns, who have had (**12**) _____ opportunities for study and spiritual practice.

TENZIN PALMO: Yes, I run the school now and travel widely speaking about the rights of girls to achieve the same status as men in Tibetan Buddhism.

INTERVIEWER: I hope my book will bring you (**13**) _____ publicity and attention for your mission. Thank you, Ani-la, for speaking with me.

TENZIN PALMO: It's been a pleasure. Let's have more tea, OK?

C STYLE: Telling an Anecdote

Everyone loves to hear a good anecdote or short story. Storytelling is one of the oldest, most basic methods for sharing information, knowledge, and experiences. In this short excerpt, the interviewer skillfully encourages William Claassen to share a few of his experiences visiting monasteries around the world.

 1 *Read the questions below, then listen to the excerpt.*

1. What phrase does the interviewer use to encourage Claassen to tell his story?

2. Claassen tells his story frequently using the word *would*. How many times does he use *would*? Keep a tally: _____

3. What purpose does the repetition of *would* serve?

2 *Look at the box on page 140 for other expressions to encourage someone to speak and to tell a story.*

Encouraging someone to tell a story	Telling the story
• (Name), give me an idea of …	• Well, I'll …
• Why don't you talk briefly about …	• I remember when …
• Tell me …	• I don't remember all the details, but …
• I want to draw you out on the subject of …	• Let me begin. What I would do is …
• Tell me about the time you …	• Well, I'll pull in one example of the time …

3 *Prepare and tell an anecdote.*

1. Think of a story about a time you trained for something or disciplined yourself to accomplish a challenge over time.

   Examples: training in martial arts, practicing a musical instrument, preparing for an exam, performing athletics, giving a big presentation

2. Make notes about the experience and give your story a title. Rehearse your story by yourself. Use the "Telling the story" expressions above. Use gestures, and practice good eye contact by looking in the mirror.

3. Work with a partner. Write down the title of your story and give it to your partner. Your partner will encourage you to begin your story using an expression from the left column. Then tell your story using expressions from the right column. When you are done with your story, encourage your partner to tell a story. Listen and take notes. Then tell your partner's story to another person in the class or to the whole class. Keep a tally of the number of times your partner uses the word *would*: _____

D   SPEAKING TOPIC

PREPARATION

Work in a small group. Read the information and case study, which are based on a real story. Then work in a small group, and follow the directions for the speaking activity.

BACKGROUND

Mepkin Abbey, located in the southeastern state of South Carolina, sits on 3,000 acres of beautiful country property. Since 1949, life there has been dedicated to the Trappist monastic traditions of solitude, prayer, work, and community. People on retreat to Mepkin learn the daily routine of the 45 monks who live there. However, retreats are not enough to keep the abbey financially stable. Economic renewal is proposed for the abbey—but will it change a centuries-old way of life?

The Monks' Schedule

3:20 A.M.	Wearing hooded robes, the monks awaken in deep darkness. They gather in the church for two hours of prayer, chanting, singing, and meditation.
5:30 A.M.	The monks greet the new day with more prayer, reading, breakfast, and simple chores.
7:30 A.M.	They return to the church for more prayer.
8:30 A.M.	The monks begin the morning work. Work includes:

- gathering eggs or making organic compost* for sale
- preparing food for the community of monks and guests
- working in the gift shop
- managing the hospitality—answering e-mail, updating the Web site, arranging for guests to visit Mepkin

NOON	Lunch is held in complete silence and is concluded by prayer and a reading.
1:45 P.M.	The monks rest.
3:30 P.M.	They work or study.
6:00 P.M.	They pray, meditate, or walk alone around the grounds.
7:35 P.M.	Closing prayer in the church is followed by sleep.

A New Abbot** Arrives

For many years, Mepkin Abbey was not well known. It is located in an obscure corner of the state notorious for its extreme heat, humidity, and abundance of snakes. The buildings and gardens were not maintained, and the chicken farm was outdated.

After decades of gradual decline, however, a new abbot assumed leadership, and slowly things began to change. First he crafted a mission statement and a business plan. He convinced well-established financial institutions to contribute millions of dollars to Mepkin's renewal efforts. The result was the addition of a new chapel, library, air-conditioned dining room, and sleeping quarters for guests. Famous horticulturists revitalized the gardens, and zoologists humanely managed the snake population.

Mepkin now has more than 15,000 visitors a year who take advantage of its greatest resource: solitude. Its chicken farm generates annual revenues of more than $500,000, producing about 9 million eggs and 270 tons of organic compost. Mepkin recently won an award as the "Best Non-Profit of the Year."

---

* *compost:* a mixture of plants, leaves, etc., used to improve the quality of soil
** *abbot:* a monk in charge of a monastery

The Conflict

The abbot is now proposing another ambitious project, one that will require another $20 million in fundraising. He would like to build a state-of-the-art, revenue-producing, retirement community on Mepkin land. The complex will support Mepkin's own aging community as well as provide limited housing to other elderly people wishing to live the contemplative life. The community will include an apartment building, 30 cottages, and a small health-care clinic with 80 beds.

The abbot's most recent proposal has generated a great deal of debate. A group of monks within the Mepkin community, as well as some residents in the area, feel that no further development should be allowed. Some monks feel that the Abbey is financially stable and should not try to expand. They feel that the fundraising will distract monks from their spiritual activities. These monks, as well as some local residents and farmers, worry that construction and possible over-development will ruin the pristine landscape.

The abbot and another group of monks feel the facility is needed. They believe that it will serve the retired monks and other elderly people, as well as help Mepkin become even better known and attract more visitors. A group of local business owners also supports the expansion because they hope it will bring more tourists and business activity to the area.

SPEAKING ACTIVITY

Divide into two groups: those in favor of a retirement complex (Pro) and those against it (Con). Take on specific roles such as abbot, monk, resident, farmer, or business owner. Discuss your feelings or tell anecdotes from that point of view. List the pros and cons. Debate the issue.

Pro	Con
a. _____	a. _____
b. _____	b. _____
c. _____	c. _____
d. _____	d. _____
e. _____	e. _____

SHARING INFORMATION

Discuss your reactions to the case with the entire class.

E RESEARCH TOPICS

Choose one of the following projects:

1. Work in pairs. Using resources found on the Internet or in the library, find out more about a topic related to monasticism. Take notes. Prepare a 5- to 10-minute presentation on your topic for the class.

   Suggested topics

   - Thomas Merton
   - Tenzin Palmo
   - Mt. Athos
   - Trappist monasteries
   - Buddhist monasteries
   - New Skete monasteries
   - Meditation
   - Fasting

2. Research spiritual retreat centers or monasteries in your areas. Write, call, or visit for more information. Present your findings to the class.

For Unit 6 Internet activities, visit the NorthStar Companion Website at http://www.longman.com/northstar.

Workplace Privacy

1 Focus on the Topic

A PREDICTING

1. Look at the cartoon. The man says he is willing to give up civil liberties in order to gain security. However, he is worried that doing so might mean there will be few civil liberties left. Can you guess what he means by "civil liberties" and "security"?

2. What do you think of when you hear the word *privacy*? What does it mean to you? Brainstorm topics or words that may come up when discussing this issue, such as *snooping*, *confidential*, and *wiretapping*.

B SHARING INFORMATION

In a small group, discuss your answers to the following questions.

1. Our ability to enjoy privacy often depends on the physical nature of the space we inhabit. Think about the home you grew up in and the home you are living in now. How does your sense of privacy compare in the two places? What factors make it easy or difficult to find privacy?

2. Think of different cultures you are familiar with. Comment on how the sense of privacy may differ. Think of home, school, and workplace. How much privacy do people expect? How is privacy protected?

3. When do you feel your privacy is being invaded? For example, would you feel your privacy was being invaded if _____?

   a. an employer opened and read your office mail or e-mail

   b. a colleague looked through your files, either on paper or on computer

   c. someone you just met asked your age, marital status, or salary

C PREPARING TO LISTEN

BACKGROUND

Read the information about workplace privacy.

"At first, it was just the supervisor coming around to take a look. Then they installed the video cameras in the corner of the office to keep watch. Now the boss is tapping our phones to monitor calls. What's next?"

—Scott Trower, computer programmer

Employees

As Scott Trower's comments indicate, Americans have begun to feel that their privacy is being invaded—especially at work. New, more sophisticated technology is being used to check up on, or monitor, people as they do their jobs. Sometimes employers even want to know about how employees spend their leisure time.

Most employees, from production line workers to managers, believe that employers have the right to evaluate the quality of their work. However, they feel that watching over people with cameras, computers, or wiretaps is invasive and unnecessary. Furthermore, trying to control people's off-the-job behavior is clearly wrong.

Employers

Employers argue that they need information about employees in order to make important decisions about quality and safety on the job. Information about employees' physical and psychological health, political preferences, and so on allows employers to give help to those who need it and reward those who are especially productive and healthy.

Moreover, improvements in technology are making it quite simple to obtain information about behavior both on and off the job. Scott Trower's employer did not inform the employees about the new monitoring mechanisms. The devices simply appeared one day.

The Law

In the United States, there are few protections against invasions of privacy. The Fourth Amendment (1791) to the Constitution prevents the government from searching or removing things from one's home without proper permission. The Electronic Communications Privacy Act (ECPA) of 1986 prevents an employer from listening to personal telephone conversations that take place during the work day. However, the act permits monitoring of business calls. The American Civil Liberties Union (ACLU) and other organizations are promoting ways to expand protections for Americans' privacy in the workplace.

Many countries have no laws about workplace privacy; others have some protections. In France, laws forbid the collection of information about an employee's political, religious, or union memberships. In Germany, laws require that every company hire a "privacy" officer whose job is to make sure that only a minimum amount of information is collected. Under Canadian law, employers must tell employees how personal information will be used. Under Swiss law, employers must justify to employees any camera surveillance or monitoring of the workplace. Hong Kong has a Privacy Commissioner for Personal Data to raise awareness of privacy issues for businesses and individuals. In a 2000 survey, the people of Hong Kong ranked privacy the third most important social issue, behind air pollution and unemployment.

The Facts

According to a recent survey of American companies:

- 78 percent monitor employees in some way
- 63 percent monitor Internet use
- 47 percent monitor e-mail use
- 18 percent view employees by video
- 12 percent review phone messages
- 8 percent review voicemail

The Issue

Where should we draw the line between the employer's right to run a business and earn a profit, and the employee's right to privacy? This issue is being hotly debated in the press, on radio talk shows, and in online discussion groups on the Internet.

*Read the following statements about the rights of employers and employees. Next to each statement, write **A** (agree) or **D** (disagree). Then, working in small groups, compare your answers with those of other students. Give reasons to support your opinions.*

An employer should have the right to _____.

_____ **1.** listen in on employees' work-related phone calls *without* telling them

_____ **2.** listen in on employees' work-related phone calls *but* tell the employees

_____ **3.** test employees for drug use if they hold *high-risk positions* such as airplane pilot, police officer, or firefighter

_____ **4.** test employees for drug use if they hold *low-risk positions* such as secretary, teacher, or computer programmer

_____ **5.** videotape employees to monitor performance

_____ **6.** videotape employees to prevent theft of equipment

_____ **7.** videotape employees in rest areas such as locker rooms, employee lounges, and so on

_____ **8.** see employees' health records

_____ **9.** read employees' e-mail or office mail

VOCABULARY FOR COMPREHENSION

Work in groups of four or five. Read aloud the opinions of the callers who phoned in to a radio talk-show program to comment on workplace privacy. Match each underlined word with a similar expression in the list that follows the dialogue.

HOST: Hello. You're on the line with *Talk of the Town*.

CALLER 1:   Hi. I'm Bob from Tallahassee, Florida. I just wanted to say that I have a sneaking suspicion that there's a lot of (**1**) <u>surveillance</u> in our office, but I don't always know when and how it's done. Sometimes our boss scans our office with video cameras to see whether we're doing a good job. I mean, talk about (**2**) <u>Big Brother</u> watching. Snooping into our private lives is really outside the (**3**) <u>scope</u> of responsible business. The thing we need to look at is why companies want to control our lives and restrict our freedom.

HOST :   Thanks, Bob. Now, let's move on to Mary from Minneapolis.

CALLER 2:   Hello. Thanks for taking my call. I love your show. I used to work in a company where they (**4**) <u>kept an eye on</u> the workers constantly. They kept (**5**) <u>a log</u> of all outgoing long-distance and local calls of each employee. In this suspicious atmosphere, it was impossible to have a sense of pride and (**6**) <u>dignity</u> in my work. I felt (**7**) <u>demeaned</u>. I just felt they didn't respect me. My boss had no (**8**) <u>legitimate</u> reason to know whom I called. It was a clear invasion of my privacy. The point I want to make is that employers have gone too far.

HOST :   OK, thank you. Hello, Louis. You're on *Talk of the Town*.

CALLER 3:   Good afternoon. I'm calling from my cell phone on the New Jersey Turnpike. I can't understand what's (**9**) <u>driving</u> this increase in employee monitoring. It's unfair. Employers just (**10**) <u>eavesdrop on</u> employee phone calls whenever they want, listening to both personal and business calls. They also do drug testing (**11**) <u>willy-nilly</u>, without warning, and for no good reason. I mean, you'd have to agree our privacy deserves some (**12**) <u>safeguards</u>.

HOST :   OK. I think we have time for one more call . . . Susan from Little Rock, Arkansas.

CALLER 4:   Hello. Great show! I am the owner of a company that manufactures highly sophisticated computer chips. There's nothing harmful or (**13**) <u>sinister</u> about these monitoring practices. As an employer, I have the right to know how my employees are using their time. On top of that, we have a lot of expensive equipment in our offices. I use the video cameras to (**14**) <u>deter</u> theft. And in addition, my managers and directors use e-mail to handle a great deal of business. I have sophisticated monitoring equipment to check their e-mail to watch for any abusive language or (**15**) <u>racial slurs</u>. This is for the employees' own protection.

_____   **a.** lawful; reasonable

_____   **b.** evil

_____   **c.** true worth and nobleness of character

_____   **d.** watched closely

_____   **e.** listen to secretly

_____   **f.** prevent

_____   **g.** insulted

_____   **h.** the act of watching carefully or secretly

_____   **i.** insulting comments about a person's race

_____   **j.** causing

_____   **k.** unpredictably; without our choosing

_____   **l.** an official written record

_____   **m.** authorities that control people[*]

_____   **n.** protections

_____   **o.** range

[*] ***Big Brother:*** a reference to George Orwell's novel *1984*, in which an all-powerful government controlled the minds and behavior of its citizens

2 Focus on Listening

You will hear an interview from the radio news program *Weekend Saturday* that aired on National Public Radio in the United States. The interviewer, Elaine Korry, reports that secret workplace monitoring has increased dramatically in the United States.

 Work with another student. Make a list of the reasons you think workplace monitoring may be increasing. Then listen to the excerpt to check your predictions.

LISTENING FOR MAIN IDEAS

 Read the following questions. Then listen to Part One of the interview, and write short answers to the questions. Do the same for Parts Two and Three. Compare your answers with those of another student.

Part One

1. How common is it for companies to monitor their employees at work?

_____

2. What warning does Eric Greenberg, of the American Management Association, issue to employees?

_____

3. According to Greenberg, what three things do employers have a right to know?

_____

Part Two

4. According to Larry Finneran, of the National Association of Manufacturers, what are some positive aspects of monitoring?

_____

5. Why does Rebecca Locketz, a lawyer with the American Civil Liberties Union, oppose surveillance?

_____

6. According to Locketz, what two safeguards should employees be entitled to?

_____

Part Three

7. How does the 1986 Electronic Communications Privacy Act safeguard employee privacy?

_____

8. According to some studies, what is the effect of electronic monitoring on worker performance?

_____

LISTENING FOR DETAILS

*Listen to Part One of the interview again. Read the sentences, and write **T** (true) or **F** (false) in the blank. Correct the false statements. Do the same for Parts Two and Three. Then compare your answers with those of another student.*

Part One

_F_ 1. Many attorneys believe that employees ~~should~~ give up *their* privacy rights when they go to work.
      do not

____ 2. One-third of the 900 U.S. companies surveyed said they use surveillance methods to monitor their employees.

____ 3. Greenberg is worried that 25 percent of companies spy on their work force without telling them.

____ 4. In the last five years, the number of employees being monitored has increased by 50 percent.

____ 5. Greenberg thinks workplace surveillance is morally wrong and should be stopped.

____ 6. The U.S. Postal Service monitors the number of pieces of mail delivered correctly.

Part Two

____ 7. The National Association of Manufacturers keeps a log of all employee phone calls for quality control purposes.

_____ 8. Sometimes employers listen in on phone calls to protect employees from sexual harassment and racial slurs.

_____ 9. Employees from the Chevron Corporation sued the company for sexual harassment.

_____ 10. Rebecca Locketz believes there are no legitimate reasons for workplace surveillance.

_____ 11. The ACLU believes that employees don't have to be told when they are being monitored.

Part Three

_____ 12. Few states allow surveillance in private places such as locker rooms or employee lounges.

_____ 13. Under the Electronic Communications Privacy Act (ECPA), an employer cannot eavesdrop on an employee's personal phone calls.

_____ 14. Under the ECPA, an employer cannot monitor the duration of an employee's phone call.

_____ 15. According to attorney Penny Nathan Cahn, many employees are going to court to sue their employers if they think their privacy rights are being violated.

_____ 16. Cahn believes that most juries are not going to be sympathetic, or favorable, toward companies that use surveillance methods without good reason.

REACTING TO THE LISTENING

 1 *Listen to four excerpts from the interview in which the speakers express opinions on the topic of workplace privacy. Decide how strongly these opinions are expressed, and circle N (not very strongly), S (somewhat strongly), or V (very strongly) below the first question in each pair on page 153. Then discuss your answers to the second question with a partner.*

Excerpt One

1. Eric Greenberg warns that employees may be watched at any time. How strongly does Greenberg express his warning?

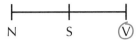

N   S   Ⓥ

2. How do Greenberg's choice of words and tone of voice support your decision?

Choice of words: "Any employee," "anytime."
Tone: Stresses "any," clear and decisive.

Excerpt Two

3. Greenberg suggests that companies are acting like Big Brother when they do performance monitoring. How strongly does he believe this?

N   S   V

4. How does his choice of words support your decision?

Excerpt Three

5. Rebecca Locketz feels it's unnecessary to monitor employees' word processing output. How strongly does she believe this?

N   S   V

6. How do her choice of words and tone of voice support your decision?

Excerpt Four

7. Locketz believes there should be no monitoring in company rest areas. How strongly does Locketz express her opinion?

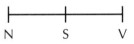

N   S   V

8. How do her choice of words and tone of voice support your decision?

2 *Discuss the following questions with the class.*

1. In your workplace or in workplaces you know, describe the amount and nature of employee monitoring. To what extent does the employer monitor computer, phone, or e-mail use? How do you feel about this?

2. Some workplaces implement surveillance devices (such as video cameras or telephone monitoring) for security reasons. How can companies balance the need for security with the individual's right to privacy? How would you feel about losing some of your privacy for the sake of security?

3. As an employee, how much and what kinds of monitoring would you be comfortable with?

B   LISTENING TWO: *Managers and Employees Speak Out*

You are going to hear several people give their opinions on whether employers should monitor their employees while at work.

 Listen to the four viewpoints on workplace monitoring. Listen again, and complete the chart as you listen. Then share your notes and reactions in small groups.

POSITION	SUPPORTS OR OPPOSES	MAIN ARGUMENT	SUPPORTING ARGUMENTS	YOUR REACTIONS
1. *Owner of small data-processing company*	*Opposes*	*By trusting employees, they will perform better.*	• *Surveillance causes loss of trust and morale.* • *People need freedom.* • *Happy people make happy, productive employees.*	Do you agree or disagree? Explain.
2.				How would you feel if you worked in this law firm?
3.				What's your position on making personal calls at work?
4.				Does an employer have the right to have access to your files and papers on your desk? Explain.

C   LINKING LISTENINGS ONE AND TWO

Work in small groups. Read the scenarios based on real cases involving workplace privacy. Choose Scenario 1 or Scenario 2. Evaluate the case in light of what you've learned in Listenings One and Two, and discuss the questions that follow.

Scenario 1: Is This Job Really Worth It? Pre-Employment Background Check

Matthew Smith applied for a job as a physical education teacher at a small private school in California. Before the interview, the school asked him to sign a form in which Matthew had to agree to:

- a background check by a private investigator
- a credit check by an authorized bank
- interviews with friends and neighbors
- completion of a lengthy, written personality questionnaire on both personal and work-related topics

Matthew is now wondering whether to continue the interview process.

1. Why is Matthew hesitating? What could he be worried about?

2. What could be the school's rationale for conducting this type of interview process?

3. How would you feel in this situation? What would you do? What do you think Matthew should do?

Scenario 2: How Much Stress Is Too Much Stress? On-the-Job Surveillance

Harriet Callas is an airline reservations clerk. She is monitored by:

- a telephone headpiece that records the length of each call
- a computer that tracks her success at booking flights
- a supervisor who makes sure she follows sales procedures

The stress from this monitoring has caused Harriet to develop a panic disorder, a condition that makes her feel anxious and worried most of the time. She is thinking about either leaving her job or organizing her fellow colleagues to complain.

1. What is Harriet's dilemma?

2. What could be the airline's rationale for conducting this form of monitoring?

3. How would you feel in this situation? What would you do? What do you think Harriet should do?

3 Focus on Vocabulary

1 *The online* Privacy Rights Journal *printed information on the Internet about a workplace privacy case at Nissan Motor Corporation. Working with another student, fill in the blanks in the newsletter with the correct form of the following expressions from the box below. Use the cues to help you.*

be all well and good	keep tabs	scope
cheap shot	leave . . . at the door	step up
concede	legitimate	subject to
fine line	morale	think twice about
go that extra mile		

Privacy Rights Journal—*Cyberspace Issue*   Volume 4   Number 2   Page 1

Fact Sheet 27: Bourke v. Nissan Motor Corporation

WATCH OUT! Assume you are being observed in some way in anything that you do or say at your office!

That is the warning that Rhonda Hall and Bonita Bourke should have listened to five years ago. The two women worked as employee trainers at Nissan Motor Corporation. Traveling throughout the United States, they conducted training sessions for car dealers, sales staff, and mechanics. The women were competent, hard-working employees. Their supervisors had often commended them for _____. They
1. (making extra effort)
had handled a great deal of their business-related communication via e-mail. However, they did _____ that at times, "there's
2. (admit)
a(n) _____ between business and personal matters." So,
3. (unclear distinction)

---

occasionally their online communications were chatty and informal,

beyond the _____ of business. They never really
                4. (range)

_____ sharing gossip or complaining about their boss.
5. (considered the problems with)

   Their way of communicating _____ until doubts about
                                    6. (be satisfactory)

the content of their e-mail were raised. Having become suspicious, their

boss uncovered their passwords and began monitoring their e-mail,

which was full of insulting comments about him. Furious and offended,

he immediately _____ his spying: He tapped their
                    7. (increased)

phones and snooped around their offices. For several weeks he

_____ on them.
    8. (observed carefully)

   Then, one day, Ms. Hall and Ms. Bourke were called in and fired. The

news came totally out of the blue. Nissan claimed they were being fired

for poor performance. Bourke and Hall immediately filed a formal

complaint with top management. They said that the supervisor's

surveillance was unfair, that it was "a(n) _____." They
                                                9. (unfair attack)

claimed they had reasonable expectations that their e-mail would not be

_____ monitoring. The women explained that the
    10. (open to)

eavesdropping practices create low _____ among
                                        11. (confidence; pride)

workers: "Workers can't just _____ their pride
                                  12. (forget)

_____ when they come to work," said Bourke.

   Nissan executives defended themselves by maintaining that the

monitoring was _____ because they owned the company
                    13. (lawful; reasonable)

system and the employees' messages were written on company time.

Unwilling to give up, the women sued Nissan Motor Corporation for

invasion of privacy.

2 *Work with a partner. Write the dialogue that may have occurred when Ms. Bourke met with a senior manager at Nissan company headquarters to issue a formal complaint. Refer to the newsletter on pages 156–157. Assume the role of the Nissan manager or Ms. Bourke, and use the directions and vocabulary in the chart below. Then give a dramatic presentation of the dialogue to the class.*

ROLE, DIRECTIONS, VOCABULARY	DIALOGUE
1. Nissan manager: Restate reasons for dismissal. **concede** **go that extra mile** **scope**	Manager:
2. Bourke: Express shock and surprise at monitoring. **keep tabs on** **think twice about** **morale**	Bourke:
3. Nissan manager: State position on e-mail privacy. **be subject to** **step up**	Manager:
4. Bourke: Express anger, and protest policy. **cheap shot** **fine line** **leave at the door**	Bourke:
5. Nissan manager: Restate position more firmly. **that's all well and good** **legitimate**	Manager:

3 *Work in a small group. Discuss what you think happened in the* Bourke v. Nissan *case. After you speculate, refer to page 243 for an explanation.*

4 Focus on Speaking

A PRONUNCIATION: Stress on Two-Syllable Words

Certain two-syllable words are stressed on the first syllable when they are used as nouns and on the last syllable when they are used as verbs.

1 *Listen to the following statements. As you listen, place a stress mark (´) over the stressed syllable of the underlined words. The first pair of statements has been done for you.*

- Companies <u>recórd</u> service calls.

- They keep <u>récords</u> of personal phone calls made by employees.

- The <u>object</u> of installing the surveillance equipment was to create a top-notch security system.

- I don't understand why any employee would or should <u>object</u> to that.

2 *Work with a partner. Take turns reading. Mark the stress (´), and write **N** (noun) or a **V** (verb) after the underlined word. Then listen to the sentences to check your answers.*

1. The ACLU director was shocked by the <u>increase</u> (_____) in monitoring and was afraid that willy-nilly surveillance would continue to <u>increase</u> (_____).

2. We decided to <u>conduct</u> (_____) a comprehensive survey to measure employee <u>conduct</u> (_____).

3. The <u>object</u> (_____) of my presentation is simply to <u>object</u> (_____) to the use of secret surveillance.

4. The boss <u>suspects</u> (_____) that she is the only <u>suspect</u> (_____) in the case involving the stolen computer files.

5. She got a special <u>permit</u> (_____) that would <u>permit</u> (_____) her to see confidential employee information.

6. We all had to keep a special <u>record</u> (_____) in order to <u>record</u> (_____) all personal phone calls.

7. Why do you always <u>insult</u> (_____) me with all those <u>insults</u> (_____)? Just tell me how to fix the mistakes.

8. We're pleased with your <u>progress</u> (_____) in the job so far, but you'll have to <u>progress</u> (_____) even further before getting promoted.

9. As hard as I tried to settle the <u>conflict</u> (_____) with my boss, our opinions continued to <u>conflict</u> (_____) over certain key issues.

10. The company <u>projects</u> (_____) big profits from these <u>projects</u> (_____).

3 *Work with a partner.*

Student A: Cover the right column. Use the cues to form a statement or question. Use the underlined word in the form indicated (verb or noun), being careful to clearly stress the appropriate syllable. An example has been provided.

*Student B: Cover the left column. Listen to the statement or question. Mark the stress (⌐) of the key word. Then decide whether the word was used as a noun or a verb, and write **N** or **V** on the line. Switch roles after statement 5.*

Student A

1. Question: <u>conduct</u> (verb) / survey / computer needs?

   Do you plan to conduct a survey to check the computer needs of the employees?

2. Statement: <u>increase</u> (noun) / theft / employee monitoring.

3. Question: boss / <u>suspect</u> (verb) / bug the phones?

4. Question: <u>insult</u> (verb) / in front of everyone?

5. Statement: make / <u>progress</u> (noun) / protect / privacy.

Now switch roles.

6. Statement: employees / <u>object</u> (verb) / video surveillance / locker rooms.

7. Question: manager / <u>permit</u> (verb) / personal phone calls / company time?

8. Question: boss / keep / <u>record</u> (noun) / long-distance calls / a log?

9. Statement: lawsuit / <u>conflict</u> (verb) / privacy issues.

Student B

1. conduct: ___V___

2. increase: _____

3. suspect: _____

4. insult: _____

5. progress: _____

6. object: _____

7. permit: _____

8. record: _____

9. conflict: _____

B   GRAMMAR: Verb + Gerund or Infinitive—Two Forms, Two Meanings

1 *Examine the sentences, and discuss the questions that follow with a partner.*

- When she found out she was subject to willy-nilly surveillance, she <u>stopped calling</u> her friends during office hours.

- When she realized how late it was, she <u>stopped to call</u> home and said she'd leave the office in ten minutes.

1. What is the difference in meaning of the verb *stop* in the two sentences?

2. What other verbs can be followed by either a gerund or infinitive with a change in meaning?

Verbs Followed by the Gerund or Infinitive with a Change in Meaning

Some verbs must always be followed by a **gerund** (base form of verb + *-ing*). Other verbs must be followed by an **infinitive** (*to* + base form of verb). Others can be followed by either a gerund or an infinitive with *no* change in meaning.

However, certain verbs that can be followed by either a gerund or an infinitive *do* have a change in meaning. Sometimes the difference in meaning is subtle; sometimes it is very obvious. For example, the meanings of the verbs **forget** and **stop** change when they are followed by a gerund or an infinitive.

- He will never **forget having** his calls monitored. The experience was so demeaning. (= recall or remember the experience)

- The manager was fired because he **forgot to have** his staff's phone calls monitored. (= remember to do something)

- She **stopped calling** her friends during office hours. (= stopped the activity of calling)

- When she realized how late she was working, she **stopped to call** home. (= stopped doing something else in order to call)

Some other verbs whose meaning changes when they are followed by gerunds or infinitives are **mean, quit, regret, remember,** and **try**.

2 *Read the sentences. From the context, choose the best meaning of the underlined verb. Write the letter of the appropriate sentence next to the correct definition.*

1. **a.** To improve customer service, the company <u>tried</u> telephone monitoring for six months. Unfortunately it didn't work, so the company gave up.

   b. By increasing surveillance, the company <u>tried</u> to improve customer service.

   _____ experimented with

   _____ intended

2. a. The attorney convinced them to <u>stop</u> monitoring secretly.

   b. Even though he was very busy with his own work, the supervisor would <u>stop</u> to monitor the new employee's calls every few hours.

     _____ finish in order to do something else

     _____ quit

3. a. The experience was extremely demeaning. Even after several years, he couldn't <u>forget</u> having been snooped on all day at his previous job.

   b. She was fired because she would always <u>forget</u> to record her personal calls in the telephone log.

     _____ forget about something unpleasant

     _____ forget to do a task or duty

4. a. In court, he told the judge that he <u>remembered</u> having sent the e-mail message but he didn't remember what was in it.

   b. Before he went home, he <u>remembered</u> to send his colleagues an e-mail message about the project.

     _____ remembered to do something (task or duty)

     _____ recalled

5. a. To some extent, he <u>regretted</u> having to sue his employer because he had worked there for 20 years. But there was no other way to resolve the dispute.

   b. The judge <u>regretted</u> to inform him that the employer has every right to monitor workers.

     _____ regretted to tell someone something or do something

     _____ regretted something that happened in the past

6. a. After three years of being subjected to willy-nilly surveillance, he <u>quit</u> working there.

   b. Things were not going well at her job. Her morale was low, so she <u>quit</u> to travel around the world.

     _____ stopped

     _____ stopped in order to do something else

7. a. The employees knew that their top-secret work <u>meant</u> intense monitoring from the boss.

   b. The bosses <u>meant</u> to monitor only for security.

     _____ intended; planned

     _____ signified; involved

3 *For this role play, work with a partner. Fill in the blanks with the correct words. Then choose roles.*

Student A: You are a television news reporter interviewing a workplace privacy expert on the issue of pre-employment testing and workplace privacy.

Student B: You are Rebecca Locketz, legal director of the Workplace Privacy Project.

Read the dialogue aloud. Listen to each other carefully, look up as much as possible, and say your lines like you mean them. Be dramatic.

Putting Job Seekers to the Test

REPORTER: Thanks for taking the time to speak to me, Ms. Locketz. I've

heard that more and more businesses today are turning to

pre-employment tests to try _____ workers to jobs.
                                        1. (match)

MS. LOCKETZ: No problem. I'm glad to be here. Yes, that's right. The employee-

testing business is booming. Employers are scared. They don't

want to regret _____ the wrong person.
                      2. (hire)

REPORTER: Yes, actually, I remember _____ about Lori
                                              3. (read)

Miller, director of Boeing Aircraft's Child Care Center, a while

ago. Miller had to hire 40 childcare workers in 3 weeks. This

monumental task meant _____ and
                                4. (test)

_____ 200 candidates. Do you know this story?
   5. (interview)

MS. LOCKETZ: Yes, I do. I spoke to Miller at that time. She said the test was meant

_____ her with insight into the candidates. She
      6. (provide)

worried she would forget _____ certain questions.
                                7. (ask)

REPORTER: Uh-huh, that's right. The test really simplified the hiring process.

She didn't have to remember _____ specific
                                        8. (question)

details about the applicant's background.

MS. LOCKETZ: Exactly. In Miller's case, the tests were used fairly. However, in

some cases, pre-employment testing violates workers' privacy

rights. So, our organization is now trying _____
                                                9. (make)

tests legal.

REPORTER: Are you suggesting employers stop _____ the tests
              10. (administer)
              completely?

MS. LOCKETZ: No. You misunderstood me. What I am suggesting is that they

              stop _____ the tests willy-nilly and
                   11. (use)
              _____ highly personal and inappropriate questions.
              12. (ask)

REPORTER: So, would you suggest that applicants simply quit

              _____ the pre-employment test if certain
              13. (take)
              questions make them feel uncomfortable?

MS. LOCKETZ: Absolutely. If they don't, I guarantee they will soon regret

              _____ information that could later be used
              14. (reveal)
              against them. These tests are an invasion of privacy.

REPORTER: Yes, thanks for the information, Ms. Locketz. We appreciate
              your taking the time to be on our show today.

MS. LOCKETZ: My pleasure.

C   STYLE: Framing an Argument

Speakers use special expressions to introduce their main ideas and to frame or
focus their key arguments. Framing your argument makes it stronger and more
sophisticated. Here are some examples from Listening Two. Notice that these
expressions are more interesting than "I think . . ." or "In my opinion . . ."

- <u>The real question is</u>, if we're not doing anything wrong, what do we have
  to worry about?

- <u>I mean, you would have to agree that</u> when you're in the office, you're not
  conducting your private life.

- <u>The point I want to make</u> has to do with trust.

- <u>Let me just pose a question here</u>: Isn't it a fact that we all take work home
  once in a while?

Other interesting phrases used to frame an argument are:

- <u>I would say specifically that</u> most employees have no idea their bosses are
  snooping on them.

- <u>The thing we need to look at is</u> the fact that balancing privacy and
  security is really a delicate matter.

Work with a partner.

Student A: Cover the right column. Ask Student B the question.

Student B: Cover the left column. Answer Student A's question. Argue your point, using the cues listed. Add your own ideas. Using several of the expressions on page 164, frame your argument. Then switch roles after question 3.

Student A

1. Should employers have the right to snoop into employees' e-mail?

2. Should employers have the right to monitor employees' off-the-job activities such as smoking, drinking, and engaging in dangerous hobbies like skydiving?

3. Should employers be allowed to have employees wear an "active badge," a small electronic card that is clipped onto the employees' clothing to keep track of their movements?

Now switch roles.

4. Should employers be allowed to install computer software that enables them to monitor employees' computer work?

5. Should employers do legitimate monitoring?

Student B

1. Of course. E-mail _____.
   - systems belong to the company
   - monitoring discourages gossip
   - is really like a postcard

   I would say specifically that e-mail systems belong to the company. I wouldn't care if my boss snooped in my e-mail. I have nothing to hide, anyway. If we all know that our e-mail may be read, we wouldn't be likely to gossip or write love letters. I mean, you would have to agree that e-mail messages are really just like postcards.

2. Definitely. These activities _____.
   - affect the health of the employees
   - cause employees to miss work
   - lead to high insurance rates

3. Sure. Why not? The badge will _____.
   - allow workers to use time better
   - tell supervisors where an employee is at all times
   - eliminate the need to look for workers if necessary

4. I don't think so. Electronic searches create an atmosphere of _____.
   - Big Brother is watching
   - mistrust and fear
   - stress

5. Absolutely. It's necessary to _____.
   - deter theft
   - control quality
   - enhance profits

D   SPEAKING TOPIC

 Listen to a recording of an interview about the Employee Monitoring Law that recently appeared in the Star Daily *newspaper. Then refer to the transcript below as you prepare a debate.*

BIG BROTHER IS WATCHING YOU!
A new Illinois law permits employers to listen in on workers' phones. Watch what you say!

Star Daily Reporter Ann Riley interviews the governor of Illinois to find the truth behind this controversial new law.

Riley: Governor, I appreciate your taking the time to meet with me.

Governor: My pleasure.

Riley: The employee monitoring law has received a great deal of media attention recently. However, many Illinois citizens are still very confused. What exactly does the new law allow?

Governor: This law permits employers to listen in on their workers' phone conversations. The law permits any listening that serves educational, training, or research purposes. It allows for both computer and phone monitoring.

Riley: How did this law come about?

Governor: Well, it was originally conceived by the telemarketing industry. This industry, which uses the telephone to sell its products and services, needed a way to monitor its employees' sales performance. The retail industry is also a big proponent of the law. Recently, I spoke with the president of the Illinois Retail Merchants Association. He told me the law is helping to make sure that Mrs. Smith gets the red dress in size 6 rather than size 16, which may have been entered into the computer by mistake.

Riley: So, in other words, the law is meant to monitor the quality of customer service calls.

Governor: Yes, for courtesy, efficiency, and overall service.

Riley: Well then, why all the opposition? I hear many groups—from labor unions to the ACLU—are clearly furious about this law.

Governor: Yes, I know. Our office has been flooded with calls and letters. The problem is, the law does not specify whether or not employers must tell employees each time they are being monitored, or just issue a one-time blanket warning. Also, only one person must agree to the monitoring, but the law does not state who must agree—the employee or the supervisor. The scope of the law is so broad that some people find it frightening.

Riley: Yes, it sounds like there are many unanswered questions. I appreciate your speaking with me, Governor. Thank you very much.

Governor: You're welcome.

DEBATE PROCEDURE

1. Divide into two teams, and debate the controversial Illinois law.

   Team A: As telemarketing and retail representatives, you support the law.
   Team B: As ACLU and union representatives, you oppose the law.

2. Working in your teams, analyze the interview for arguments. Add additional arguments, using information from the entire unit.

   Team A: Supporters of the Law
   necessary for quality control

   _____

   _____

   Team B: Opponents of the Law
   invasion of privacy

   _____

   _____

3. Start the debate.

   a. Make an opening statement.

   b. Take turns presenting arguments.

   c. Frame your arguments, using expressions from the Style section on page 164. Try to use the gerunds and infinitives from the Grammar section on page 161.

E   RESEARCH TOPIC

As a roving reporter, you will ask several people their opinions on the topic of workplace privacy. Follow the steps outlined below to conduct your interviews and prepare your summary.

Step 1: Choose two different workplaces, and try to arrange interviews with both employees and employers. If you cannot, interview people you know who work or run businesses.

Step 2: Working with another student, brainstorm a list of questions to use in your short interviews. Here are some questions you may want to include.

   • Are you aware of any monitoring practices done in your company?

   • Does your company have a privacy policy? If so, what is it?

   • Do you think employers have the right to bug the phones?

Step 3:   Practice the following introduction. Then conduct your short interviews. Try to talk to both employers and employees.

Excuse me. I'm doing a brief survey for my English class on the topic of workplace privacy. Could I ask you a few questions?

Step 4:   While you interview, take notes on the answers to your questions.

Step 5:   Present a summary of your findings to the class.

For Unit 7 Internet activities, visit the NorthStar Companion Website at http://www.longman.com/northstar.

Warriors without Weapons

TODAY THERE ARE 4 GENEVA CONVENTIONS
THEY PROTECT :

THE WOUNDED AND SICK
IN THE FIELD

THE WOUNDED, SICK AND
SHIPWRECKED AT SEA

PRISONERS OF WAR

CIVILIANS IN TIME
OF ARMED CONFLICT

1 Focus on the Topic

A PREDICTING

1. Work in a small group, and look at the sequence of drawings and the title of the unit. What do you know about the International Committee of the Red Cross (ICRC) or local Red Cross organizations? What do you think the Geneva Conventions might be?

2. ICRC volunteers have been referred to as *warriors without weapons*, or *unarmed warriors*. In your group, discuss why you think they are referred to in this way.

B SHARING INFORMATION

Work with a partner. Check (✓) whether you have had any of the following experiences. Then discuss your experiences.

Have you ever _____?

_____ **a.** done volunteer work

_____ **b.** given or received first aid (temporary medical treatment given in an emergency)

_____ **c.** witnessed or experienced a natural disaster such as fire, flood, famine, earthquake, hurricane, typhoon, tornado, or volcano

_____ **d.** fought in a war or lived in a country during wartime

C PREPARING TO LISTEN

BACKGROUND

1 *Read the information. Then take the quiz that follows to see what facts and figures you can guess about the International Committee of the Red Cross (ICRC). Circle the letter of each appropriate answer, and then check your answers on page 243.*

Almost everyone recognizes the symbol of the ICRC. It looks like the Swiss flag. Although the Red Cross was started by a Swiss citizen, and its headquarters are in Geneva, the organization has no official ties to Switzerland. It is not related to the United Nations (UN), either. It is a completely independent organization which is funded by donations from public and private agencies and from governments. The ICRC is also the oldest humanitarian relief organization in the world.

Symbol of the ICRC

Have you ever given blood or taken swimming lessons through a Red Cross–sponsored program? These are the best-known peacetime activities of the organization. The Red Cross also aids refugees and victims of such natural disasters as floods, fires, and famines.

Much more controversial are the Red Cross's activities during wartime. Unlike most relief organizations, the ICRC helps the wounded and sick on both sides of an armed conflict. Red Cross relief workers are dedicated to neutrality. Also, they believe that war cannot be abolished, but it can be controlled. To civilize conflict, they promote the Geneva Conventions (1949), which are international agreements, or laws of war, that protect prisoners of war, wounded soldiers, and civilians.

Other humanitarian relief organizations disagree with the Red Cross's position. Instead of promoting the neutrality principle and the laws of war, these human rights organizations promote the UN's Universal Declaration of Human Rights (1948). If people's human rights are violated—as in torture, slavery, or lack of freedom of speech or religion—then these human rights organizations do not remain neutral. Instead, they denounce the abusers and help the victims. Among the best known of the human rights organizations are Amnesty International, Doctors Without Borders, and Human Rights Watch.

Facts and Figures about the ICRC

1. In about how many countries around the world are ICRC volunteers working?
   a. 30
   b. 80
   c. 150

2. Which of the following activities would the ICRC *not* do?
   a. carry out clean water programs
   b. remove land mines (explosive devices hidden underground)
   c. organize a protest for equal rights for women

3. ICRC workers are *not* involved in teaching _____.
   a. health care
   b. agriculture
   c. English

4. Who can become an ICRC relief worker?
   a. only single men between the ages of 25 and 35
   b. single men and women between 25 and 35
   c. single or married men and women between 25 and 45

5. Each year, ICRC volunteers visit approximately _____ prisoners of war.
   a. 300,000
   b. 500,000
   c. 700,000

6. The ICRC reunites family members separated by war. In a recent 18-month period, the ICRC reunited _____ families.
   a. 160
   b. 1,600
   c. 16,000

7. The ICRC forwards messages to family members who may be separated as a result of war or other disasters. Yearly, approximately _____ messages were sent.
   a. 400
   b. 40,000
   c. 400,000

2 *Think about the information in the reading and the quiz. Then, working with a partner, complete the following sentences:*

   1. I was surprised to find out that . . .

   2. The information that interested me most was . . .

   3. I would now like to learn more about . . .

VOCABULARY FOR COMPREHENSION

Read the passage. Then, working with a partner, match each underlined word in the passage to the synonym or definition on page 173.

Jean-Henri Dunant

In 1864, the wealthy Swiss businessman Jean-Henri Dunant wanted to create an international volunteer organization to care for the wounded on both sides of a battle. He wanted an international agreement that would give protection and (1) <u>legitimacy</u> to these tireless volunteers. Dunant had been inspired by the (2) <u>devastating</u> scene of thousands of dead Austrian and French soldiers in a (3) <u>volatile</u> regional conflict of the time. He witnessed firsthand the horrific battlefield: bloody corpses, severed body parts, and wounded and dead horses. Shocked by the (4) <u>barbarism and savagery</u> he had witnessed, Dunant wrote a book in which he explained his ideals.

With his influence, Dunant persuaded the Swiss government to organize an international meeting to discuss his proposals. In 1864, representatives of 12 governments met and (5) <u>ratified</u> an agreement. It was the first version of the Geneva Conventions, or the "rules of war." As the first attempt to (6) <u>institutionalize</u> guidelines for wartime behavior, it was the beginning of the modern humanitarian law movement.

Dunant's ideas were controversial then, just as they are today. Some people thought his beliefs were (7) <u>counterintuitive</u>, going against a natural way of thinking. Critics did not believe that (8) <u>codes</u>, or laws of war, could help

Red Cross Volunteers on Nineteenth-Century Battlefield

(9) <u>restrain</u> soldiers during conflicts. Yet Dunant argued that these laws are basic (10) <u>human universals</u>, with roots in every culture.

The original 1864 Conventions (11) <u>prevailed</u> until 1949, when four more were added. One of these requires the (12) <u>sparing</u> of civilian lives during wartime. Now more than 180 countries (13) <u>subscribe</u> to the Geneva Conventions. The Red Cross devotes a great deal of effort to (14) <u>disseminating</u> information about the conventions.

_____ **a.** likely to explode; tense

_____ **b.** communicating widely

_____ **c.** rules

_____ **d.** signed; officially approved

_____ **e.** saving

_____ **f.** support and follow

_____ **g.** moral and legal acceptability

_____ **h.** existed; lasted

_____ **i.** values shared by all human beings

_____ **j.** completely destructive

_____ **k.** cruel and extremely violent behavior

_____ **l.** make generally acceptable; establish

_____ **m.** control

_____ **n.** illogical; unexpected

2 Focus on Listening

A LISTENING ONE: *Warriors without Weapons*

You will hear an interview from a radio news program, *Fresh Air with Terry Gross,* that aired on National Public Radio in the United States. Terry Gross interviews Michael Ignatieff, author of a magazine article, "Unarmed Warriors," and a book, *The Warrior's Honor.*

Working with a partner, predict what topics Ignatieff might deal with in his article. Make a list of the topics. Then listen to Terry Gross's introduction to check your predictions.

_____   _____

_____   _____

LISTENING FOR MAIN IDEAS

 Look at the following key phrases. Then listen to Part One of the interview. When you hear the key phrases, add information about these topics. Do the same for Parts Two and Three. Share your notes with a partner.

Part One

1. volatile regional wars: *how war is changing—what that means for relief workers*

2. controversies: _____

_____

3. two traditions in the humanitarian movement: _____

_____

Part Two

4. Geneva Conventions: _____

_____

5. the Gulf War, for example: _____

_____

6. standards of decency: _____

_____

Part Three

7. warrior tradition: _____

_____

8. men have to be trained: _____

_____

9. war and morality: _____

_____

10. warrior's honor: _____

_____

LISTENING FOR DETAILS

 Read the statements below. Then listen to each part of the interview, and circle the letter of the correct answer. Compare your answers with those of another student.

Part One

1. Ignatieff reported on the safety of _____.
   a. Red Cross workers
   b. regional armies
   c. civilians in war zones

2. Ignatieff wrote about the Red Cross because he wanted to _____ humanitarian relief work.
   a. understand
   b. get involved in
   c. recruit volunteers for

3. The tradition of the "laws of war" and the tradition of "international human rights" are _____.
   a. the same
   b. slightly different
   c. very different

4. The humanitarian movement does *not* include _____.
   a. laws of war
   b. human rights
   c. workers' rights

5. The Red Cross wants to enforce the "laws of war tradition," which means that the Red Cross _____.
   a. opposes war
   b. accepts war if fought with rules
   c. accepts only traditional war

Part Two

6. The Geneva Conventions have been ratified by _____ countries.
   a. 100
   b. more than 100
   c. fewer than 100

7. The Geneva Conventions do not protect _____.
   a. combatants who are not injured
   b. prisoners of war
   c. civilians

8. During the first Gulf War, the United States _____ the Geneva Conventions.
   a. did not follow
   b. followed
   c. questioned

9. Ignatieff refers to human universal values, which he believes you can find in _____.
   a. only European cultures
   b. all cultures
   c. only cultures with warrior traditions

10. To educate people about the Geneva Conventions, the Red Cross uses many methods. One thing it does *not* do is _____.
   a. tell the story in comic books
   b. read the Conventions on the radio
   c. translate the Conventions into many languages

Part Three

11. According to Ignatieff, in all societies the warrior's primary responsibility is to protect his _____.
   a. community
   b. traditions
   c. honor

12. In the tradition of warrior's honor, warriors are trained to _____.
   a. wound, not kill
   b. kill aggressively
   c. kill selectively

13. According to Ignatieff, many people in the modern world think war is _____ moral.
   a. sometimes
   b. never
   c. always

14. The warrior's honor is one of the oldest moral traditions in the world. The Red Cross wants to use this tradition to get combatants to _____.
   a. stop fighting completely
   b. fight with honor
   c. fight with control

REACTING TO THE LISTENING

 1 *Read the questions. Then listen to the excerpts from the interview with Terry Gross, where Michael Ignatieff speaks about complex, abstract ideas such as war, warriors' honor, and human rights. Focus on the meaning of these concepts. Discuss the questions that follow with a partner, and share your own ideas about war and human rights.*

Excerpt One

1. What does Ignatieff mean by the "tradition [of] international human rights"?

2. Why does he think most Americans can identify with the tradition of international human rights?

Excerpt Two

3. What are examples of "standards of decency" that should be followed during war?

4. What are some examples of human universals that exist in every culture?

Excerpt Three

5. What is Ignatieff's attitude toward the work of the Red Cross? How do you think he feels about their position? How do you know? What words does he use to indicate his viewpoint?

6. How can elements of the "warrior's honor" restrain people in war?

2 *In the interview, Ignatieff discusses important controversies surrounding the ICRC. Recall the issues he discusses. Then read the statements below, and decide whether you agree or disagree. Write **A** (agree) or **D** (disagree) next to each statement. Then, working in small groups, discuss the reasons for your answers.*

_____ 1. In order to do his or her job, a relief worker cannot take sides in a conflict.

_____ 2. War involves killing. Killing is morally wrong. Therefore, war cannot be made civilized by any codes.

_____ 3. The Geneva Conventions sound good on paper; however, they are impossible to enforce. A soldier's aggression cannot be restrained, controlled, or disciplined.

_____ 4. The ICRC should be working toward abolishing war, not civilizing it.

_____ 5. "War should always be waged with a view to peace."
—seventeenth-century Dutch scholar and diplomat, Hugo de Groot

B LISTENING TWO: *Michael Ignatieff's Views on War*

Listening Two is from the second part of Terry Gross's interview with Michael Ignatieff. Here Ignatieff discusses the ways in which his study of the ICRC affected his views on war.

 *Listen to four more excerpts from the interview. As you listen, mark **T** (true) or **F** (false) next to each statement. Then compare your answers with those of another student.*

Part One

Michael Ignatieff _____.

_____ 1. protested against the Vietnam War during the 1960s

_____ 2. was drafted into the Vietnam War

_____ 3. changed his views on war after witnessing the Red Cross in action

Part Two

In the Red Cross's approach, Ignatieff discovered that war _____.

_____ **4.** is necessary to human culture

_____ **5.** is never a good way to solve conflicts

_____ **6.** can sometimes free oppressed people

Part Three

The rules that the Red Cross enforces are that armies must not _____.

_____ **7.** capture prisoners   _____ **9.** kill anyone

_____ **8.** shoot at civilians   _____ **10.** torture prisoners

Part Four

Michael Ignatieff believes that the Red Cross's rules of war are _____.

_____ **11.** too simple and unrealistic

_____ **12.** barbaric because war itself is barbaric

_____ **13.** moral

C LINKING LISTENINGS ONE AND TWO

Working in a small group, discuss the answers to these questions.

1. The ICRC strictly adheres to the principle of absolute neutrality. It takes no sides in a conflict; it makes no judgments, and its sole concern is the welfare of war's victims. On the other hand, Doctors without Borders, another international human rights organization, will not assist countries or groups that violate basic human rights. If you were going to join one of these groups, which would you join and why? Discuss your reasons for your decision.

2. Should the ICRC be involved in helping both sides of a terrorist conflict?

3. Can people be taught about the "rules of war" through comic books and radio soap operas? What would be another effective means of education?

4. What would motivate someone to join the ICRC? What qualities, experience, background, or education do you think a new recruit should have? To check your guesses, go to www.icrc.org, and look for information about jobs with the ICRC.

5. Doctors Without Borders does not adhere to the position of neutrality. Dr. James Orbinski, former head of that organization, said, "We don't know for sure whether words save lives, but we know for sure that silence kills." What does this mean? Do you agree or disagree? Support your ideas with specific examples.

3 Focus on Vocabulary

1 *Read the following statements, and then read about confusing pairs of words.*

- "There's a distinction between war and barbarism. And we should keep to that distinction and struggle to <u>ensure</u> it, and that's what the Red Cross tries to do."—Michael Ignatieff

- The Red Cross volunteer <u>assured</u> the families that food and water would be coming soon.

Ensure and **assure** are words that are often confused. To *ensure* means to make sure or certain that something happens. To *assure* means to tell someone that something will happen to lessen their worries.

 Here are some other confusing pairs. Some differ in pronunciation; others do not. Listen to the pairs, and repeat each one.

1. accept/except	6. council/counsel
2. access/excess	7. disinterested/uninterested
3. advice/advise	8. eminent/imminent
4. affect/effect	9. imply/infer
5. assure/ensure	10. principal/principle

2 *Read the sentences. From the context, identify the meaning of each underlined word. Then write the letter of the appropriate sentence next to each definition.*

1. **a.** The volunteer <u>advised</u> his friend not to go into that volatile war zone.
   b. Although she felt she should have gone onto the battlefield, she took her colleague's <u>advice</u> and her life was spared.

   _____ an opinion about what someone should or shouldn't do

   _____ give an opinion about what someone should or shouldn't do

2. **a.** Red Cross workers must <u>accept</u> the ICRC's position of neutrality.
   b. Some people support all the ICRC's ideas <u>except</u> the principle of neutrality.
   c. Jean-Henri Dunant, founder of the ICRC, <u>accepted</u> the Nobel Peace Prize in 1901.

   _____ apart from

   _____ receive

   _____ agree to

3. a. According to the Geneva Conventions, the ICRC must remain a
      <u>disinterested</u> group in any conflict.
   b. In law school, she was <u>uninterested</u> in studying international codes of law.

   _____ impartial

   _____ not curious about

4. a. The <u>principal</u> reason that Ignatieff wrote about the ICRC was to
      understand its controversial position on neutrality.
   b. The ICRC is based on universal human <u>principles</u>.
   c. The <u>principal</u> insisted that all the teachers in the school receive some basic
      first aid training.

   _____ beliefs

   _____ main

   _____ director of a school

5. a. The aid workers had no <u>access</u> to that volatile zone because it was
      blocked by soldiers.
   b. Civilians and aid workers are thrilled to receive any <u>excess</u> food or
      medical supplies.

   _____ additional; extra

   _____ way to enter

6. a. The ICRC has a duty to <u>ensure</u> respect for international humanitarian law.
   b. The president <u>assured</u> the ICRC that the Geneva Conventions would
      prevail.

   _____ make sure or certain that something happens

   _____ tell someone something to lessen their worries

7. a. Ignatieff <u>implies</u> that he has become wiser since his antiwar days.
   b. From the interview, we can <u>infer</u> details about Ignatieff's past.

   _____ form an opinion; derive meaning

   _____ suggest indirectly

8. a. The original ICRC consisted of a small <u>council</u> of five Swiss citizens.
   b. The ICRC volunteer <u>counseled</u> the civilians not to drink the water until
      the wells were cleaned.
   c. The prisoner of war asked for some legal <u>counsel</u>.

   _____ give an opinion

   _____ opinion

   _____ official group

9. **a.** Traveling in war zones <u>affected</u> Ignatieff's views on war.

b. He didn't realize that the experience would <u>effect</u> such a huge change in his thinking.

c. Critics believe that the Geneva Conventions will have little <u>effect</u> on the conduct of warfare in the twenty-first century.

_____ influence

_____ cause to happen

_____ consequence

10. **a.** On October 15, 1999, the <u>eminent</u> director of Doctors Without Borders, Dr. James Orbinski, accepted the Nobel Peace Prize on behalf of his organization.

b. Once the terrorists attacked the water-treatment plant, everyone in the region knew that war was <u>imminent</u>.

_____ threatening to happen soon

_____ outstanding

3 *Work with a partner.*

Student A: Ask Student B a question. Check Student B's answer by referring to the correct answer in the parentheses.

Student B: Cover the left column. Answer Student A's question using the cues provided. Choose the correct form of the word provided. Spell it if necessary. Add additional words to the cues when necessary. Then switch roles after question 5.

Student A

1. I heard you got typhoid shots before you went to Africa. How did you react to them?
(Fine. They didn't affect me at all.)

2. What did your parents call you about?
(They advised me not to go into that volatile war zone.)

3. What did the Red Cross workers tell the civilians?
(They counseled them to stay inside until further notice.)

4. What drew you to the ICRC?
(I respected the principle of neutrality.)

Student B

1. Fine. They didn't (affect/effect) me at all.

2. They (advice/advise) me not to go into that volatile war zone.

3. They (council/counsel) them to stay inside until further notice.

4. I respected the (principal/principle) of neutrality.

5. Did you hear about the demonstrations planned by Doctors Without Borders and UNICEF*?
(Yes. I heard the protest against women's rights violations was imminent. It will happen tomorrow.)

5. Yes. I heard the protest against women's rights violations was (imminent/eminent). It will happen tomorrow.

Now switch roles

6. Did she take sides in the negotiations?
(Absolutely not. She remained disinterested.)

6. Absolutely not. She remained (disinterested/uninterested).

7. Have you completed all the necessary first aid training?
(I finished everything except the part about treating a snake bite.)

7. I finished everything (accept/except) the part about treating a snake bite.

8. Why was the reporter angry?
(He couldn't get access to the ICRC files. They were top secret!)

8. He couldn't get (excess/access) to the ICRC files. They were top secret!

9. Did you understand Ignatieff's point about warriors?
(Yes. He implied that every culture has a warrior tradition that restrains soldiers during war.)

9. Yes. He (infer/imply) that every culture has a warrior tradition that restrains soldiers during war.

10. What did the Red Cross worker tell the prisoner of war?
(He assured him that his message would be delivered.)

10. He (ensure/assure) him that his message would be delivered.

4 *Read the open letter that Dr. Sandra Martino wrote to the* Star Daily. *A physician with the ICRC, Dr. Martino has been working in Africa for the past three months. After you read the letter, match each underlined word with a synonym or definition.*

---

* *UNICEF:* acronym for United Nations International Children's Emergency Fund.

To the Editor:

For years, I had been **(1)** <u>drawn</u> to the idea of doing relief work. So, last year, after receiving my medical degree, I joined the International Committee of the Red Cross.

As I had grown up in a wealthy San Francisco suburb, I wondered whether I could do the job. Could I truly relate to and **(2)** <u>identify</u> with the **(3)** <u>devastating</u> misery of victims in war-torn regions? I questioned my ability to **(4)** <u>do without</u> the comforts of home and family that I took for granted. But more important, could I truly **(5)** <u>live by</u> the principles of the ICRC, especially the principle of neutrality?

My parents were firmly opposed to my decision to join the ICRC. My father had been a **(6)** <u>draft evader</u> and had participated in many antiwar demonstrations in Berkeley, California, during the 1960s. Raised as a pacifist, my mother has always **(7)** <u>equated</u> war with barbarism and believes that war has no **(8)** <u>legitimacy</u> whatsoever.

My parents had advised me to join the group Doctors without Borders, a human rights group which provides medical relief to populations in **(9)** <u>volatile</u> war zones. Unlike the ICRC, Doctors without Borders takes a firm position against those that **(10)** <u>unleash</u> aggression and hostility against innocents. Doctors without Borders does not claim to remain neutral at all times.

However, I had studied the ICRC and the Geneva Conventions in college and was fascinated by the **(11)** <u>alternative ethic</u> of neutrality. What I'd like to **(12)** <u>get at</u> here is that the Red Cross is trying to remind people that we all share one moral tradition: the warrior's honor. In other words, "warriors" in all human societies must be trained to **(13)** <u>tame</u> and discipline their aggression. The **(14)** <u>codes</u> of the ICRC, the Geneva Conventions, are really simply **(15)** <u>house-and-garden</u> rules that remind people to follow the tradition of the warrior's honor.

In the ICRC, my role is not only to provide medical services, but also to **(16)** <u>disseminate</u> information in a clear, meaningful way. It's important that people all over the world be aware of the valuable work of the ICRC.

Sandra Martino, M.D.

_____ **a.** potentially violent

_____ **b.** follow

_____ **c.** express

_____ **d.** rules

_____ **e.** completely destructive

_____ **f.** attracted

_____ **g.** release

_____ **h.** understand

_____ **i.** live without

_____ **j.** legal acceptability

_____ **k.** distribute; spread

_____ **l.** common-sense

_____ **m.** different moral principle

_____ **n.** strongly associated

_____ **o.** someone who illegally avoids the military

_____ **p.** control

5 *Another* Star Daily *reader, Dr. David Chan, responded "on air" to Dr. Martino's letter in a radio call-in show. Work with a partner.*

Student A: Read the first half of Dr. Chan's "on-air" letter to your partner. Pause or say "blank" when you come to a blank space. Wait for your partner to fill in the missing word. Check Student B's answers with the correct answer in parentheses. Give your partner a hint if necessary.

Student B: Cover the letter. Listen to Student A, and fill in the on-air letter as Student A reads it. Choose from the words in the box. Then switch roles after the first half of the letter.

Student A

Student B

To the Editor

I would like to respond to Martino's comments from a different perspective. As a physician working for the organization Doctors Without Borders, I too have seen the _____ (devastating) effects of war going on in _____ (volatile) war zones. I agree with the ICRC in that soldiers must try to obey "_____ (codes) of honor," or rules of war. I do not _____ (equate) war with _____ (barbarism) and savagery. However, we members of Doctors Without Borders disagree with the ICRC in an important way.

barbarism
codes
devastating
equate
volatile

Now switch roles, and continue reading the letter.

We do not believe that a soldier's aggression can always be _____ (tamed) and controlled, since war by its nature _____ (unleashes) instincts and behavior that cannot always be restrained. It's simply unrealistic to think that soldiers will always _____ (live by) "rules of war," simple _____ (house-and-garden) rules that tell them how to behave. War is much more than that. We do not hesitate to denounce human rights violations. We do much more than just _____ (disseminate) basic health-care information or bandage up the wounded. As doctors, there are times when we cannot and will not be neutral.

disseminate
house-and-garden
live by
tamed
unleashes

4 Focus on Speaking

A | PRONUNCIATION: Vowels /æ/—/ɑ/—/ə/

 1 *Look at the diagrams of the mouth, and listen to the words.*

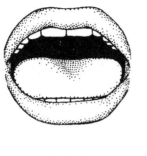   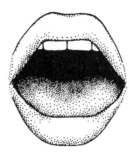   

/æ/ c<u>a</u>t   /ɑ/ c<u>o</u>t   /ə/ c<u>u</u>t

Your mouth is open.   Your mouth is open wide.   Your mouth is almost closed.

Your lips are spread.   Your lips are not spread.   Your lips are not spread.

 2 *Listen to the words, and repeat them.*

	/æ/	/ɑ/	/ə/
1.	cat	cot	cut
2.	cap	cop	cup
3.	lack	lock	luck
4.	Nat	not	nut
5.	hat	hot	hut
6.	lag	lock	lug

 3 *Listen to the words from Exercise 2 above, and circle the words that you hear.*

4 *Work in pairs.*

1. Choose a set of words from Exercise 2, and say them to your partner. Your partner will check the shape of your mouth with the diagrams at the top of the page.

2. Say any word from Exercise 2. Your partner will point to the word. Then switch roles.

5 *Listen, and repeat the phrases. Then, working with a partner, write the phrase under the correct vowel pattern in the chart below.*

government funding	gun shots	a practical discovery
public controversy	a bloody struggle	love of country
natural disasters	floods and famines	a challenging task
cultural values	a bloody battle	a tough job
lack of money	savage attack	combatants' conduct

Vowel Patterns

CUP–CUP /ə/ – /ə/	CAP-CAP /æ/ – /æ/	CUP–COP /ə/ – /ɑ/	CUP–CAP /ə/ – /æ/	CAP–CUP /æ/ – /ə/
government funding				

6 *A tongue twister is a phrase with many similar sounds that is difficult to say quickly. Listen to these tongue twisters. Practice saying them as quickly as possible.*

1. A block from the gun battle, the cops found a black bottle full of gasoline.

2. A lack of love and trust made him lock the clock in the closet.

3. Nat did not eat the nuts.

4. The big black bug bled black blood.

B GRAMMAR: Direct and Indirect Speech

1 *Examine this passage, which includes both direct and indirect speech. Then answer the questions that follow.*

The interviewer Terry Gross asked Michael Ignatieff why he wanted to write about the ICRC. He replied, "As a group I was very drawn to them because I thought they could take me into the whole world of what involves people into that kind of humanitarian relief work." Terry wondered if he had always believed in the ICRC's principle of neutrality. He responded, "I was very involved in the anti-Vietnam protests that were centered in Toronto during the '60's."

1. Why do you think some of the statements have quotation marks and some do not?

2. What do you think are some of the differences between the direct quotations and the other statements?

Direct and Indirect Speech

To add variety and interest when you tell a story or report information, use a combination of direct and indirect speech. **Direct speech** is a quotation of someone's exact words. **Indirect speech** reports or tells what someone said without using the person's exact words. When you use indirect speech, try to vary the reporting verbs. Choose expressive verbs such as *complain, mention, remark, answer, reply, predict, deny, explain, wonder, question, add, respond, comment, observe,* and *continue*.

To Change	Direct Speech ⟶	Indirect Speech
Statements		
Shift tense back (for example, from past to past perfect). Make appropriate pronoun and adverb changes.	Dunant remarked sadly, "Yesterday we lost another 50 soldiers right here."	Dunant reported that on the previous day they had lost another 50 soldiers right there.
Questions		
<u>Yes/No questions</u>: Use *if* or *whether*. Do not use *say*.	Ignatieff asked the ICRC representative, "Can I tape-record my interviews with the volunteers?"	Ignatieff asked the ICRC representative if he could tape-record his interviews with the volunteers.

(continued)

Wh- questions:	Ignatieff asked the volunteer, "How did you survive the tough Red Cross training?"	Ignatieff asked the volunteer how he had survived the tough Red Cross training.
Use statement word order. Do not use **say**.		
Commands		
Use **not** + **infinitive** with negative commands.	Dunant warned the soldier, "Don't shoot!"	Dunant warned the soldier not to shoot.
Introduce with **tell, order, command, warn, direct.**		

2 *Work with a partner.*

Student A: Read silently Part One of the conversation between an ICRC volunteer and the prisoner of war (POW) he is visiting in a detention camp. Then retell the story to Student B using direct and indirect speech and a variety of reporting verbs.

Student B: Read Part Two of the conversation silently. After Student A has finished retelling Part One, retell the second part of the story using direct and indirect speech and a variety of reporting verbs.

Part One

VOLUNTEER: Hello. How are you doing? I'm here to collect your messages for your family.

POW: Thanks so much. But I have a question. Can I attach photos to my message?

VOLUNTEER: Yes, you can. However, let me warn you: Do not attach more than two photos, and you must protect them with something so they don't get damaged.

POW: Oh. Then, does that mean I can staple a little plastic bag to the message?

VOLUNTEER: Well, this is the first time anyone has ever asked me this question. Let me think. Yes, I guess it's all right with me. I can't imagine the prison censor would object.

Part Two

VOLUNTEER: But where did you get the plastic bag? You know, plastic bags are against prison rules.

POW: I traded ten cigarettes with the prison cook.

VOLUNTEER: Hmm. Well, what exactly are you going to put into this bag?

POW: Please, please, trust me. Don't worry. But I have to tell you: It's not for photos. It's for something more special than that.

VOLUNTEER: What do you mean?

POW: You see, I've been working in the prison gardens this year. I grew the most lovely azaleas in the world. I want to send some of the seeds to my wife. It's as simple as that.

C   STYLE: Responding to Complex or Controversial Questions

Sometimes people ask complex or controversial questions that require thought before they are answered. To respond, use expressions to signal that the answer is complex and that the speaker needs time to think, and/or to give a partial answer.

In the interview, Terry Gross and Michael Ignatieff discuss complex issues such as war, neutrality, humanitarian law, and human rights. In this imaginary exchange between Gross and Ignatieff, notice the expressions he uses to respond to her questions. He uses an *opening phrase* to buy time, and then *follow-up phrases* to explain his answer.

TERRY GROSS: Michael, why is the ICRC spending so much time and money these days educating people about the Geneva Conventions?

IGNATIEFF: Well, Terry, <u>there's no simple answer to that</u>. <u>You might say</u> they are doing that to let people know how important their work is. <u>But you could also say</u> they feel they must inform people about the "rules of war" in order to lessen the amount of violence in certain conflicts.

Here are additional expressions you can use:

Opening Phrases	Follow-up Phrases
Well, there's no simple answer to that …	You might say … (but you could also say …)
Well … that's a complicated issue …	One way to look at it is … (another way …)
Hmm … that's a tough one …	You could think that … (but perhaps …)

Work with a partner.

Student A: Ask Student B the complex or controversial question.

Student B: Answer the question, using an opening phrase to buy time and follow-up phrases to answer. Then switch roles after question 4.

Student A

1. Do you think soldiers can really follow "rules of war"?

2. How can Red Cross workers witness horrible, unjust scenes and not take a stand?

3. Should the ICRC allow its volunteers to work in highly volatile and dangerous areas?

4. Working for the ICRC is so risky. Why would anyone want to do it?

Student B

1. Hmm . . . that's a complicated issue.

2.

3.

4.

Now switch roles.

5. Can people really learn about the Geneva Conventions and the "rules of war" through comic books, radio soap operas, or posters?

6. Shouldn't ICRC workers be allowed to carry weapons as a form of self-defense?

7. Don't you think the ICRC should work harder to eliminate war and not just limit war?

8. The ICRC says it's not concerned with "justice," but simply "good treatment." What does this really mean?

5. Well . . . that's a tough one.

6.

7.

8.

D   SPEAKING TOPIC

Public Service Announcements (PSAs) are short messages that are broadcast on television and radio. Their purpose is not to advertise a product. Instead, they inform the public of important health and safety issues. Generally, in the United States, non-profit organizations produce public service announcements, and television and radio stations are required to broadcast them.

🎧 **1** *Listen to the American Red Cross's PSA about blood donations. The announcement is about a gift that would "go over really big," or be highly appreciated. Work with a partner, and discuss these questions:*

1. What is the message and tone of this PSA? _____

2. What title would you suggest for the PSA? _____

🎧 **2** *Listen again. Then fill out this outline of the PSA.*

Purpose: _____

Sound effects: _____

Opening line (used to grab the listeners' attention): _____

_____

Reasons for giving blood: _____

Suggested action: _____

3 *Working in groups of two or three, write and present your own PSA about blood donations.*

1. Decide on a target audience, such as college students, first-time donors, or businesspeople.

2. Write your PSA. Use the outline of the Red Cross PSA from the previous section as a guide. Include some of the following facts about blood donations in the United States in your announcement:
   - Fewer and fewer people are donating blood.
   - Blood is needed every day, not only for emergencies.
   - There are 40,000 units of blood needed daily
   - The Red Cross needs donations most during the holiday season (November to January).
   - If donors gave twice a year, there would be no blood shortages.
   - Some people donate blood in order to get cookies, candy, or doughnuts that are given after the blood is drawn.

3. Select music and sound effects to fit your target audience. Record your PSA.

4. Present your PSA to the class. Ask the other students to listen and discuss how effective its message is for your target audience. Use techniques you learned in the grammar (direct and indirect speech) and style (responding to complex or controversial questions) sections of this unit.

E   RESEARCH TOPICS

FIRST AID

1. Visit a Red Cross office. Find out what its main activities are.

2. Learn how to give one kind of first aid treatment. Find information at your local Red Cross office, at the library, or on the Internet.

   Examples of first aid treatment are:
   - bandaging a wound
   - handling a snake bite or other animal bite
   - treating a burn
   - treating someone who is poisoned

3. Teach your class how to give the treatment, and have the class practice the techniques. Provide supplies if needed. Use visual aids.

INTERNET RESEARCH

1. Use the Internet to research human rights groups such as Doctors without Borders (www.doctorswithoutborders.org), Oxfam (www.oxfam.org), UNICEF (www.unicef.org), or Human Rights Watch (www.hrw.org) to learn about relief agencies that do not adhere to strict positions of neutrality. Organize your research into three parts:
   - purpose and philosophy of the organization
   - recent activities (for example, countries the organization is now working in, projects in those countries, new approaches to the work in the face of terrorism)
   - volunteer opportunities and qualifications

2. Compare this organization to the ICRC, and present your findings to the class. Support your oral presentation with a poster, handout, short video clip, audio recording, or photos.

For Unit 8 Internet activities, visit the NorthStar Companion Website at
http://www.longman.com/northstar.

Boosting Brain Power through the Arts

"When I listen to Mozart, the numbers just seem to crunch themselves."

1 Focus on the Topic

A PREDICTING

Look at the title of this unit. The *arts* refers to all the arts, including music, painting, sculpture, theater, dance, and so on. Look at the cartoon. *To crunch numbers* is a popular idiom meaning "to calculate." Why do you think listening to Mozart might make this man's job easier? Do you think this cartoon is funny? Why or why not?

B SHARING INFORMATION

 1 *Some scientists have suggested that listening to classical music, particularly music composed by Mozart, may improve our ability to perform certain tasks. Listen to the excerpt from a piano sonata by Mozart, and discuss the following question.*

- What skills or abilities (for example, drawing pictures) may be helped by listening to such music?

Compare your ideas with those of a partner.

2 *Work in a small group, and discuss your answers to the following questions.*

1. Think back. Did you have music and art lessons in primary and secondary school? How often? How important were they in the overall school program? Did you like them? Why or why not?

2. Outside of school, what other music or art training have you had?

3. What role do music and art play in your life today?

C PREPARING TO LISTEN

BACKGROUND

Scientists in many parts of the world are conducting experiments to explore the relationship between art and music, and intelligence. You are going to learn about three of these studies. Three important terms will be used in the descriptions of the studies:

- *control group:* a group studied in a scientific experiment; this group's behavior is not changed

- *experimental group:* another group studied in a scientific experiment; this group's behavior is changed and compared to the standard, the control group

- *spatial reasoning:* the ability to understand how things fit together in space and time (for example, putting together a puzzle)

1 *Work in groups of three.*

Student A: Read about Experiment 1 on page 245.

Student B: Read about Experiment 2 on page 245.

Student C: Read about Experiment 3 on page 246.

On the chart, take notes about the experiment that you read about. Then describe the experiment to the other members of your group so that they can complete their charts.

	EXPERIMENT 1 SWITZERLAND AND AUSTRIA	EXPERIMENT 2 UNIVERSITY OF CALIFORNIA, IRVINE, USA	EXPERIMENT 3 UNIVERSITY OF CALIFORNIA, IRVINE, USA
Researchers' Name(s)			
Research Subjects (age and number)			
Length of Study (years or months)			
Purpose of Study			
Control Group			
Experimental Group			
Results of Study			

2 *In your groups, discuss your answers to these questions:*

1. Which results were the most surprising? Interesting? Explain.

2. In the University of California studies, the researchers chose the music of Mozart because it is complex, repetitive, and structured.

   a. Do you agree with the choice of Mozart? Why?

   b. What other composer or style of music could have been chosen? Why?

   c. What kind of music would not fit these criteria? Why?

VOCABULARY FOR COMPREHENSION

1 *Work with a partner. Read the sentences below, and try to guess the meaning of the underlined expressions from the context. Write a synonym or definition on the lines.*

1. A <u>well-rounded</u> education includes the study of many subjects, including music and art.

   _____

2. The students scored much higher on the statewide exams this year, indicating that their math <u>proficiency</u> had improved.

   _____

3. In most U.S. elementary schools, the <u>curriculum</u> includes math, science, language, social studies, physical education, art, and music.

   _____

4. The <u>building blocks</u> of a musical education include instruction in reading music, playing an instrument, and understanding music theory.

   _____

5. Children can develop <u>sequential</u> skills through activities such as counting and putting the events of a story in order.

   _____

6. To solve problems in their work, professionals depend on their <u>abstract reasoning</u> skills as well as their specific knowledge of the field.

   _____

7. Exposure to music and art in school and at home <u>enhances</u> one's enjoyment of the arts.

   _____

8. A person with low <u>self-esteem</u> may be afraid to try new things or m
   people.

   _____

9. When the child did not walk at a normal age, her parents had her examined.
   Doctors discovered a serious <u>neurological</u> disorder in the child's brain and
   spinal cord.

   _____

10. Bright colors, vivid images, and thickly painted surfaces are the <u>hallmarks</u> of
    Van Gogh's paintings.

    _____

11. Because of the child's learning difficulties, the teacher recommended
    <u>intervention</u> by a reading specialist.

    _____

12. Most psychologists <u>underscore</u> the importance of the role that parents have
    in teaching their children.

    _____

2 *Working with a partner, match the words and expressions on the left with a definition or
synonym on the right. Write the appropriate letter in the blank. Compare your answers
with those of other students.*

__I__	**1.** abstract reasoning	**a.** parts; pieces
_____	**2.** building blocks	**b.** related to nerves
_____	**3.** curriculum	**c.** self-confidence
_____	**4.** enhance	**d.** list of subjects taught
__L__	**5.** hallmarks	**e.** special activities to prevent bad results
__E__	**6.** intervention	**f.** improve
_____	**7.** neurological	**g.** emphasize
_____	**8.** proficiency	**h.** in a particular order
__K__	**9.** self-esteem	**i.** ability to understand general concepts that cannot be immediately seen or felt
_____	**10.** sequential	**j.** complete and varied
_____	**11.** underscore	**k.** ability and skill
__J__	**12.** well-rounded	**l.** outstanding features

2 Focus on Listening

A ▌ LISTENING ONE: *Does Music Enhance Math Skills?*

You will hear an interview from the radio news program *All Things Considered*, which airs on National Public Radio in the United States.

NPR

 Working with a partner, brainstorm some answers to the question, "Why do you think music may enhance mathematical skills?" Make a brief list. Then listen to a short segment of the interview to check your answers.

LISTENING FOR MAIN IDEAS

 Read the questions. Then listen to Part One of the interview, and circle the letter of the correct answer to each question. Do the same for Part Two. Compare your results with those of another student.

Part One

1. According to a recent study, music and art education can _____.
   a. increase students' appreciation of nature
   b. improve reading and math skills
   c. improve math, but not reading skills

2. The purpose of the special arts program in Rhode Island was to _____.
   a. help students appreciate the arts
   b. make students' education more well-rounded
   c. investigate the impact of arts training

3. The special arts program in Rhode Island took advantage of children's natural inclination to master skills in _____.
   a. sequencing
   b. testing
   c. building

4. At the end of the test period, the researchers checked the children's _____.
   a. attitude
   b. test scores
   c. attitude and test scores

Part Two

5. Children who benefit from arts training are those with _____.
   a. involved parents
   b. artistic talent
   c. no special talent

6. Scientists have made some guesses as to how music may enhance mathematical skills. One factor *not* mentioned is that arts training _____.
   a. increases self-esteem
   b. relaxes nervous students
   c. teaches students how to learn new things

7. Scientists and educators are now more aware that a rich learning environment can help children _____.
   a. learn more
   b. become more artistic
   c. become more musical

LISTENING FOR DETAILS

 Listen to the interview again. As you listen, fill in the chart on page 200 with the information about the two experiments described.

		PART ONE	PART TWO
Researcher's Name			
Experiment Location			
Research Subjects (age/number of subjects)			
Purpose of Study			Impact of arts education on math ability
Frequency of Classes	Control Group	Standard curriculum music: ____ x/month art: ____ x/month	
	Experimental Group	Special arts classes ____ x/week	
Style of Instruction	Control Group	music lessons were: [check (✓) one] ____ active ____ passive	
	Experimental Group	arts program was: [check (✓) one] ____ active ____ passive	
Skills Taught: Art and Music	Control Group	Check (✓) two items: ____ went to concerts ____ listened to concerts ____ played music ____ talked about music	
	Experimental Group	Check (✓) two items: ____ sang together ____ sang alone ____ drew portraits ____ drew shapes	
Results		1. 2. 3.	1. 2.

REACTING TO THE LISTENING

1 *Work in a small group. Review the chart on page 200. Then listen to the excerpts about the two experiments. Based on these studies, make judgments as to how schools and parents might enhance children's brain power. For each excerpt, rank the items below in order of importance. Use the number **1** as the most important and **6** as the least important. Then discuss your judgments with those of the other groups.*

Excerpt One

1. If schools want to apply the Rhode Island research, they should _____.

   _____ **a.** offer more music and art classes than math classes in the curriculum

   __1__ **b.** offer intensive music and art classes in kindergarten (age five)

   __2__ **c.** organize art and music exhibitions

   _____ **d.** encourage parents to arrange for private music lessons

   __3__ **e.** invite visiting artists and musicians to lecture to the children

   _____ **f.** have students write reports about famous musicians

Excerpt Two

2. If parents want to apply the results of Rauscher's research, they should _____.

   _____ **a.** have pregnant mothers listen frequently to Mozart's music

   __1__ **b.** provide intensive music and art classes for children under age five

   _____ **c.** provide computer lessons along with music lessons

   __3__ **d.** sing with their children

   _____ **e.** give at-home tutorial math instruction

   __2__ **f.** take their children to recitals, operas, and concerts

2 *In a small group, discuss the answers to the following questions.*

1. What new or surprising information did you find out from the interview with Michelle Trudeau?

2. Besides art and music, what other "external" factors might boost intelligence? Games? Food? Explain.

3. In your opinion, in addition to increasing intelligence, how else might art and musical experiences help children?

4. The research results indicate the importance of arts education in schools. However, many U.S. schools emphasize reading and math much more than art and music. In your view, is arts education only a "frill"—a supplementary activity to be added only if there's time and money?

B   LISTENING TWO: *Music, Art, and the Brain*

Listening One contains reports on scientific studies on school-age children. We learned that music has been shown to enhance mathematical and spatial ability, as well as analytical skills. Michelle Trudeau reported that something neurological may happen in the brain to create this connection.

Listening Two focuses on studies of babies. Here, David Alpern and Warren Levinson, hosts of the weekly radio broadcast, *Newsweek on Air,* interview Sharon Begley, *Newsweek* magazine's science editor, about the relationship between music and art, and the brains of very young children.

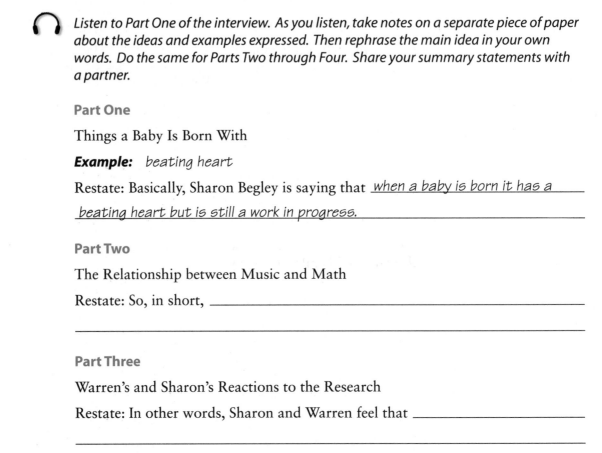

Listen to Part One of the interview. As you listen, take notes on a separate piece of paper about the ideas and examples expressed. Then rephrase the main idea in your own words. Do the same for Parts Two through Four. Share your summary statements with a partner.

Part One

Things a Baby Is Born With

Example: *beating heart*

Restate: Basically, Sharon Begley is saying that *when a baby is born it has a*
beating heart but is still a work in progress.

Part Two

The Relationship between Music and Math

Restate: So, in short, _____

_____

Part Three

Warren's and Sharon's Reactions to the Research

Restate: In other words, Sharon and Warren feel that _____

_____

Part Four

Things to Do with Your Child

Restate: In other words, Sharon suggests that _____

_____

C LINKING LISTENINGS ONE AND TWO

Work in groups of three. Imagine you are advisers to a candidate running for governor. Education is a major issue. Some education leaders want to apply the new research linking music and intelligence. You want to use the new research to help get your candidate elected. Evaluate the proposals below, and choose one to use in the upcoming campaign.

1. Read and discuss the pros and cons of each proposal.* Modify the proposals if necessary, or add one of your own. Use the information you learned so far in the unit.

2. In your groups, come to a consensus.

3. Present your proposal for the candidate to the class. Have one student from your group play the role of the candidate. He or she will discuss the proposals with you.

Suggested Proposals

- Distribute free classical CDs to all families of newborns.

- Give out books about and music by Mozart to all families with children under the age of four years.

- Require 15 minutes of Mozart's music to be played prior to any standardized statewide examination.

- Offer free, once-a-week private piano or violin lessons for every two- or three-year-old child, for one year.

- Require all public preschools and day care centers (schools with children under the age of five) to play 30 minutes of classical music each day.

- Your own idea: _____

_____

3 Focus on Vocabulary

1 *Working with a partner, read the sentences on pages 204–205. Put an **L** next to the sentence if the underlined word is being used in a **literal** way, and put an **F** next to the sentence if it's being used in a **figurative** way. Then, using the context clues, explain what the word means in the sentence.*

---

* Some of these are actual ideas and have already been implemented.

_F_ **1a.** Early interventions might be having some effect in children knowing how to <u>attack</u> new material (Andrea Halpern, Listening One)

Explanation: **Attack** *is used in a nonphysical way. The word creates a picture in your mind. In this sentence,* **attack** *means "set to work on" or "approach."*

_L_ **b.** The army <u>attacked</u> the opposing forces.

Explanation: **Attack** *is used in a concrete, physical way. It means "used violence against."*

_F_ **2a.** After the performance, the audience gave the singer <u>a big hand.</u>

Explanation: a big hand is the audience giving the singer applause

_L_ **b.** The pianist's <u>big hands</u> allowed him to play the difficult chords in romantic music.

Explanation: The pianist has big hands

_L_ **3a.** The composer <u>orchestrated</u> his pieces for only string and brass instruments.

Explanation: The Composer write music.

_F_ **b.** The museum director <u>orchestrated</u> the contract with intelligence, skill, and persistence. Her strategy was successful.

Explanation: _____

_L_ **4a.** The <u>wiring</u> in this lamp is so old it could start a fire.

Explanation: _____

_F_ **b.** Warren Levinson said that the <u>wiring</u> for music and math is in the same part of the brain right next to each other.

Explanation: No wiring in the brain

L **5a.** When speaking to the architects who were designing her art studio, the artist said that she needed many <u>windows</u> in order to see color in natural light.

Explanation: _____

_____

F **b.** According to Warren Levinson, the notion that so many <u>windows</u> in the child's brain are closed so early may be frightening for <u>parents</u>.

Explanation: _____

_____

F **6a.** Levinson and Begley both felt that parents may have already <u>blown</u> it if their children have not been introduced to music and art by the <u>age</u> of seven.   *miss the change*

Explanation: _____

_____

L **b.** While she was practicing the electric organ, the electricity went out. The instrument may have <u>blown</u> a fuse. *light off*

Explanation: _____ *don't blown a fuse. don't get so upset*

_____

F **7a.** Parents will inevitably <u>blow up</u> at their children when they misbehave. *get angry*

Explanation: _____

_____

L **b.** Police suspect that the terrorist group may <u>blow up</u> another car.

Explanation: _____

_____

L **8a.** The pianist's hand was <u>scarred</u> after he burned it.

Explanation: _____

_____

F **b.** The father forced his child to practice eight hours a day. That experience was painful and <u>scarred</u> the child for life.

Explanation: _____

_____

2 *Work with another student.*

Student A: Ask Student B questions 1 through 4.

Student B: Cover the left column. Answer Student A's questions. Respond in as much detail as possible, using the cues given and incorporating figurative language as much as possible. Then switch roles after question 4.

Student A

1. When was the last time you went to a concert or show and gave the performers <u>a big hand</u>? Describe the performance.

2. Have you ever <u>orchestrated</u> anything? A party? A meeting? A sports event? What did you have to do?

3. What is your strategy for <u>attacking</u> new material in English?

4. Were you interested in the fact that the <u>wiring</u> for both music and math is in the same area of the brain? Why?

Now switch roles.

5. Do you agree with Warren Levinson that it's a bit scary to find out that <u>windows</u> for learning close so early in life? Why?

6. Have you ever <u>blown</u> an important test, presentation, job interview, business deal, etc.? Describe what happened.

7. When was the last time you <u>blew up</u> at someone? What happened?

8. Very scary movies often frighten young children out of their wits. Do you think these experiences <u>scar</u> them for life? Why or why not?

Student B

1. Hmm. Let me see, . . .

2. Yes, I remember . . .

3. Well, one idea I have . . .

4. Yes, because . . .

5. Well, maybe . . .

6. Of course. One time . . .

7. Hmm. I'm not sure I remember all the details, but . . .

8. Let me see . . .

3 *Work with another student. Match the underlined words in the sentences with a similar expression from the list below. Write the corresponding letter in the blank.*

___E___ **1.** Scientists are <u>advancing</u> slowly toward an understanding of brain development in children.

___D___ **2.** The students' intensive preparation in reading and vocabulary helps <u>boost</u> their test scores.

___C___ **3.** The university applied the new rules to the student body <u>as a whole</u>, not just to the first-year students.

___F___ **4.** After the accident, he fell behind in piano studies and never <u>caught up to</u> the level of the other children in his group.

___H___ **5.** Twentieth-century painting is <u>dramatically</u> different from that of earlier centuries.   *Big different*

___I___ **6.** The parents of the young cellist want to buy the best instrument available, <u>regardless</u> of the price.   *don't care*

___G___ **7.** A sculptor's <u>works in progress</u> often reveal more about the creative process than the finished sculpture does.

___A___ **8.** Playing piano <u>did more for</u> the young woman's self-esteem than getting good grades in school.

___B___ **9.** The student insisted that the wrong notes <u>had nothing to do with</u> lack *no* of practice. The piece had sounded much better at home.

    a. benefited

    b. didn't involve ไม่รวมถึง

    c. entirely โดยสิ้นเชิง, ทั้งหมด

    d. increase ทำให้มากขึ้น

    e. progressing ความก้าวหน้า

    f. reached บรรลุ, ไปถึง

    g. unfinished products

    h. very; noticeably ชัดเจน, อย่างมาก

    i. without considering with out thinking of

whole = everything

hole s ð

4 *Divide the class into several teams of two to four players. All teams will play the game described below.*

WORD GAME: CLEAN THE BOARD

Object of the Game: To be the first team to "clean the board," or remove all cards from the large piece of paper, the "game board."

How to Play the Game

1. Each team copies the game board onto a larger piece of paper. It should be two columns and three rows as shown in the picture on the left below.

2. Each team chooses six words from the list below and places them face up. Write each word on a small card, and place each card over a different box on the game board. Each team may choose different words.

a big hand	curriculum	self-esteem
attack	do more for	sequential
blow	enhanced	well-rounded
blow up	have to do with	windows
boost	orchestra	work in progress
catch up to	proficiency	

3. All teams play at the same time, competing against one another. One student on each team asks the teammate(s) a question that elicits one of the words on the board. In other words, the student tries to get his teammate(s) to answer his question using one of the words on the board. The teammate(s) listen to the question and then answer it. If the teammate(s) choose the correct word to answer the question, they remove the card from the board.

Example

Teammate One: "How do you feel about winning the math contest?" (Teammate One is thinking of the word *boosted* and wants one of his teammates to answer the question using that word.)

Teammate Two: "Great! It *boosted* my self-confidence."

The correct word, *boosted*, was chosen, so Teammate One removes the word from the board.

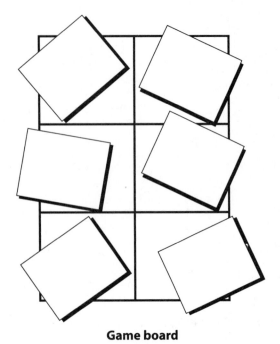

Game board

4. The winning team is the one that cleans the board (removes all its cards) first.

5. Play again and start over, using different words from the list.

4 Focus on Speaking

A PRONUNCIATION: Joining Final Consonants

Words that end in final consonants join to following words in different ways.

- When the next word starts with a vowel: Join the final consonant and vowel clearly.

    Self-esteem   works in progress

- When the next word starts with the same consonant or sound: Hold one long consonant (" "). Do not say the consonant twice.

    Art teachers   enhance skills

- When the next word starts with a different consonant: Keep the final consonant short. Hold it (") "), and then immediately say the next word.

    Crunch)numbers   attack)problems

 1 *Listen, and repeat the phrases. Then practice saying them with a partner. Pay attention to how you join the two words together.*

1. music appreciation
2. art education
3. critical ingredients
4. parental involvement
5. music class
6. top performance
7. math theories
8. abstract topics
9. math proficiency
10. reap benefits
11. research findings
12. geometric shapes

2 *Listen, and repeat the phrases. Using the rules for joining consonants, mark each phrase: ⌣ or ⌢ or). Then complete the sentences with the correct phrases. Compare your answers with those of a partner. Take turns saying the sentences.*

standard curriculum   boost brain power   an interactive approach
a critical ingredient   research challenge   logical thinking
art classes   typical lesson   self-esteem

1. In most music classes around the country, listening to tapes or a lecture is really the ___typical lesson___ .

2. The researchers found that music has a general effect of improving a child's self-image and ___self-esteem___ .

3. Just how and why music and art enhance certain mathematical skills continues to be a ___research challenge___.

4. Some classes got the special arts curriculum; others received the ___standard curriculum___ .

5. The children learned to draw shapes and deal with colors and forms in the ___art classes___ .

6. Arts education seems to be ___a critical ingredient___ in improving analytical reasoning.

7. Studies done in the past seven years indicate that studying music and art can significantly ___boost brain power___ .

8. Communication, discussion, and involvement are hallmarks of ___an interactive approach___ to education.

9. Neuroscientists believe the brain works similarly when people perform tasks requiring spatial reasoning and ___logical thinking___ .

B   GRAMMAR: The Passive Voice and the Passive Causative

1 *Working with a partner, examine the sentences on page 211, and discuss the questions that follow.*

- In one study, a group of three-year-olds <u>was given</u> singing lessons while another group <u>was given</u> piano lessons.

- A lot of the brain research <u>has been done</u> on animals.

- A mistake <u>was made</u> in the printed program. The sonatas by Mozart <u>will not be played</u>.

- Before the concert, we had the piano <u>tuned</u> and <u>got</u> the lights <u>repaired</u>.

1. In each sentence, why do you think the speaker is choosing the passive voice for the verbs?

2. In the fourth sentence, who is performing the action?

The Passive Voice and the Passive Causative

How to Form the Passive Voice

The **passive voice** is formed by using a form of the verb **to be** plus the past participle of the main verb. The verb *to be* can be used in any tense, as illustrated below.

Subject	Form of the Verb *To Be*	Past Participle	Complement
The students	**are**	**given**	a well-rounded education.
His self-esteem	**was**	**enhanced**	by the new arts curriculum.
Intervention	**will be**	**needed**	if things don't improve.
The curriculum	**is going to be**	**improved.**	
The pieces	**must be**	**practiced**	before the performance.
The neurons	**might have been**	**stimulated.**	
Spatial reasoning	**is being**	**improved.**	

When to Use the Passive Voice

The passive voice is used when you:

- want to emphasize the object of the action, not the actor

- do not know the actor

- want to avoid mentioning who performed the action or to avoid blaming anyone

- want to report an idea or fact

(continued)

Passive Causative

The **passive causative** is used to speak about services arranged.

It is formed by the verbs **get** or **have** and the past participle of the main verb.

- Mrs. Diaz is organizing an art exhibition of her students' work. With special funds collected for this purpose, she <u>had</u> the paintings <u>mounted</u> on special paper. She also <u>had</u> the works <u>framed</u>. Finally, she <u>got</u> the school lobby <u>cleaned</u> and <u>set up</u>.

2 *Complete the paragraphs with the appropriate forms of the verbs provided. Choose active or passive forms, including passive causative. Keep in mind that some verbs cannot be used in the passive voice.*

Piano or Computer: Which Boosts Intelligence?

There is exciting new research about the effects of musical training on intelligence. Currently the effects of piano lessons on young children

_____ by Frances Rauscher of the University of Wisconsin.
　　　1. (research)

Whether children can learn more from a piano keyboard or a computer

keyboard _____. Last week, a report on this research
　　　　　2. (study)

_____ in the journal *Neurological Research*. It said that
　　3. (appear)

certain aspects of a child's intelligence _____ by musical
　　　　　　　　　　　　　　　　　　4. (can/enhance)

training, particularly by piano study. Spatial reasoning skills

_____ by work on a piano keyboard, but not on a computer
　　5. (can/improve)

keyboard.

In one of Rauscher's recent studies, 78 young children

_____. They _____ into four groups of
　　6. (involve)　　　　　　　　　　7. (divide)

subjects. Some of the children _____ piano keyboard lessons,
　　　　　　　　　　　　　　　　8. (receive)

some computer lessons, and others group singing lessons. No special training

_____ for the fourth group. By the end of six months, the
　　9. (provide)

piano keyboard children _____ instruction in muscle
　　　　　　　　　　　　　10. (give)

coordination, simple compositions, and musical literacy. Rauscher claimed that

the children _____ enough training to be able to play simple
　　　　　11. (give)

pieces, like Beethoven's "Ode to Joy."

The final step in the research _____ of a test of
12. (consist)

analytical reasoning skills. With the help of research assistants, Rauscher

_____ the results _____. Then she
13. (collect)

_____ the data _____ using a highly
14. (analyze)

sophisticated computer program. An important finding _____.
15. (emerge)

The children who _____ in piano keyboard training scored
16. (instruct)

significantly higher on the test than the children in the other three groups.

Therefore, Rauscher _____ that, regardless of the fact that a
17. (conclude)

keyboard _____ for the computer group, the piano keyboard
18. (use)

children still _____ higher on the test.
19. (score)

The research underscores the fact that the piano _____
20. (seem)

to be the critical ingredient. In musical training, the brain circuits

_____ in such a way that certain nerve pathways
21. (may/stimulate)

_____. These pathways _____ to be
22. (strengthen)   23. (appear)

the same ones which _____ when spatial reasoning tasks
24. (fire)

_____. Nevertheless, in order to confirm these results,
25. (perform)

Rauscher _____ the study _____ by
26. (repeat)

other researchers.

3 *For this activity on page 214, work with a partner.*

Student A: You are a reporter for Music Times Newsletter. *You are writing a story about a child who displayed extraordinary talent at a very young age. The prodigy is Tanya Chang, a thirteen-year-old violinist who could play works by classical composers at the age of four. You are interviewing Tanya's mother. Cover the right column. Read the questions in the left column. Change the underlined verbs to the passive voice as you read.*

Student B: You are Mrs. Chang, Tanya's mother. You have dedicated your life to supporting your daughter's musical career. Cover the left column. Read the responses in the right column. Change the underlined verbs to the passive voice as you read.

Listen carefully, look at each other as much as possible, and read your lines with feeling.

Student A

1. Thanks so much for taking the time to speak with me.

2. So, how <u>be</u> Tanya's interest in violin <u>spark</u>?

3. <u>Be</u> she <u>push</u> to <u>play</u>?

4. Do you mean it took two years to identify her talent?

5. I <u>told</u> that at the age of four, you <u>have</u> a tape <u>make</u> of a recital and this tape <u>send</u> to a famous school in New York City. Is that correct?

6. Have you been guiding and supporting her career, or <u>have</u> that <u>do</u> by her teachers?

7. I hear now that she may <u>have / be / choose</u> to participate in a concert at the Royal Academy Hall in London.

8. Good luck to you both. I'm sure she <u>will / select</u> and then her picture <u>will / print</u> in newspapers all over the world.

Student B

1. Oh, it's my pleasure.

2. I'm not really sure. She <u>might / inspire</u> when she <u>give</u> a violin at the age of two.

3. Absolutely not! She <u>encourage</u>, but not <u>push</u>. In fact, she had been playing for over two years before she <u>identify</u> as a gifted musician.

4. Unfortunately, yes. It <u>should / notice</u> earlier, but I just wasn't paying attention.

5. Yes, it is. Then she immediately <u>ask</u> to enter the school at the age of five.

6. No, her teachers only teach. All other details <u>handle</u> by me alone. Before a concert, we sometimes have to <u>have</u> her violin <u>repair</u>. We always <u>get</u> her dress <u>dry-clean</u> and <u>have</u> photos <u>take</u>. There's so much that <u>must / do</u>.

7. Yes, at this time she <u>consider</u> for the position. If she <u>be / choose</u>, she'll be the youngest performer ever to <u>have / invite</u>.

8. Thanks for interviewing me. I hope you'll hear Tanya play sometime soon.

C   STYLE: Expressions That Link Sentences or Ideas

Notice the underlined words or phrases in the sentences below.

- Students listened to tapes and concerts and talked about music in class. <u>In contrast</u>, the special arts classes met twice weekly and got students involved.

- Music appears to stimulate certain brain cells involved in logical thinking and spatial reasoning. <u>Likewise</u>, mathematics seems to activate these same brain cells.

- Three experiments done by the psychologist are <u>similar in that</u> in all three, spatial reasoning proficiency was enhanced. They are <u>different, however, in that</u> one involved 18- to 22-year-olds and the other two involved preschool children.

The underlined phrases are common expressions used to make **transitions of similarity and contrast** that link sentences and ideas. When we speak, it's important to use these transitions to show how ideas are similar or different.

Similarity	Contrast
Likewise,	In contrast,
Similarly,	However,
…is similar to …in that	…is different from …in that

Working with a partner, examine the chart summarizing four studies. Make statements about the information under each heading. Compare and contrast the experiments using the transitional expressions above. Share your responses with each other.

Example: *The University of California, Irvine study is similar to the Harvard study in that it was conducted over a period of eight months.*

EXPERIMENT LOCATION	RESEARCHER'S NAMES	AGE OF RESEARCH SUBJECTS	LENGTH OF STUDY	PURPOSE OF STUDY	RESULTS OF STUDY
#1 Switzerland Austria	Maria Spychiger and Jean-Luc Patry	7 to 15 years old	3 years	Effect of music on math and language ability	Math and language skills improved
#2 University of California, Irvine, USA	Frances Rauscher and Gordon Shaw	3 years old	8 months	Effect of music (singing and piano) on intelligence	Abstract and spatial reasoning skills improved
#3 Providence, Rhode Island, USA	Martin Gardiner	6 to 7 years old	7 months	Effect of arts education (music and art) on math and language ability	Math and language skills improved
#4 Harvard University, Cambridge, Massachusetts, USA	Christopher Chabris	18 to 22 years old	8 months	Effect of Mozart's music on intelligence	Spatial reasoning skills did not significantly improve

D SPEAKING TOPIC

Read the background information and case study based on a real news report. Then do the activity that follows. You will be planning and conducting a meeting.

BACKGROUND

In the United States, public schools are administered and financed by local governments. Each local district has a school board, a group of citizens who are elected by the voting residents of the town. One of its most significant responsibilities is to determine the local school budget, the yearly financial plan of how the school district will spend money allocated for the local school.

Money to support public school education comes from a variety of sources: local taxpayers, state governments, and the federal government. In recent years, many public schools have had to deal with smaller and smaller budgets. The cost of services is rising, and the state and federal governments are contributing less financial support. Therefore, many districts are struggling to maintain a high-quality educational program.

Case Study: School Board Proposes Drastic Cuts in Arts Program

One school district in Illinois is in the process of developing its yearly budget. However, this year the district must work with 30 percent less money than it has had in the past. The state of Illinois has severely cut back on the amount of money it usually gives to the local districts. In order to save money, the local school board has already decided on a number of actions:

- forced early retirement for 17 teachers

- elimination of physical education classes in the middle school and high school

- elimination of foreign language instruction in the elementary school (kindergarten through sixth grade)

However, now the board is saying that these cuts are not enough. Now they have proposed to eliminate all art and music classes from the elementary school curriculum. Parents are outraged. Angry discussion can be heard everywhere throughout the town: on downtown streets, in supermarkets, at the YMCA and soccer fields, and so on. Parents are demanding that the board reconsider its decision.

Because of all the complaints, the board has agreed to hold open forum meetings to discuss the proposal. It has invited representatives from three groups to attend the meetings: (1) parents, (2) art and music teachers, and (3) school board members.

PREPARING FOR THE MEETING

Everyone in the class should choose a role: parent, teacher, or school board member. Divide into groups of students all playing the same role. In your role groups, study the descriptions that follow, and brainstorm other supporting arguments. Write your arguments on separate pieces of paper.

Parents

- want to keep art and music classes in the school curriculum

- do not wish to pay extra to provide private art or music lessons

- feel art and music instruction inspires appreciation of the arts and provides a break from academic instruction

Art and Music Educators

- believe in the research findings from California and Rhode Island

- feel that it's important for children to have many ways to express themselves

- feel that arts instruction can improve perceptual skills and motor coordination

School Board Members

- feel that art and music instruction is a frill, a non-academic extra

- feel the arts do not have the rigor or importance of math, science, or reading

- think parents should be responsible for this instruction

CONDUCTING THE MEETING

1. One student leads the meeting. This leader:
   - opens the meeting by introducing the participants and explaining the purpose
   - conducts the meeting by eliciting comments and questions from the participants
   - closes the meeting by summarizing the main arguments

2. During the meeting, all students should use the passive voice and expressions of similarity and contrast whenever appropriate.

SUMMARIZING THE ISSUE

Write an editorial letter to the local newspaper voicing your concerns about the cuts to the arts education program. Emphasize the important role that art and music play in the lives of all children.

E   RESEARCH TOPIC

You will organize an experiment on "The Mozart Effect." The experiment will try to determine if listening to music by Mozart can increase the speed of performing simple math, logic, or spatial problems.

PREPARING FOR THE EXPERIMENT

1. Choose four to six people to participate, or divide the class into two groups.

2. Divide the participants into two groups: Group A: control group, and Group B: test group.

3. Explain to the participants the purpose of the experiment, and give a little background that you have learned in this unit. Then present the experiment rules.

   Group A will sit in silence for 10 minutes. Group B will listen to 10 minutes of music by Mozart (you can use the music from the beginning of the unit). After 10 minutes, you will all be given problems to do.* Do them as quickly and as accurately as possible. Work alone. You will do three problems.

Conducting the Experiment

1. Participant groups go into two rooms. Group A sits in silence. Group B listens to Mozart. After 10 minutes, all participants do the problems.

2. Compare the two groups' problem-solving skills in terms of speed and accuracy.

Reporting the Results

1. Report the results to the class. Compare the results. Use the expressions of contrast and similarity and the passive voice to explain the process.

2. Work in small groups, and discuss the answers to these questions:
   • Did you see evidence of the Mozart effect? Why or why not?
   • If you were to repeat the experiment, how would you do the experiment differently?

For Unit 9 Internet activities, visit the NorthStar Companion Website at
http://www.longman.com/northstar.

---

* Use the sample problems on page 245, or find or design your own.

Television and Freedom of Expression

1 Focus on the Topic

A PREDICTING

Discuss these questions in a small group.

1. Look at the title of the unit and the cartoon. What point is the cartoonist trying to make about television ratings?

2. Do you think there is too much violence, sex, and strong language on TV? Explain.

3. Do you believe that watching violence on TV causes children to behave more violently? Why?

B | SHARING INFORMATION

Read this brief description of the movie ratings system. In a small group, discuss the questions that follow.

Rating Movies

The impact of television is one concern of parents. But what about the impact of movies? This, too, is an ongoing issue. Since 1968, movies have been rated by the Motion Picture Association of America (MPAA). The MPAA is a group of independent reviewers who are not connected to the film industry. The group rates movies according to the amount of sex, violence, and strong language they contain. Then it decides for which age group the movies are suitable:

> **G:** suitable for **G**eneral audiences of all ages
>
> **PG:** suitable for all ages, but **P**arental **G**uidance is suggested
>
> **PG-13:** suitable for all ages, but **P**arental **G**uidance is suggested for children under age **13**
>
> **R:** **R**estricted to persons age 17 or older, unless accompanied by a parent or guardian
>
> **NC-17:** **N**o **C**hildren under age **17** allowed

1. Do you think this age-based rating system is useful? Explain. Are the movies you see rated? If so, how?

2. Some people say that any form of rating or classifying system is censorship, a limit on freedom of speech. Why might they think so?

C | PREPARING TO LISTEN

BACKGROUND

The movie rating system in the United States is well established, but the rating of TV programming is still an issue. People are concerned about the effect of violent TV shows on children. Most research[1] has shown that watching violent TV shows often leads to more violent behavior in children. As a result, many people believe that the amount of violence shown on TV should be decreased.

---

[1] One study proved that the average American child will have watched 8,000 murders on television by the age of 12.

How can violence on TV be reduced? Whose responsibility is it to regulate the content shown on television? Who is responsible for protecting children from viewing content that may be harmful or lead to harmful behavior? The government? Parents? The television industry? A neutral group of citizens?

One proposed solution is for the government to regulate the content of television programming. In the United States, however, this is not always a popular solution. Several influential groups are opposed to such regulation.

First, there are some Americans who oppose government regulation in general—they do not like laws that tell them what they may or may not listen to, read, or watch. They are in favor of individual choice and self-regulation. Some people think that if you don't want your children to watch violent TV shows, you should just turn off the TV.

In general, the television industry also disagrees with government regulation. Industry leaders fear that a television ratings system will have an impact on the number of viewers watching certain shows. As a result, industry profits will be reduced. Television program writers feel that a TV ratings system will affect the creativity and content of their work. Pressured by this system, they may produce shows that are less interesting, less entertaining, and less provocative.

Finally, civil liberties groups[2] take a strong stand against government regulation of TV programming. They feel that government control of TV program content may be illegal and a violation of the First Amendment right to free speech, a right guaranteed by the U.S. Constitution. The First Amendment is based on the belief that in a free and democratic society, individuals must be free to decide for themselves what to read, write, see, hear, paint, draw, and so on. The whole idea of the First Amendment is to protect all media (television, newspapers, movies, art, books) from the political process. These civil liberties groups believe that the Constitution guarantees Americans freedom of expression, meaning expression without censorship from the government. This is a highly important and valued freedom.

So how can TV violence be controlled without the government censoring TV content? This is an issue that parents, the television industry, civil liberties groups, and the federal government are struggling with. It is very difficult to resolve.

*Working with a partner, read the ten statements of opinion that follow. Decide whether the point of view expressed represents the opinion of the U.S. government **(USG)**, the television industry **(TI)**, parents **(P)**, or free-speech supporters **(FSS)**. Some statements may be the point of view of more than one group. Write the initials of the group(s) next to each statement. Then summarize the point of view of each group.*

_____   **1.** "We know our content, so only we can rate it."

_____   **2.** "We are disgusted with the amount of sex, violence, and strong language on television."

_____   **3.** "It is our responsibility to protect the public. We have a right to control television content if the content is harmful to society."

---

[2] ***Civil liberties groups:*** groups that try to protect the rights of Americans that are set forth in the U.S. Constitution.

_____ 4. "Television is a form of freedom of expression. Government cannot control the freedom of expression in any way."

_____ 5. "We are a business whose primary goal is to make a profit. We cannot allow ratings to affect our profits."

_____ 6. "If a show is rated for mature audiences only (e.g., TV-MA), only adults can watch the show. There will be fewer viewers. Advertisers will not want to advertise during that show. We will lose money."

_____ 7. "We must pass a law requiring that the television industry rate its programming. We have the right to regulate its programming."

_____ 8. "Detailed information about television content can help us make informed choices."

_____ 9. "Television writers and producers will change their content in order to receive a certain rating. Therefore, these ratings are a form of control of creativity."

_____ 10. "The government has forced the television industry to implement the ratings system. This mandate (insistence) is direct government intervention in television content."

VOCABULARY FOR COMPREHENSION

Look at the underlined words in the following sentences. From the context, circle the letter of the best definition of the word. Compare your answers with those of another student.

1. The U.S. <u>media</u> and the entertainment industry recently agreed to a ratings system for TV programs.

   a. broadcast organizations   **b.** government agencies

2. In some countries, a TV rating system is <u>voluntary</u>. Broadcasters are not required to rate their TV programs.

   a. forced   **b.** not forced

3. To avoid government regulation, the U.S. television industry has <u>pledged</u> that it will develop its own rating system.

   a. discussed   **b.** promised

4. In the United States many people are against violence on TV, yet they also dislike government regulation of TV. This attitude is <u>hypocritical</u>.

   a. contradictory   **b.** unfair

5. All over the world, in recent years, there has been <u>a tidal wave</u> of violent programming on TV.

   a. a huge increase in   **b.** an increase in

6. Violence on TV is a big problem. Although the ratings system may help, it's not a <u>panacea</u>.

    a. perfect solution   **b.** possible solution

7. Most people are concerned about violence on <u>prime-time</u> shows because those shows attract the largest audiences.

    a. late afternoon   **b.** early evening

8. Sex and violence on TV are <u>offensive</u> to many people.

    a. disturbing   **b.** aggressive

9. Studies have shown that TV violence may make children behave violently. A television ratings system is designed to <u>counteract</u> this effect.

    a. cancel out   **b.** limit

10. If you treat something like <u>forbidden fruit</u>, young people usually want it more.

    a. something that looks enjoyable because it is not allowed   **b.** something you enjoy that cannot be eaten

2 Focus on Listening

A   LISTENING ONE: *Interview with* Newsweek *Entertainment Editor*

You will hear an interview from the radio news broadcast *Newsweek on Air*. Host David Alpern interviews Rick Marin, *Newsweek* magazine's entertainment editor. They discuss a system of regulating TV content: on-screen ratings combined with an electronic blocking device such as a V-chip.

Working with a partner, listen to the first sentence of the interview. Predict three questions that David Alpern might ask Rick Marin. Write your questions on the lines below, and compare your answers with those of another student.

_____

_____

_____

LISTENING FOR MAIN IDEAS

 Read the questions. Then listen to the interview, and write short answers to the questions. Compare your answers with those of another student.

Part One

1. The television industry has agreed to develop a TV ratings system. Why is the ratings system necessary? _____

2. The industry was responding to pressure from two groups. Who are they?
   _____Gaverment , public_____

3. Will the ratings end the trashy tidal waves of TV programming? _____
   _____No_____

Part Two

4. Check (✔) the correct answer. The television ratings will cover _____.

   _____ news

   _____ sports

   ___✔___ prime-time shows

   _____ movies

5. How much of a show is the V-chip supposed to block out? _____

Part Three

6. The V-chip and ratings systems may have problems. Rick Marin mentions some of them. Check (✔) the ones he mentions.

   _____ It'll take time for the V-chip to be accepted throughout the culture.

   _____ It'll take ten years to manufacture V-chips.

   _____ It'll take time for people to buy new TV sets with V-chips.

   _____ Television shows that are forbidden will interest young people.

7. What are the results of the Canadian experiment with the V-chip and ratings system? _____

   _____

LISTENING FOR DETAILS

 *Listen to the interview again. Then read the sentences, and write **T** (true) or **F** (false) in the blank. Correct the false statements. Then compare your answers with those of another student.*

Part One

__T__ **1.** The U.S. television ratings system will be developed by the television industry.

__F__ **2.** The president wants a ratings system developed by the ~~government~~. *TV industry*

__T__ **3.** The television industry decided to use the V-chip/ratings system partly because of government pressure.

_____ **4.** The president thinks the new V-chip/ratings system is a panacea that will eliminate all violence on television.

Part Two

_____ **5.** [Entertainment shows are rated.] Rick Marin thinks that talk shows are a form of entertainment.

_____ **6.** Rick Marin isn't sure whether TV news magazines, such as *Hard Copy* and *A Current Affair*, will be rated.

_____ **7.** Because the V-chip blocks out shows permanently, parents cannot watch any show that has been blocked out for their children.

Part Three

_____ **8.** People can install V-chips in their old television sets.

_____ **9.** A ratings system can be used before a V-chip is installed.

_____ **10.** Canadians experimented with 215 families.

_____ **11.** The V-chip system in Canada was too complicated for people to use.

_____ **12.** Canadians enjoy violent programming more than Americans do.

REACTING TO THE LISTENING

 1 *The speaker's choice of grammar and vocabulary, as well as responses such as laughter and sighs, are often clues to the speaker's intention. Focusing on these features, listen to these excerpts from the interview, and answer the questions that follow. Discuss your answers with a partner, then with the class.*

Excerpt One

1. In Rick Marin's view, what's the quality of the talk shows he mentions?

2. What words and structures reveal his opinion?

3. How do you know what David Alpern thinks?

Excerpt Two

4. In Marin's view, what kind of show is *NYPD Blue*?

5. What words and grammatical structures reveal his view?

Excerpt Three

6. Does Rick Marin feel that other people have the same opinion of "forbidden fruit" that he has? How do you know? What expressions reveal his opinion?

7. How do you know what David Alpern thinks?

2 *Answer these questions. Discuss your answers with a partner.*

1. When you were a child, did your parents let you watch anything you wanted on TV? If you have children, do you let them watch whatever they want on TV? Why? If you don't have children, how would you manage what your children watch if you did?

2. If you were going to take a stand on the issue of television content regulation, which group would you most likely side with—the government, parents opposed to violence, free speech and civil liberties supporters, the TV industry—or none of these? Why?

3. What do you know about the regulation of television content in other countries?

B ▌ LISTENING TWO: *Interview with Former Chairman of MPAA Ratings Board*

In the second interview, David Alpern, *Newsweek on Air* host, interviews Richard Heffner, Professor of Communications and Public Policy at Rutgers University in New Jersey and former chairman of the screen ratings board of the Motion Pictures Association of America (MPAA). Heffner has always supported movie ratings. However, he is clearly opposed to a ratings system for television.

Read the statements below. Listen to the interview. Then listen again, and put a check (✓) next to the reasons that Heffner gives to support his opinion that a voluntary television ratings system will not work.

_____ 1. There is no box office (ticket buying) between children and the harsh content aired on televisions in the home.

_____ 2. Children are surrounded at home, at school, in the community with all kinds of media. It is impossible to control everything.

_____ 3. The television ratings system is voluntary, and it shouldn't be.

_____ 4. The government, not the television industry, should regulate.

_____ 5. Regulation is censorship, and any censorship is bad.

_____ 6. The television industry is incapable of regulating its own TV programming, because making a profit rather than creating a wholesome media environment is its primary goal.

_____ 7. Television should be regulated by a separate group of individuals who are concerned with public safety.

C   LINKING LISTENINGS ONE AND TWO

*Think about your reactions to the two interviews that dealt with the pros and cons of regulation of television content. Read the statements below, and decide whether you agree or disagree. Mark **A** (agree) or **D** (disagree) next to each statement. Then compare your answers with those of a partner. Give reasons to support your opinions.*

_____ 1. Sex, violence, and strong language on TV can harm children.

_____ 2. Parents can effectively control their children's viewing habits with an electronic blocking device such as a V-chip.

_____ 3. News and sports should be rated too, since they often contain violent scenes.

_____ 4. On-screen ratings are enough. Viewers can simply check the warnings flashed at the beginning of a program. Electronic blocking devices, such as a V-chip, are not necessary.

_____ 5. Broadcasters should not determine ratings of their own programs. Instead, a neutral, non-governmental group, such as a panel of parents and psychologists, could provide more useful information.

_____ 6. Parents concerned about TV content and their children should take other steps to protect them from unsuitable content such as making their own guidelines, watching TV with them, or simply turning the TV off.

3 Focus on Vocabulary

1 *Match the underlined words or expressions in the sentences with a similar expression. Write the appropriate letter in the blank space from the list below. Then compare your answers with those of a partner.*

_B_ **1.** The amount of sex and violence on that show <u>disgusted</u> me.

_E_ **2.** I wouldn't waste my time reading that <u>trashy</u> newspaper. It's filled with gossip about movie stars.

_F_ **3.** I don't know what category that TV show would <u>fall under</u>.

_A_ **4.** In his speech, the television company president addressed such <u>bread-and-butter</u> issues as wages and promotions.

_G_ **5.** I only allow my children to watch <u>wholesome</u> family movies.

_D_ **6.** The government was disappointed that the ratings system didn't <u>take</u>. People were unwilling or unable to use it.

_C_ **7.** Violence is so pervasive in our society. I have a hard time <u>swallowing</u> the idea that a blocking device will be a panacea.

_j_ **8.** One study reported that children who were allowed to watch R-rated movies were <u>invariably</u> more likely to use tobacco or alcohol.

_H_ **9.** Civil liberties groups are horrified by the <u>notion</u> of censoring television content. To them, it doesn't matter who does the censoring.

_i_ **10.** The television industry makes a great deal of money from some of its trashiest shows. Allowing the industry to decide the ratings of its own shows is like <u>putting the fox in charge of the henhouse</u>.

a. very basic

b. annoyed; sickened

c. accepting; believing

d. succeed

e. poor-quality

f. be grouped with

g. morally good and healthy

h. idea

i. when a person or group that can do harm is in charge of protecting the very thing or people that can be harmed; a conflict of interest

j. almost always

2 *Complete the following article by filling in the blanks with the appropriate form of one of the expressions listed below.*

bread-and-butter	hypocritical	notion	take
fall under	invariably	panacea	trashy
forbidden fruit	media	swallow	wholesome

Blocking Out Violence or Blocking Out Freedom?

In many countries around the world, governments regulate television broadcasting. Government officials preside over the industry and control what will be shown to the public. In other countries, this industry functions freely and independently. Television stations can broadcast whatever they want without government interference. For many people, this lack of government interference in the (1) _media_ symbolizes an important freedom: freedom of speech. The V-chip/ratings system has raised important questions related to this freedom. Parents, children, the broadcasting industry, and free-speech groups all have different opinions.

Parents, disgusted with television programming, complain that too many shows are (2) _trashy_ and offensive, rather than (3) _____ and educational. Many feel that a V-chip/ratings system will protect their children from viewing inappropriate programs. Moreover, they are pleased that the government has finally forced the television industry to clean up the airwaves. Many parents do not think that the (4) _wholesome_ of a government-controlled television ratings system is censorship. They mistrust the industry's ability to regulate itself. To them, it is like putting the fox in charge of the henhouse. So parents are hopeful. A parent of one child said, "Boy, I hope the new system will (5) _take_ here as well as it did in Canada."

However, not everyone sees the ratings system as a (6) _panacea_, a cure-all for the whole problem of TV violence. Teenagers in particular view the blocked-out shows as (7) _forbidden fruit_. The fact that they can't watch a particular show (8) _invariably_ makes them want to watch it even more.

Broadcasters feel that the V-chip/ratings system is only a quick technological fix. They worry that parents who use the V-chip will block out prime-time shows, profitable evening programs which serve as their (9) _bread and butter_ programming. Moreover, broadcasters don't trust the public to use the system. Even though parents say they want less sex and violence on TV, shows containing such scenes are often the most popular. Broadcasters think the public is (10) _hypocritical_ and doubt that any electronic blocking device or ratings system will actually be used.

Supporters of freedom of speech, or First Amendment rights, are the loudest protesters against the V-chip/ratings system. They can't (11) _swallow_ the idea of blocking out certain programs. For them, this system (12) _fall under_ the category of censorship. In the Telecommunications Act, the government ordered the television industry to establish a ratings system. The law also ordered television manufacturers to install blocking devices in all new sets. The FCC (Federal Communications Commission), a government agency, is responsible for approving the implementation of the V-chip/ratings system. It can reject the broadcasters' ratings system and set up its own. Free speech supporters feel that the government has ultimate power and control over what is shown on television. Therefore, they see this power as full-fledged censorship.

3 *Politicians, public interest groups, the television industry, parents, and free-speech supporters continue to discuss television programming and who should control the TV set. Recently, leaders of all groups met in Washington, D.C., to discuss television content regulation. A well-respected magazine journalist moderated the session. The following are brief key exchanges taken from the session.*

Work in pairs.

Student A: You are the moderator leading the session and asking the questions.

Student B: Think about each group you represent (underlined). Read the response given and elaborate on it, using the words in parentheses. Create a response that is longer than one sentence.

Switch roles after question 3.

Student A

1. Moderator: How do you feel about the government's role in mandating the ratings system?

2. Moderator: You have 600,000 hours of programming each year. The ratings do not even apply to news, sports, or talk shows. What is your take on the new system?

3. Moderator: Studies have shown that you ignore movie ratings and consequently will also ignore television ratings. Is that right?

Now switch roles.

4. Moderator: You know that most electronic blocking devices are a little difficult to use. Do you think they are useful?

5. Moderator: I know that regulation of television content is a subject near and dear to your heart and that you and your colleagues are passionate about controlling it.

6. Moderator: You are a neutral group, citizens interested in the public good. Who do you think owns the responsibility?

Student B

1. Civil libertarian: Clearly, we are opposed to it because it is a violation of free speech rights. (invariably, fall under, full-fledged)

2. Television industry representative: Of course, it is ridiculous. We can't possibly rate all of these shows. (hypocritical, media)

3. Teenager: Of course, even though a movie is rated R, restricted for viewers under age 17, most of my friends and I see a lot of videos rated R at home. (forbidden fruit, panacea)

4. Parent: No way. I will never use it. It is way too complicated. (disgusted, take)

5. Government representative: Absolutely, we have a responsibility to protect the children of this country. No other group— not parents, not the industry, not public interest groups—will take charge. (trashy, wholesome)

6. Public interest group: We think that a panel or group of people from government, the television industry, and parent organizations should be formed to discuss the ratings system. (swallow, notion)

4 Focus on Speaking

A   PRONUNCIATION: Word Stress of Phrasal Verbs

A **phrasal verb** is a verb and preposition combination that has a special meaning. Phrasal verbs are common in informal, spoken English.

- *Newsweek* entertainment editor Rick Marin <u>looked into</u> the debate over TV ratings.

- The focus of the ratings involves the bread-and-butter programming and the movies that TV <u>picks up</u> from Hollywood.

Word Stress and Joining of Phrasal Verbs

Stress the preposition of a two-word phrasal verb.

   turn óff   look úp

Stress the second part (syllable or word) of a three-word phrasal verb.

   take cáre of   run óut of

Join the words of the phrasal verb together. Say them as a unit.

   Turn it off .   Look into it.

Phrasal verbs can be categorized in two groups: **inseparable** and **separable**. Inseparable phrasal verbs cannot be separated by an object. Separable phrasal verbs can be either separated or not separated.

Separable: Turn the TV off. (*Turn off* can be separated by the object, *TV*.)

Inseparable: Look into the debate. (*Look into* cannot be separated by *debate*. You cannot say: Look the debate into.)

Here is a list of some common phrasal verbs used in the interviews.

Separable	Inseparable
block out	catch up with
pick up	look into
put in	stick with
take up	
try out	

1 *Listen to the following sentences and phrases. As you listen, underline the phrasal verbs. Put a stress mark (⌐) over the stressed syllable. Then check your answers with those of another student, and take turns reading the sentences aloud.*

1. Will the ratings and electronic blocking devices <u>block óut</u> whole shows, or just offensive parts?

2. So you could presumably program your TV to pick up shows that were either G or PG rated.

3. . . . but if you stick with your old set for another ten years . . .

4. All the families that tried it out, loved it.

5. We caught up with him in Sydney, Australia.

6. You should be flattered that TV is taking up your model.

7. Rick Marin, a magazine editor, looked into the debate over TV ratings.

8. Manufacturers are reluctantly putting them in.

2 *Work with a partner.*

Student A: Cover the right column. Ask Student B a question. Then listen to Student B, and check the answer.

Student B: Cover the left column. Listen to Student A's question, and answer the question choosing one of the phrasal verbs from the box. Use the appropriate form of the word. Then switch roles after question 4.

try . . . out	put . . . in	stick with	pick up	look into	take up

Student A

1. Will other countries also adopt a content-based TV ratings system? (taking up)

2. Do you think you'll drop that broadcasting course because its so hard? (stick with)

3. Do you ever listen to radio broadcasts from overseas? (pick up)

4. Does your computer have a software program that blocks out offensive material? (put . . . in)

Student B

1. Yes, France is considering _____*taking up*_____ the Canadian model.

2. No, I think I'll _____ it.

3. No, my radio can't _____ any foreign broadcasts.

4. No, not yet. But I may _____ one _____ soon.

Now switch roles.

5. Are you using your V-chip? (try out)

5. Are you kidding? I _____ it _____, but it was much too complicated.

6. Are psychologists and sociologists sure that TV violence leads to violence in real life? (look into)

6. No, they're not 100 percent sure. I think they'll be _____ it for years.

7. Have you spoken to your film studies professor recently? (catch up with)

7. No. He's so busy, its impossible to _____ him.

8. Can your children access everything on the Internet? (block out)

8. No. I have a special screening device that _____ inappropriate material.

B GRAMMAR: Modals—Degrees of Certainty

1 *Working with a partner, examine the following statements, and discuss the questions that follow.*

- The V-chip will block out the whole show. With it, you <u>could</u> program your TV and you <u>could</u> lock your TV as well.

- The V-chip <u>should be able to</u> save the entertainment industry from full-fledged censorship.

   a. Which statement is more certain?

   b. What words could you substitute for the underlined words and keep the same meaning?

Modals: Degrees of Certainty

Use **modal verbs** to express different **degrees of certainty** about the present, the past, and the future. The modal you use shows how strongly you believe something is true or not true.

Almost Certain

| Present | *must* | The show has such explicit language that I think it **must** be rated MA. |
| Past | *must* + *have* + past participle (*must've*)* | They walked out in the middle of the movie. They **must have (must've)** been disgusted. |

Almost Certain, Negative (Impossible)

| Present | *can't / couldn't* | TV ratings **can't** possibly work as well as movie ratings. |
| Past | *can't / couldn't* + *have* + past participle (*couldn't've*)* | Oh no! The government **couldn't have (couldn't've)** censored that harmless children's movie. |

Quite Sure

| Future | *should / ought to* | Parents **should** be able to program the V-chip. It'll be easy to use. |
| Past | *should* + *have* + past participle (*should've*)* | He left at 4:30. He **should've** arrived by now. He's late. |

Less Certain

| Present | *could / may / might* | There are some violent scenes in the movie, which **might** be why it was censored. |
| Past | *could / may / might* + *have* + past participle (*might've*)* | That movie never came to my town. It **might have (might've)** been censored. |

---

* In speaking, the auxiliary *have* [modal + *have* + past participle] is pronounced /əv/ and is joined to the preceding word.

2 *Work with a partner.*

Student A: Cover the right column. Ask a question or make a comment.

Student B: Cover the left column. Respond, using the cues and a present or past modal verb of certainty. Refer to the box on page 234. Be sure to pronounce the reduced modal forms (must've, couldn't've, should've, might've) correctly. Then switch roles after question 4.

Student A	**Student B**
1. Do you think the ratings system will really eliminate TV violence?	1. (less certain) It's possible. It (help) to reduce TV violence, but not completely.
2. Will the public be able to understand the ratings system?	2. (quite sure) Yes, they (able / understand) it. It's not that difficult.
3. Do the police know what motivated the child to commit that awful crime?	3. (less certain) They're not sure. They think he (copy) a crime he saw on TV.
4. I can't believe it! This little chip has blocked out all my favorite shows.	4. (impossible) Really? I wouldn't believe that! It (happen).

Now switch roles.

Student A	**Student B**
5. That scene was included in the movie theater version, but not in the television version.	5. (almost certain) Hmm . . . it (block out [passive]).
6. Did that new drama get an MA* rating?	6. (quite sure) Yes, it (gotten) an MA rating since the actors used some fairly strong language.
7. Will the television industry be able to rate all shows on television?	7. (impossible) It's not at all likely. They (rate) all of them.
8. Will parents make the effort to consult the TV ratings?	8. (less certain) Yes, some (make) the effort, but most parents won't bother.

---

* *MA:* mature audiences

3 *Work with a partner.*

Student A: Cover the right column. Ask the question. Check Student B's answer against the words in parentheses.

Student B: Cover the left column. Answer the question, using an appropriate past modal of certainty in short-answer form from the box on page 234. Be sure to pronounce the modal perfect forms correctly. Then switch roles after question 4.

Student A

1. Did the price of a new television go up because of the V-chip? (must've)

2. Was the TV program writer angry about the Telecommunications Law, which requires ratings? (must've been)

3. Did that record store really refuse to sell the rock group's latest CD? (could've been/ might've been/may've been)

4. Did she resign from her writing position at the television network because of her opposition to the ratings system? (couldn't've)

Now switch roles.

5. Did he attend the free-speech group meeting last night? (must've)

6. Were those children allowed to see that movie rated for children over 13 only? (could've/might've/may've)

7. Has your child's school installed the Internet blocking device in all the computers? (should've)

8. Were the shareholders of that broadcasting company pleased with the quarterly earnings report? (couldn't've been)

Student B

1. (almost certain) Yes, it _____*must've*_____.

2. (almost certain) Yes, he _____. He stormed out of the meeting when he heard the news.

3. (less certain) I don't know. They

_____. I heard that store has a policy of not selling music with offensive lyrics.

4. (impossible) No, she _____. It's a rumor. I saw her in the office yesterday.

5. (almost certain) Yes, he _____. He wasn't home when I called, and I know he's protesting the Telecommunications Law.

6. (less certain) It's possible. Their parents are not very strict, so I guess they

_____.

7. (quite sure) Yes, by now they

_____. Its been required by law for over a year.

8. (impossible) No, they _____. Profits have been down 75 percent since the ratings system started.

C STYLE: Expressing Doubts or Reservations

When answering a complex question, you may not be able to give a definite answer. Sometimes you may want to express a **doubt** or **reservation**. Look at the following underlined expressions that are used in the interviews to express doubts or reservations regarding the proposed television V-chip/ratings combination.

DAVID ALPERN: We hear the ratings won't cover news or sports, but what about raunchy news magazines . . . talk shows?

RICK MARIN: That's unclear. I think talk shows would fall under the category of entertainment.

DAVID ALPERN: Adult ratings actually attract young audiences, but isn't that exactly what the V-chip is supposed to counteract?

RICK MARIN: Yeah, [but] the problem is . . .

RICK MARIN: The Canadian results have been encouraging. . . . We've got to remember that the Canadians . . . have always loved violence less than Americans. . . . So who knows if [the V-chip/ratings will] take here as well as it has there.

The following sentences contain other expressions commonly used to express doubts and reservations.

- **I can see what you're getting at,** but the age-based ratings provide little information.

- **I have some doubts about that.** For example, the content-based ratings used in Canada give parents information about the program.

- **The thing I question is whether** parents will actually care enough to use any kind of electronic blocking device.

Work with a partner.

Student A: Read the strong opinion. Say it like you mean it.

Student B: Use an expression from the following list to express a doubt or a reservation about the opinion expressed by Student A. Add further comments to explain your hesitation. Then switch roles after question 5.

> That's unclear. I think . . .
> Yes, but . . .
> Yes, but who knows if . . .
> I can see what you're getting at, but . . .
> I have some doubts about that. For example . . .
> The thing I question is whether . . .

Student A

1. Sex and violence are everywhere. Blocking out TV shows is useless.

2. Music CDs should be rated just like TV or movies. Offensive lyrics are harmful to teenagers.

3. Give kids reality: sex, violence, whatever. Why hide the truth?

4. Cartoons are too violent for children.

5. Advertisements can be violent. The V-chip should block them out, too.

Now switch roles.

6. TV is a form of art. It shouldn't be censored.

7. Broadcasters rating their own shows— that's like putting the fox in charge of the henhouse.

8. The answer to TV violence is simple: Turn off the tube, and take your children to the library!

9. Not rate the news! Are you kidding? The news is full of violence.

Student B

1. **I can see what you're getting at, but** *we really don't need even more sex and violence on TV.*

2. I have some doubts about that. For example, . . .

3. Yes, but . . .

4.

5.

6. The thing I question is whether . . .

7. That's unclear. I think . . .

8.

9.

D SPEAKING TOPIC

1 *Divide into two teams to debate a First Amendment issue:*

Team A (Pro): Supporters of the Telecommunications Law

Team B (Con): Supporters of First Amendment rights

1. Debate the following question:

> Does the government have the right to regulate TV programming content with the Telecommunications Law?

Supporters of the Telecommunications Law believe that the government has the right to:

- insist that the television industry rate television programming
- approve the television industry's ratings system
- implement a government-controlled ratings system if the television industry's system is not satisfactory
- require that TV manufacturers install V-chips in all new TV sets

Supporters of First Amendment rights believe that the government does not have the right to regulate TV programming. They believe that:

- the law violates free-speech rights
- free and open broadcasting is protected by the First Amendment, which prevents direct government intervention in TV content
- by mandating the V-chip/ratings system, the government is controlling TV content

2. Work in your teams, and brainstorm four more arguments. Write them on a separate piece of paper.

Team A (Pro)	Team B (Con)
Example	**Example**
The government must do something about sex and violence on TV. The industry refuses to regulate itself.	*The industry has the right to regulate its own product.*

3. Start the debate:

    1. Make opening statements.

    2. Take turns presenting arguments.

    3. Use expressions from section C (Style) as well as from the Style sections of previous units.

2 *Write a letter to the editor of your local newspaper, and give your opinion on this debate issue.*

E   RESEARCH TOPIC

A roving reporter is a reporter who asks several people their opinions on a current issue in a very short interview. The reporter roves, or moves from person to person, in order to solicit opinions. You are going to act as a roving reporter by interviewing several individuals on the topic of content controls, such as the V-chip and TV ratings.

1. Working with a partner, brainstorm a list of questions to use in your short interviews. Two have been provided for you.

    a. *Do you think there is too much violence on television?*

    b. *Have you heard of the V-chip and ratings system? If so, what do you think of them?*

    c. _____ ?

    d. _____ ?

    e. _____ ?

2. Select four of the questions to ask your interviewees.

3. While you interview, try to take notes as the interviewees answer your questions.

4. Present a summary of your findings to the class.

5. Discuss your experience as a roving reporter.

For Unit 10 Internet activities, visit the NorthStar Companion Website at http://www.longman.com/northstar.

Student Activities

BACKGROUND, page 49

1. 40%   **2.** 40%   **3.** 15%   **4.** 5%

D. SPEAKING TOPICS

ROLE PLAY 1, page 71

Interview with Suzanne Vega, singer-songwriter

Student B

Since I was a child, everyone has always said, "Yes, she is really shy." And they have always described me as withdrawn, aloof, or reserved. They have sometimes used the word "timid" too, but I have a problem with that because I really don't consider myself timid.

In 1989, I performed in front of 100,000 people at a music festival in Scotland. Being able to perform in front of so many people was something I had to work on for many years. Since I was a young child, I loved singing and everyone said I was good at it, but I hated being in front of an audience. I hated everyone looking at me and only wished they would look somewhere else. But finally I knew I just had to do it, in the same way that some people who are afraid of heights take up skydiving.

My earliest memory was when I was three years old and I dressed up for Halloween as a blue ghost. I remember walking into the room, and my family all looked at me. My face turned red, my heart started beating quickly, and all I wanted to do was disappear!

As a celebrity, I often get asked to give an autograph to fans. I try to be pleasant and appreciative and usually provide the autograph. But I don't look for a lot of interactions with strangers. I usually still don't like making contact with strangers.

ROLE PLAY 2

Interview with Dr. Cardoza, psychologist

Student A

The "successfully shy" person is the person who truly understands his or her shyness. He has taken the time to admit his shyness to others, openly discuss his shyness with family and friends, gets advice from them and takes action. The successfully shy person controls his own shyness. Shyness does not control him.

Successfully shy people don't try to change themselves. They accept themselves. They are often kind and considerate folks who are good listeners rather than talkers. They enjoy observing rather than being the center of attention. The world needs people like this!!

When it comes to shyness, we tell people that if the shyness is really preventing them from realizing their dreams, they should attend an individual or group counseling session. There they can begin to understand and finally control their shyness. They can check the Internet for different groups in their area.

UNIT 4

C. PREPARING TO LISTEN, page 76

When confronted with the same problem, Yale University health officials distributed another set of booklets that included a map of the campus, with the university health building circled and the times that shots were available clearly listed. The vaccination rate then increased from 3 percent to 28 percent.

UNIT 6

C. PREPARING TO LISTEN, page 123

1. Most monks are quiet, introverted people.

   Myth: The personality of monks around the world is as diverse as the personality of human beings around the world. There are monks who have all kinds of temperaments: quiet, gregarious, aloof, friendly, reserved, and so on. Because monks do live in a community with others, it is necessary that a monk enjoy being with other people.

2. Monks and nuns never retire and generally work until they die.

   Fact: There is a saying among one group of monks called the Trappists: "Live, work, and die in place." Monks are expected to work hard and rest while being vitally interested in everything. Becoming a monk is a lifelong commitment that must be nurtured by work and play.

3. Monks and nuns have made few contributions to the outside world since they devote themselves to an inner, spiritual world.

   Myth: Monks and nuns throughout history have excelled in scientific research, healing arts, agricultural development, architecture, politics, poetry, and social work. Community service is a major part of the work of many monasteries throughout the world.

4. It is not necessary for monks to be vegetarians, shave their heads, or wear special robes called *habits*.

   Fact: Some monasteries are vegetarian only; some groups of monks, particularly in Asia, must shave their heads, and many monks do wear habits. However, these practices vary widely from monastery to monastery throughout the world.

5. Monks and nuns are chosen from birth to become monks by the family or the community.

Myth: People can become monks or nuns at any time in their lives. Men and women who have entered a monastery come from a wide range of backgrounds, both religious and secular, or non-religious. Many monks had well-established careers—such as airline pilot, corporate executive, or physician—but chose to give up those careers for life in the monastery.

6. Although most monks follow strict daily schedules, most monasteries are open to outside visitors.

Fact: Hospitality and a friendly, open attitude toward visitors are important elements of the mission for most monasteries. They welcome individuals regardless of their religious background and invite them to experience monastic life—daily chanting or praying, solitude, meditation, walking, and community work. There are, however, monasteries which are totally separated from the outside world and do not allow visitors.

UNIT 7

3. FOCUS ON VOCABULARY, page 158

The court ruled in favor of Nissan, saying that the electronic mail system is owned by the company. In addition, the e-mail messages were written on company time. Therefore, management has the right to read anything created on that system.

The judge in the case, however, recommended that Nissan come up with a privacy policy that informs employees of the fact that their e-mail may be monitored from time to time without notice.

UNIT 8

BACKGROUND, page 170

1. b
2. c
3. c
4. b
5. a
6. c
7. c

UNIT 9

BACKGROUND, page 194

Student A

Experiment 1 (Alpine Experiments)

Maria Spychiger and Jean-Luc Patry conducted the so-called Alpine experiments in Switzerland and Austria. The subjects were children, age 7 to 15. Approximately 1,200 children were involved in the study, which lasted three years. The researchers wanted to investigate the effect of music on math and language learning ability.

Control group: Children received one or two music lessons per week and seven or eight math and foreign language lessons per week.

Experimental group: Children received five or six music lessons per week and only two or three math and foreign language lessons per week.

The researchers found that even though the experimental group received fewer math and foreign language classes, those children scored just as well as the control group children on math tests. But more surprising, in spite of the reduction in language instruction, the experimental group scored better at foreign languages. And they worked better with each other.

Student B

Experiment 2 (University of California, Irvine)

Frances Rauscher from the University of California, Irvine,* worked with 79 college students, age 18 to 22, for two years. She wanted to find out if listening to the music of Mozart would affect the students' scores on tests of spatial reasoning. She used only one group in three sessions: two control sessions and one experimental session.

Control session 1: Students listened to a recorded message suggesting they imagine themselves relaxing in a peaceful garden.

Control session 2: Students sat in silence for 10 minutes.

Experimental session: Students listened to 10 minutes of Mozart's *Sonata for Two Pianos* in D Major.

After each 10-minute period, the students took a standard IQ (intelligence) test of spatial reasoning. Rauscher discovered that the students scored much higher on the spatial reasoning IQ test when they took it after listening to Mozart's music.

---

*Dr. Rauscher is now a professor at the University of Wisconsin–Oshkosh.

Student C

Experiment 3 (University of California, Irvine)

In another study Frances Rauscher and her colleague, Gordon Shaw, worked with nineteen 3-year-olds for eight months. They wanted to study the effect of music, singing, and piano on spatial reasoning abilities. They had one control group and two experimental groups.

Control group 1: Children received regular curriculum (no musical training).

Experimental group 2: Children received 30 minutes of singing lessons each day.

Experimental group 3: Children received 30 minutes of piano lessons each day.

At the end of the study, the children in the experimental groups scored 35 percent better on a spatial reasoning test than the children in the control group did.

E. RESEARCH TOPIC, page 218

Sample Problems

1. Study the table of numbers below for 2 minutes. Then cover it up, and try to reproduce it yourself.

2	6	6	1
3	4	2	6
6	3	6	0
4	2	1	8

2. How many rectangles are there in the figure?

(Answer: 9)

3. What is the minimum number of arrows that must be turned in some manner so that all arrows point in the same direction?

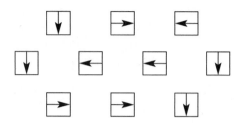

(Answer: 6)

Grammar Book References

NorthStar: Listening and Speaking, Advanced, Second Edition	Focus on Grammar, Advanced, Second Edition	Azar's Understanding and Using English Grammar, Third Edition
Unit 1 Wish Statements: Expressing Unreality	**Unit 24** Unreal Conditionals	**Chapter 20** Conditional Sentences and Wishes: 20-6, 20-10, 20-11
Unit 2 Noun Clauses after Verbs or Expressions of Urgency	**Unit 23** Noun Clauses and Phrases: Complements	**Chapter 12** Noun Clauses: 12-8
Unit 3 Adjective Clauses: Identifying and Nonidentifying	**Unit 10** Adjective Clauses: Review and Expansion **Unit 11** Adjective Clauses with Quantifiers: Adjective Phrases	**Chapter 13** Adjective Clauses: 13-5, 13-6, 13-7, 13-8, 13-10
Unit 4 Adverb Clauses of Result	**Unit 18** Adverb Clauses	**Chapter 19** Connectives that Express Cause and Effect, Contrast, and Condition: 19-4
Unit 5 Spoken Discourse Connectors	**Unit 20** Discourse Connectors	**Chapter 19** Connectives that Express Cause and Effect, Contrast, and Condition: 19-2, 19-6, 19-7, 19-9
Unit 6 Count and Non-Count Nouns and Their Quantifiers	**Unit 6** Count and Non-Count Nouns **Unit 7** Definite and Indefinite Articles	**Chapter 7** Nouns: 7-9, 7-10, 7-11

NorthStar: Listening and Speaking, Advanced, Second Edition	Focus on Grammar, Advanced, Second Edition	Azar's Understanding and Using English Grammar, Third Edition
Unit 7 Verb + Gerund or Infinitive: Two Forms, Two Meanings	**Unit 16** Gerunds **Unit 17** Infinitives	**Chapter 14** Gerunds and Infinitives, Part 1: 14-4, 14-7, 14-8, 14-9, 14-10
Unit 8 Direct and Indirect Speech	**Unit 12** The Passive: Review and Expansion **Unit 13** Reporting Ideas and Facts with Passives	**Chapter 12** Noun Clauses: 12-6, 12-7
Unit 9 The Passive Voice and the Passive Causative	**Unit 13** Reporting Ideas and Facts with Passives	**Chapter 11** The Passive: 11-1, 11-2, 11-7
Unit 10 Modals: Degrees of Certainty	**Unit 5** Modals: Certainty	**Chapter 10** Modals, Part 2: 10-1, 10-2, 10-3, 10-4, 10-5, 10-6

Audioscript

UNIT 1: The Internet and Other Addictions

2A LISTENING ONE: *Interview with an Internet Addiction Counselor*

Ira Flatow: Welcome back to *Talk of the Nation: Science Friday.* I'm Ira Flatow. We're talking this hour about how and why people might become addicted to things other than drugs . . . addicted to things like gambling, sex, even shopping. Of course, our high-tech society also offers new high-tech addictions like video games, on-line chat rooms. Jonathan Kandell is a counselor at the University of Maryland who puts together a support group for students who find themselves addicted to the Internet. Maybe you should listen carefully to this one if you are an Internet groupie. He joins me now from his office in College Park. Welcome to the program.

Jonathan Kandell: Thank you very much.

LISTENING FOR MAIN IDEAS

Ira Flatow: Welcome back to *Talk of the Nation: Science Friday.* I'm Ira Flatow. We're talking this hour about how and why people might become addicted to things other than drugs . . . addicted to things like gambling, sex, even shopping. Of course, our high-tech society also offers new high-tech addictions like video games, on-line chat rooms. Jonathan Kandell is a counselor at the University of Maryland who puts together a support group for students who find themselves addicted to the Internet. Maybe you should listen carefully to this one if you are an Internet groupie. He joins me now from his office in College Park. Welcome to the program.

Jonathan Kandell: Thank you very much.

IF: Is this a relatively new addiction?

JK: Well, for some people, I mean, some people have been involved with the Internet for years and uh . . . some of them may have been addicted for a while . . . with the widespread usage of the Internet now. . . . I mean . . . it's certainly growing especially on college campuses . . . we are seeing more and more of it.

IF: How does it present itself? Does a student come to you and say, "Doc, you gotta help me. I'm addicted to the Internet"?

JK: Well, I've seen people who have been, but they haven't presented with that particular issue. They've presented with issues like relationship problems, or they are having problems maintaining their grades because they are spending so much time doing other things and when you find out what's really going on . . . they're spending a lot of time on the Net and they're not paying attention to their studies . . . they're not devoting the attention to the relationships. These problems are coming out in other ways.

IF: Do other people turn their friends in . . . saying, "Doc, you gotta find out . . . this . . ."

JK: They haven't to this point. At this point, people still see computers as a very positive thing. And I mean, I agree. . . . I think there are many positive benefits for computers. But . . . uh . . . it's such a new idea that there is a problematic piece to

it . . . that, um . . . there haven't been many people turning other people in.

IF: This is something I worry about . . . personally, myself. I'll share this with you for a free consultation. I mean . . . whenever I get a chance and have some time, I love to go surfing on the Net. I'll be on there sometimes, very surprisingly, I'll be on there one o'clock in the morning . . . I'll send somebody an e-mail message thinking they'll get it the next morning. And I'll get an immediate response back . . . you know.

What are the symptoms? How do I know when my Internet compulsiveness is turning into an Internet addiction?

JK: Uh . . . I'm not sure the exact amount of time is really the issue, but I think when it becomes something that really begins to affect other areas of your life . . . when for instance your work performance or your school performance . . . or relationships with other people. Uh, one of the problems I see with the Internet, especially the chat rooms, is that people start developing relationships over the Net and they are very different from relationships that you have on a face-to-face basis, and you start losing some of the skills that make relationships successful . . . so that's certainly a warning signal. I think if people are beginning to say something to you like, "You seem to be spending a lot of time on-line," that's probably a good indicator as well . . .

But, I think, a real important thing is to examine what's going on with you when you are not on the Net . . . if you are beginning to feel anxious or depressed or feeling empty and lonely . . . and you know you really look forward to those times when you can be on-line to be connected with other people in that way . . . then, I think, a serious issue is starting to happen.

IF: What about if you stop giving up other things, like going out for a walk . . . is that a symptom?

JK: Uh, well, I mean, people have to make choices every day about the different activities that they're going to do. I think it's helpful to have some sort of balance in your life . . . if you can spend some time on the Internet and then go take a walk at a different time of the day. That's not an issue. In fact, that's one of the things that we suggest in the group is to somehow break the pattern . . . set an alarm clock or something. Go out and take a walk, and then come back before you get back on-line.

IF: You speak of the group, then, I mean, I'm assuming then some of the treatments you offer are group therapy sessions for these kids.

JK: Yes, this is a support group. And the group itself becomes a therapeutic tool . . . because people are getting out of their rooms, getting out of the isolation that they may find themselves in, and are dealing with other people face-to-face. They are talking about the issues that are going on with them. They are getting support from other people. Uh, they realize that it is not just them . . . that there are other people who are engaged in the same behavior and facing the same problems, and also they can help each other strategize about what's the best way for them to break the pattern . . . to figure out other things to do. Uh, also we examine people's life situations . . . it's important to figure out what's going on in the person's life that's contributing to these particular behaviors. . . . Why is the person spending so much time? Are they avoiding something? You know, what type of pain is going on in their life . . . that they are looking to find some fulfillment in this way?

LISTENING FOR DETAILS

(Repeat Listening for Main Ideas)

REACTING TO THE LISTENING

Exercise 1

Excerpt One

Jonathon Kandell is a counselor at the University of Maryland who puts together a support group for students who find themselves addicted to the Internet. Maybe you should listen carefully to this one if you are an Internet groupie.

Excerpt Two

IF: Is this a relatively new addiction?

JK: Well, for some people, I mean, some people have been involved with the Internet for years and uh . . . some of them may have been addicted for a while . . . with the widespread usage of the Internet now . . . I mean . . . it's certainly growing especially on college campuses . . . we are seeing more and more of it.

Excerpt Three

IF: How does it present itself? Does a student come to you [and] say, "Doc, you gotta help me. I'm addicted to the Internet"?

2B LISTENING TWO: *Time to Do Everything Except Think*

Exercise 1

WL: Warren Levinson of the Associated Press.

DA: I'm David Alpern of *Newsweek*.

WL: David Brooks, you argue that we already live in an over-communicated world that will only become more so in the next tech era. What exactly do you mean by that?

DB: The problem is that we've developed technology that gets us so much information that we've got cell phones ringing every second, we've got computers and laptops, we've got personal organizers and it's just—we're just being bombarded with communication and every advance and technology seems to create more and more communications at us. I do believe at the end of the day it shapes our personality because we are sort of overwhelmed by the information flow.

DA: Seriously though, just last week we reported on research suggesting that all the multi-tasking may actually make our brains work better and faster producing as its been reported a world-wide increase in IQ up to 20 points and more in recent decades. Can you see any benefit in all these mental gymnastics we now have to go through?

DB: Yeah I, I, I don't think we're becoming a race of global idiots uh, but I think certain skills are enhanced and certain are not. You know the ability to make fast decisions, to answer a dozen e-mails in five minutes, uh to fill out maybe big SAT type tests. That's enhanced. But creativity is something that happens slowly. It happens when your brain is just noodling around, just playing. When it puts together ideas which you hadn't thought

of or maybe you have time say to read a book. You are a businessperson but you have time to read a book about history or time to read a book about a philosopher and something that happened long ago or something or some idea somebody thought of long ago. Actually, you know, it occurs to you that you can think of your own business in that way, and so it's this mixture of unrelated ideas ah that feeds your productivity, feeds your creativity and if your mind is disciplined to answer every e-mail, then you don't have time for that playful noodling. You don't have time for those unexpected conjunctions so I think maybe we're getting smarter in some senses but I think it is a threat to our creativity and to our reflection.

DA: So how wired or wireless are you tied into the new technology?

DB: A total addict. When I'm out there with my kids playing in our little league or something like that, I've got my cell phone in my pocket. I'm always wondering, "Gee, did I get a voicemail?" uh and that's why I think I'm sort of driven to write about this because I do see the negative effects it's having on my own brain patterns.

DA: Could be *Newsweek on Air* calling . . . David Brooks thanks a lot.

DB: Thank you.

4A PRONUNCIATION

I've GOT to have a cigarette.

I REALLY need to check my e-mail again.

Exercise 1

1. Patty was running up <u>huge</u> sums of money on her credit cards.
2. She spent <u>thousands</u> of dollars.
3. <u>Nothing</u> could stop her.
4. She was <u>totally</u> out of control.
5. <u>Fifteen</u> cups of coffee a day was the <u>only</u> thing that kept Jim going.
6. <u>Totally</u> overwhelmed by work, he drank from <u>5</u> in the morning to 11 at night.
7. Now, addicted to both coffee <u>and</u> the Internet, his life was a <u>complete</u> disaster.
8. He couldn't get to a therapist's office <u>fast</u> enough.

Exercise 2

A: Workaholism isn't <u>really</u> an addiction. Some people have <u>no</u> choice <u>but</u> to work <u>long</u> hours.

B: Not <u>only</u> that. A <u>lot</u> of people are workaholics because they <u>love</u> what they do.

A: <u>Agreed</u>, but being <u>driven</u> to succeed at all costs may not be such a good thing.

B: Yeah, that makes me think of my father. He was <u>so</u> hooked on work, he used to <u>drive</u> talking on his cell phone and checking his <u>e-mail</u> at red lights.

A: You <u>must</u> be joking. That is multi-<u>tasking</u> at its <u>best</u>!

B: Well, not <u>exactly</u>. He just lost his <u>driver's</u> license after getting into his <u>third</u> accident and getting his <u>fifth</u> ticket.

UNIT 2: Celebration, Florida: Disney's Utopia

2A LISTENING ONE: *The Celebration Experiment*

Andrew Ross: [they] were very much looking for a town where they could fully participate and create and define the sense of community there, and for most of them, I think, initially they found that, but a lot of them got burned out because there's so much community, almost too much community. Others I think suffered a little more hardship in realizing that a lot of their expectations would be thwarted in one way or another.

LISTENING FOR MAIN IDEAS

David Brancaccio, Host: Remember the setting for the movie *The Truman Show*? It looked like a nice place to live. Well, for the most part it wasn't a set, the town actually exists and it's called Seaside, Florida, and it was built on the concept of "new urbanism"—the idea of using architecture and planning to nurture civic ties and to encourage interaction between neighbors. In Central Florida, the Walt Disney Company is running its own experiment in new urbanism—a town called Celebration. Andrew Ross is a professor of American Studies at New York University. He spent a year living in Celebration, getting to know the town and its people.

Andrew Ross: The town more or less borrows very heavily from new urbanist principles—that's the town planning movement that is pledged to create environmentally friendly alternatives to sprawl and to create communities around people rather than automobiles. But, many aspects of that kind of design of that sort of town are really aimed at maximizing social interaction between residents, not just on the streets but also in community institutions that are very much a part of public life there. So I think it's fair to say there were social goals that went along with the physical plan and I was as much interested in them as in the physical plan itself.

DB: And from your point of view these would be laudable goals, I mean you go to some horrible sprawl communities in places like Southern California and you'll see houses that only present garage doors to the street and a community setup where you absolutely have to drive to every single place and no one ever sees each other, so it's interesting when Disney planners address some of these issues.

AR: Mm-hmmm. What makes Celebration unique—there are many things that make Celebration unique, but one of them is the very high level of media scrutiny. By the time I got there to spend my year in Celebration, this was a community of folks who were already the most scrutinized people on the planet, and that generated a very high level of performance anxiety among the folks living there. Really, that trickled down all the way from the Disney boardrooms to the school restrooms, ceaselessly assessing how the community was doing; whether it was creating a vibrant sense of interaction and participation, and whether it was being a success or a failure.

DB: Now despite all the planning that went into Celebration it evolved in what turned out to be unpredictable ways; a lot of people disappointed there, some people less disappointed.

AR: It was really the first unscripted product the Disney Company has ever done, and there was no script to follow and that was part of the interest. A lot of folks who moved in there had very high expectations—a goodly number of them were Disneyphiles who had been accustomed to high levels of customer satisfaction from the company in their vacation experiences. Obviously those high expectations would be inevitably thwarted at some level. But most folks, and we are talking about a self-selecting group of pioneers who moved in there, were people who had moved from the cheerless isolation of a lot of other suburban places—were very hungry for community, very much looking for a town where they could fully participate and create and define the sense of community there, and for most of them I think initially they found that, but a lot of them got burned out because there was so much community, almost too much community. Others I think suffered a little more hardship in realizing that a lot of their expectations would be thwarted in one way or another.

DB: What about the attempts of the planners to engineer a community where there would be a mixture of incomes? Was that effective? How did that play out?

AR: Initially it was effective, and this is highly unusual in the American housing landscape to find fairly pricey houses just a spit away from multi-family rental apartment buildings, you just don't find that anywhere in the American housing landscape. The problem is that a lot of new urbanist towns like Celebration become commercially successful, and Celebration has indeed been that. What happens is the housing prices rise and the low-income folks can't afford to live there anymore. That's already beginning to happen; there were working class people who I knew in Celebration who had moved in there as pioneers and Lord knows how they made ends meet, but they did. Certainly it wasn't cheap to live in town, but increasingly those lower income folks won't be able to afford that.

DB: Professor Ross, you're now back in your life mixing with your callous sophisticate Manhattan friends. Do you miss Celebration?

AR: Oh I sure miss a lot of the people that I knew there—I made a goodly number of friends and actually am going back next week to visit Celebration. For me it was a very comfortable place to live.

DB: Andrew Ross teaches American Studies at NYU. His book is called the *The Celebration Chronicles*.

LISTENING FOR DETAILS

(*Repeat Listening for Main Ideas*)

REACTING TO THE LISTENING

Excerpt One

Exercise 1

DB: Remember the setting for the movie *The Truman Show*? It looked like a nice place to live. Well, for the most part it wasn't a set, the town actually exists and it's called Seaside, Florida, and it was built on the concept of "new urbanism."

Excerpt Two

AR: By the time I got there to spend my year in Celebration, this was a community of folks who were already the most scrutinized people on the planet, and that generated a very high level of performance anxiety among the folks living there. Really, that trickled down all the way from the Disney boardrooms to the school restrooms, ceaselessly assessing how the community was doing.

Excerpt Three

AR: What happens is the housing prices rise and the low income folks can't afford to live there anymore. That's already beginning to happen; there were working people who I knew in Celebration had moved in there as pioneers and Lord knows how they made ends meet, but they did. Certainly, it wasn't cheap to live in town . . .

Excerpt Four

DB: Professor Ross, you're now back in your life mixing with your callous sophisticate Manhattan friends. Do you miss Celebration?

2B LISTENING TWO: *Living in Celebration*

Douglas Frantz, Co-author: You know, they've tried to look backward at small-town America and take the best of those planning elements—you know, houses close together, sidewalks, front porches, tree-lined streets, easy, non-automobile-dependent access to the town center and to your neighbors and to the school and the other institutions that are vital. And they've tried to take some of those ideas and update them and come up with a livable, workable place where people can go and rekindle the sense of community that seems to be missing from suburbs all across the country.

Terry Gross, Host: So give us a sense of how this new town, Celebration was designed.

DF: Houses are all very close together. We were just 10 feet apart from our neighbors on either side of us, and that's pretty much the standard for the town. So, you have houses that are close together, houses that surround open areas. They have a lot of big parks, a lot of common areas. The theory is that you're willing to sacrifice your private yard space—you don't need a quarter of an acre or half an acre—if you have a public area where you can go and enjoy the facilities there and, most importantly, you can interact with your neighbors. That helps to create this sense of community that's so important to many of these "new town" developments.

TG: You know, this whole sense of, like, "It's going to be a new town, but we're going to do it with a sense of nostalgia for the past so nothing can be designed past what existed in the 1940s"—it seems—it just seems a little contradictory, and some of the designs from the 1940s didn't really transfer that well into the '90s. Like, a lot of the houses had porches.

DF: . . . what Disney expected with these front porches, what the planners envisioned was it would create a "front porch culture"—that people would be out on their porches talking to their neighbors next door and to people walking down the street or people riding their bikes, and there would be this culture that, you know, either existed or existed in somebody's imagination, you know, 30, 40, 50 years ago.

But that really has been one of the failures that we observed during our two years in Celebration, and the people don't spend very much time at all on their front porches. There are a couple things going on. One is it's central Florida, and it's hotter than hell a good part of the year, and sitting on your front porch, even if you have a fan going, can be a very uncomfortable thing. People prefer to be inside in the air-conditioning.

TG: What were some of the rules you had to live by in Celebration? And did any of those rules bother you?

Catherine Collins, Co-author: Well, Doug and I have different feelings about rules. His feeling is—now, if I can summarize his feelings for him—that you move in there knowing the rules, and if you don't like them, you shouldn't move in. I have a few—some problems with rules. I just sometimes like to break them. And they just bother me because they're in existence. But the rules sometimes were silly and sometimes weren't. They dictated what color your curtains could be facing the street and actually asked a woman with red curtains to remove them.

DF: They dictated where you could park your car.

CC: And for how long.

DF: And for how long. They dictated any sort of thing you could attach to your house. You couldn't attach a satellite dish to your house. They dictated forever the color of your house. And they dictate how often you have to repaint your house. They've tried to go a step further and remove plastic flowers and plastic furniture from those all-important front porches. You know, there's—there are rules, and then there are rules that seem to go a little too far.

But yeah, my point of view is that you know coming in that you're going to have to live by these rules, and if you don't like it, there are lots of other nice places to go live. I mean, I think there's a reason for most of these rules.

4A PRONUNCIATION

They <u>watch as</u> many Disney movies as I do.

My <u>watch has</u> been stolen.

My <u>watch is</u> a Disneyland souvenir.

Exercise 1

1. a. He's eating lunch /əz/ usual.
   b. Lunch /əz/ ready.
   c. I ordered two lunch/əz /.
   d. Lunch /əz/ been served.
2. a. The porch/əz/ need to be painted.
   b. The porch /əz/ in need of repair.
   c. The porch /əz/ been fixed.
   d. Please rebuild the porch /əz/ it was before.
3. a. The house /əz/ been put on the market.
   b. The house /əz/ way too pricey.
   c. They built that house /əz/ a model.
   d. The house/əz/ are very close to the street.
4. a. The garage/əz/ are hidden from view.
   b. The garage /əz/ behind the house.
   c. The design of the garage /əz/ finally been approved.
   d. They repainted the garage /əz/ fast as they could.

UNIT 3: The Bold and the Bashful

2A LISTENING ONE: *Americans Are Getting Shyer*

Philip Zimbardo: Virtually all the people that we have surveyed, certainly 75 percent of them, say shyness is undesirable, has adverse consequences. Shy people are less popular, they have fewer friends, they have lower self-esteem, they make less money, their life is more boring, they have less intimate . . . less intimacy, less sex, they have fewer leadership skills, less social support, they're more likely to be depressed and, as you get older, more likely to be lonely. That's a terrible syndrome of negative consequences.

LISTENING FOR MAIN IDEAS

Part One

Alex Chadwick, Host: Do you find these days that it's more difficult meeting people? In social situations with strangers do you wind up asking yourself, "Am I dressed wrong today or something?" Friends, take heart. A new study says it's not you at all. The problem is Americans are, generally speaking, more shy than many people would expect, and getting shyer all the time.

Philip Zimbardo is a professor of psychology at Stanford University who runs a shyness clinic in Palo Alto. He's the author of numerous studies on shyness. Good morning, Professor Zimbardo.

Philip Zimbardo: Good morning.

AC: Your earlier study showed shyness already widespread, but what about the newest figures?

PZ: Our research, which we've been conducting since 1972, focused on adults who were shy. Before our research started, of course, the interest was always in shy children and, to our amazement, we discovered that about 40 percent of all Americans label themselves as currently shy, and over the past ten years that figure has increased to about 48 percent. What that means is two out of every five people you meet think of themselves as shy, and now that figure is moving toward one out of two, which is a surprise, especially to foreigners, who think . . . think of Americans as bold and outgoing and not at all shy.

AC: Why is shyness so common, and why is it becoming even more common?

PZ: Well, shyness is a fascinating problem because at one level to be shy means to be reticent, to be self-conscious. It's a kind of social phobia, a fear of people, and it's very hard to avoid people, and there are just many things in a culture, our culture, which leads lots of people to be shy. We have a very competitive culture. We have a culture where people are constantly . . . at least feel they are being evaluated, where the . . . whole notion of testing, of . . . of individual merit that starts in school, at work, really extends for many people to their social life. But what's been happening recently is a whole series of social forces that are increasingly isolating people from normal day-to-day informal social contact, which is essential to be a social being, an extrovert, an outgoing person who can easily and comfortably relate to other people.

AC: A set of social factors, you say. What do you mean?

PZ: Well, first, the electronic revolution replaces people with computer chips wherever possible, so at every level where you replace bank tellers with ATM machines, you replace operators with direct dialing, you replace the gas station attendant with automatic gas fill-ups . . .

AC: So there's . . . there's just less opportunity for social interaction? People forget about . . .

PZ: Well, people don't forget, they don't learn . . . young people don't learn in the first place, they don't practice it, they don't see it practiced, as you have, so this gets really complicated because

computers, computer games, video games, are things people can play alone. You don't need other people the way you used to in the past and, also, as families get smaller, as both parents work, we no longer have extended families, children don't see . . . don't have the opportunity to see their parents and relatives relating in a natural, easy, friendly way. So . . . so they just . . . we are losing the . . . the . . . the social lubrication that's essential for people to feel comfortable in the presence of each other.

Part Two

AC: Professor Zimbardo, when you say shy, when you say it's a problem, what kind of shyness do you mean? Many people feel some awkwardness in social situations, especially if they get attention from others, if they're the object of attention from others.

PZ: Virtually all the people that we have surveyed, certainly 75 percent of them, say shyness is undesirable, has adverse consequences. Shy people are less popular, they have fewer friends, they have lower self-esteem, they make less money, their life is more boring, they have less intimate . . . less intimacy, less sex, they have fewer leadership skills, less social support, they're more likely to be depressed and, as you get older, more likely to be lonely. That's a terrible syndrome of negative consequences.

AC: So this is not just a momentary shyness that . . . that . . . people feel; this is something that really marks their lives?

PZ: Yeah. The momentary shyness is something we call situational shyness. That is if . . . if you're on a blind date, if you're asked to perform in public, we are not really prepared. Or if your mother says, you know, "Play the piano for Aunt Tilly." Well, you have feelings of shyness, the . . . the arousal, the negative thoughts, the . . . the physical tension, but that is situational. So you say to yourself, "Well, that's not me; that's that external situation which I have to avoid." It's when it becomes chronic and dispositional. You begin to see shyness as Quasimodo's hump, the thing you carry around with you that's always there and even . . . even if . . . if people in the world don't notice it, you know it's there ready to emerge.

AC: When . . . when you're at a cocktail party, or just in conversation with someone anywhere and you recognize that they're shy, what do you do to draw them out or try to make them more comfortable?

PZ: Essentially what we say, for example, to shy people is, "If you begin with the knowledge that maybe half the people out there are also shy, then when you're in a situation, do your best to find those other people, those kindred souls." And a great way to break the ice is to talk about how uncomfortable these situations make you feel, and you presume the other. Admitting your shyness is really an important first step because if you don't, people make misattributions. That is, if you don't perform in a situation where people expect you to perform, to smile, to be outgoing, to start a conversation, people assume you're dumb, you're unmotivated, you're boring, or you're not interested in them. You're bored or boring, and those are terrible misattributions, especially if you're attractive as a man, or beautiful as a woman, and shy. Then it's a double handicap because people then assume you are aloof, you are condescending, you think you're too good for them.

AC: Professor Zimbardo?

PZ: Yes?

AC: Are you shy?

PZ: No, not at all. In fact, I'm a firstborn from a big Sicilian family, so my job was making all the other kids feel comfortable, and so I . . . I am more like a Zorba the Greek-type person whose job in the world it is to make people feel comfortable, you know, at life's party.

AC: Professor Zimbardo, thank you very much.

PZ: It's been a joy, thank you.

AC: Stanford University psychologist Philip Zimbardo runs a shyness clinic at Palo Alto. He spoke to us from member station KQED in San Francisco. This is NPR's *Morning Edition*; I'm Alex Chadwick.

LISTENING FOR DETAILS

(*Repeat Listening for Main Ideas*)

REACTING TO THE LISTENING

Exercise 1

Excerpt One

AC: Do you find these days that it's more difficult meeting people? In social situations with strangers do you wind up asking yourself, "Am I dressed wrong today or something?" Friends, take heart.

Excerpt Two

PZ: Our research, which we've been conducting since 1972, focused on adults who were shy. Before our research started, of course, the interest was always in shy children and, to our amazement, we discovered that about 40 percent of all Americans label themselves as currently shy, and over the past ten years that figure has increased to about 48 percent. What that means is two out of every five people you meet think of themselves as shy.

Excerpt Three

AC: Professor Zimbardo: Are you shy?

PZ: No, not at all. In fact, I'm a firstborn from a big Sicilian family, so my job was making all the other kids feel comfortable.

2B LISTENING TWO: *The Pollyanna Syndrome*

Exercise 1

If you're the sort to divide people into two groups, consider the division between those who always see the bright side and those who'd rather wallow in their misery.

Julie Danis tackles the Pollyanna syndrome in today's *Tale from the Workplace*.

Hi, this is Julie Danis with *Tales from the Workplace*.

Arriving at the office after a visit to the eye doctor with no diagnosis for my blurred vision, I was in a grouchy mood. "No time to be cranky," a co-worker said, "we have a project due." "Besides," she continued, "now you have a prescription to skip the mascara and rest your eyes, every two hours."

She'd done it again, I realized. She had made lemonade out of lemons. We all know people like this. They find the silver lining inside the darkest cloud . . . all the time . . . without fail . . . driving others to distraction with their "find the bright side" philosophy.

"Oh well," they say, "a stop-and-go commute is perfect for listening to language tapes while doing relaxation exercises, *mais oui*?"

They may emit an occasional, "Oh, no," when the computer crashes and the hold time on the 1-800-HELP line promises to be hours. But that is soon replaced by an, "Oh good, time to purge the files."

This optimistic outlook does have its merits. When you're snowed in with no hope of flying for twenty-four hours or more, take it as a sign you should catch up on some movies.

But don't get carried away. Nothing will take away the ache in your mouth or fill the void in your pocketbook from two root canals, not covered by your company's health plan.

So, the next time someone says, "You can't cry over something that can't cry over you," assert yourself in the face of their sunny-side-up point of view. State firmly, "Yes I can, and I plan to do just that." Then go suck on some lemons and feel better in your own way.

I'm Julie Danis with *Tales from the Workplace*.

4A PRONUNCIATION

Exercise 1

1. We discovered that about 40 percent of all Americans label themselves as currently shy.

2. Over the past ten years, that figure has increased to about 48 percent.

3. Do you find these days that it's more difficult meeting people?

4. Two out of every five people you meet think of themselves as shy.

5. There are just many things in a culture, our culture, which lead lots of people to be shy.

6. Children don't see . . . don't have the opportunity to see their parents and relatives relating in a natural, easy, friendly way.

7. When you're at a party, or just in a conversation with someone anywhere and you recognize that they're shy, what do you do to draw them out or try to make them more comfortable?

8. Admitting your shyness is really an important first step because if you don't, people make misattributions.

Exercise 2

1. "Phillip," said the doctor, "doesn't suffer from shyness."

2. My sister who lives in California is a Pollyanna.

3. Suzanne's manager told me she's gotten over her shyness.

4. Zimbardo interviewed the students who had admitted they were shy.

5. Everything he said was based on research.

6. The therapy, which the clinic provides, gets people to be more outgoing.

4D SPEAKING TOPICS

Exercise 1

Left of Center
by Suzanne Vega

If you want me
You can find me
Left of center
Off of the strip

In the outskirts
In the fringes
In the corner
Out of the grip

When they ask me
"What are you looking at?"
I always answer
"Nothing much" (not much)
I think they know that
I'm looking at them
I think they think
I must be out of touch

But I'm only
In the outskirts
And in the fringes
On the edge
And off the avenue
And if you want me
You can find me
Left of center
Wondering about you

I think that somehow
Somewhere inside of us
We must be similar
If not the same
So I continue
To be wanting you
Left of center
Against the grain

If you want me
You can find me
Left of center
Off of the strip
In the outskirts
In the fringes
In the corner
Out of the grip

When they ask me
"What are you looking at?"
I always answer
"Nothing much" (not much)
I think they know that
I'm looking at them
I think they think
I must be out of touch

But I'm only
In the outskirts
And in the fringes
On the edge
And off the avenue
And if you want me
You can find me
Left of center
Wondering about you
Wondering about you

UNIT 4: The Tipping Point

2A LISTENING ONE: *The Tipping Point*

Malcolm Gladwell, author: Well there are, I you know in the book I profile them, they are these extraordinarily social people with a lot of energy who are consumed by, with kind of the task of getting to know people. Of meeting people, of knowing them, of keeping in touch with them. They're the people who write little notes. They're the people who keep in touch with you after they've left town. They're the people who make, you know, phone calls all day long. And these people—

LISTENING FOR MAIN IDEAS

Malcolm Gladwell, author: I think that same idea holds for word-of-mouth epidemics—that there is a small number of exceptional people who play a huge role in the transmission of epidemic ideas. I call them mavens, connectors, and salesmen.

Christopher Lydon, host: Say it again . . . Mavens, connectors, and salesmen.

MG: Mavens, connectors, and salesmen. Connectors are um, the kind of people who know everybody. There are a handful of people in any group, in any social group who have extraordinary social ties. Well above . . . I mean if the average . . . I do this names test in the book, which is 200, I have 350 names in the Manhattan, last names in the Manhattan phone book and you go down the list and every time you see a last name you know, you give yourself a point. Well, the average score, most people score like 25, 30. There is in every group someone who scores 120 or 130. That kind of person is incredibly powerful in generating word-of-mouth epidemics. Because if they like something and get a hold of some idea, they can spread it five or six times, you know, further than anybody, than most of . . . than the average person.

CL: Who are those people? What defines them?

MG: Well there are, I you know in the book I profile a lot of them, they are these extraordinarily social people with a lot of energy who are consumed by, with kind of the task of getting to know people. Of meeting people, of knowing them, of keeping in touch with them. They're the people who write little notes.

MG: They're the people who keep in touch with you after they've left town. They're the people who make, you know, phone calls all day long. And these people—

CL: I'm afraid I'm one of them.

MG: I think you might be one of them—they, you know, this is not typical behavior. This is behavior that's actually rare.

Most of us don't do that, and you know I'm someone who is not that way. If I like, go to a movie, a new movie, and like it, I can't start a word of mouth epidemic because I simply don't know enough people. I can't get it outside my own immediate circle of friends. Someone who has friends all over the place, they can and someone you know who is sort of relentlessly social, they can spread the news about a new restaurant or a new movie or something far and wide in a very very short time.

CL: These are the connectors. Who are the mavens and who are the salesmen?

MG: The mavens are people who have specialized knowledge. If you examine why you make certain decisions, why do you shop somewhere, why do you go to a certain movie, why do you go to a certain restaurant, what you find is that you are relying on the same person over and over again for recommendations. Those people I call mavens. And mavens, I always give the example of this friend of mine Ariel who knows all about restaurants in lower Manhattan. If I want to know about the hot new restaurant I call Ariel. Well all of Ariel's friends call Ariel and if you go to restaurants in lower Manhattan and look around the room, you will see friends of Ariel. The restaurant market in Manhattan, which is an epidemic market, right?—restaurants come and go—is controlled by a group of Ariels. I don't think there's very many of them, I think there's probably you know, two dozen of them. If you knew who the Ariels were, you could, you know—that's an extraordinarily powerful piece of information if you're interested in restaurants in Manhattan. Well, that's true of lots of things. That's true of shopping and books and movies, and um, you know the Ariels of the world, the mavens uh, and if you think about it if a maven gets together with a connector, than you begin to see why a word of mouth epidemic might happen. Um, someone who knows everyone, in combination with someone who knows everything, is a really powerful connection.

CL: And then introduce the salesman.

MG: Well there's also, I think there's also a role played by people who are incredibly persuasive, and again, that's a very rare and unusual trait and—

CL: Leaves me out you see, I connect but I can't sell.

MG: You can't sell. Well—these are—they're separate categories. I have—I've met with this guy in the book, a guy I called Tom Gau—who I—who is known as one of the greatest salesmen in America today and tried to get at the root of what was, you know, why he's so persuasive and you know it's a really fascinating question, and—but you—you know when you meet someone like that you begin to realize as well, why do trends happen? They happen because someone like this, who has this extraordinary natural ability to win you over, gets a hold of an idea, and when they get a hold of an idea, they can really make it go a long way.

LISTENING FOR DETAILS

(Repeat Listening for Main Ideas)

REACTING TO THE LISTENING

Exercise 1

Excerpt One

Malcolm Gladwell, author: I think that same idea holds for word-of-mouth epidemics—that there is a small number of exceptional people who play a huge role in the transmission of epidemic ideas. I call them mavens, connectors and salesmen.

Christopher Lydon, host: Say it again . . . Mavens, connectors and salesmen.

Excerpt Two

MG: The restaurant market in Manhattan, which is an epidemic market, right?—restaurants come and go—is controlled by a group of Ariels. I don't think there's very many of them, I think there's probably you know, two dozen of them.

Excerpt Three

MG: They're the people who keep in touch with you after they've left town. They're the people who make, you know, phone calls all day long. And these people—

CL: I'm afraid I'm one of them.

MG: I think you might be one of them—they, you know, this is not typical behavior. This is behavior that's actually rare.

Excerpt Four

MG: Well there's also, I think there's also a role played by people who are incredibly persuasive, and again, that's a very rare and unusual trait and—

CL: Leaves me out you see, I connect but I can't sell.

MG: You can't sell. Well—these are—they're separate categories. I have—I've met with this guy in the book, a guy I called Tom Gau—who I—who is known as one of the greatest salesmen in America today

2B LISTENING TWO: *Tipping Points in Fighting Crime*

Exercise 1

Todd Mundt, host: Let's talk about a social condition that you wrote about then, there are a few that I want to touch on but the first one is the one I mentioned in the introduction, crime in New York City. Crime was a problem for a very long time in New York City and it was rising and rising and rising and then it started dropping and um, I suppose there could be a number of different reasons for it but I can't really find that anybody really knows exactly for sure what caused it.

Malcolm Gladwell, author: Crime is so—is such a fundamentally contagious thing that once we reached a kind of tipping point and once certain influential people in communities hard hit by crime stopped behaving in that way, it was contagious, and there was a kind of sea change that happens all at once.

TM: Maybe we can go into those little triggers, because I find this really interesting because we're talking about such a big change that takes place uh, being triggered by very small things, uh, what do you think some of those were?

MG: Well, I'm very impressed by this idea called "the broken windows theory" which is an idea George Kelling has put forth in New England. He's argued for some time that criminals and criminal behavior is acutely sensitive to environmental cues and he uses the example, the broken window—that if you—if there is a car sitting on the street with a broken window, it is an invitation to someone to vandalize the car. Why? Because a broken window on a car symbolizes the fact that no one cares about the car. No one's in charge, no one's watching, no one's . . . and if you think about it, this is a fundamentally different idea about crime than the kind of ideas that we've been carrying for the past 25 years. We have been told by conservatives over and over again that crime is the result of moral failure, of something deep and intrinsic within the hearts and souls and brains of criminals, that a criminal is by definition in the sort of conservative topology, someone who is insensitive to their environment, right? They just go out and commit crimes because that's who they are, they're criminals. Well, Kelling came along and said well no no, a criminal is like all of us, someone who is acutely sensitive to what's going on in the environment, and by making subtle changes in the environment, you can encourage and induce much more socially responsible behavior.

Well in New York we had the perfect test case of that idea. It starts in the subway. You know, in the early '80s they decided to clean up the subway. Well, how did they do it? The subway was a complete mess, right? It was . . . crime rates were going through the roof. They bring in a man who is a big disciple of this idea, of "broken windows," and what does he do? Well, the first thing he does is he picks up all the litter. The second thing he does is he cleans up the graffiti, and the third thing he does is he says from now on, no one will ever jump a turnstile in a New York City subway station again. He puts cops by the turnstiles and if someone jumps, he arrests them. Everybody said he was crazy, but you've got a subway system where people are killing, and robbing, and assaulting and raping each other and what do you do? You go after the two kinds of criminality that, the only two kinds of criminality that in fact don't hurt anybody else, right? Turnstile jumping and graffiti, you know, littering and graffiti . . . but it turns out that those were tipping points. Once they put those three changes in place, the subway starts to come around really quite dramatically. It's because if you're on a subway that's clean and if you're walking into the subway and no one's allowed to jump the turnstile anymore, all of a sudden, everyone gets the message that someone's in charge, and somebody cares about this. It's not a space that permits this kind of criminal behavior.

4A PRONUNCIATION

Exercise 1

1. sensitivity, criminality, responsibility, popularity

2. energetic, fantastic, realistic, apologetic

3. transmission, organization, decision, documentation

4. financial, artificial, commercial, influential

5. logical, musical, critical, theoretical

Exercise 2

1. a. able
   b. possible
   c. public
2. a. invite
   b. inoculate
   c. complicate
3. a. president
   b. benefit
   c. office
4. a. category
   b. chaos
   c. symbol

4D SPEAKING TOPIC

Exercise 1

Announcer: Looking to do something good? Well, there's lots teenagers can do. Like saving the rare speckled Burmese Bear Cub.

Girl: Oh, isn't he cute and furry!

SFX: (Bear coos)

Guide: Okay, okay, be careful Susie. That's too close. Don't feed him . . .

Girl: C'mere little fellow.

Girl: C'm . . .

Bear: Roar!

Girl: (starts screaming)

SFX: (RIP!)

Guide: Whoa!

Girl: He's got my arm!

Guide: Wow, that's gotta hurt.

Announcer: Or how about just saving something closer to home, like your neighborhood? Tutor. Mentor. Volunteer. Help change your community and change the way the world sees you. Click on weprevent.org or call 1-800-722-TEENS. A message from McGuff, the U.S. Department of Justice, the Crime Prevention Coalition of America and the Ad Council.

Exercise 2

(*Repeat Exercise 1*)

UNIT 5: Feng Shui: Ancient Wisdom Travels West

2A LISTENING ONE: *Interview with a Feng Shui Expert*

Sedge Thomson, Host: When you walk into a building, are you able to sort of immediately sense whether it has good feng shui or not . . . a good flow of the ch'i?

Kirsten Lagatree, author: Yes, and so are you. Anytime you walk into any room, you get a feeling about it, whether you feel good about being there or not so good. So everyone has experienced good feng shui. Anytime they've walked into anybody's home or even an office where suddenly they think, "Oh, this is pleasant. I feel good." You know, maybe their mood's a little peppier or maybe they're more relaxed . . . whatever. It's just a positive reaction you get when you're in the midst of good feng shui.

LISTENING FOR MAIN IDEAS

Part One

Sedge Thomson: So, feng shui is exactly, what, a way of ordering buildings, rooms, corridors in your life to keep out evil spirits?

Kirsten Lagatree: Well, I wouldn't say to keep out evil spirits. That sounds so superstitious. But I would say, it's a system of arranging all the objects around you at home or at work in such a way that they are in harmony and balance with nature in the way that feng shui teaches us to do . . . then, therefore, you are in harmony and balance, and so is your life.

ST: Now this is something that's very important in Asia. In fact, it's part of the architecture of buildings . . . how the staircases go up, where buildings are aligned, how people are . . . how live . . . what is your particular interest in it? You sound as if you have a Scandinavian background. I mean, is feng shui something important in Scandinavia?

KL: Well, there's a huge digression coming. My name is Scandinavian. I was named for a Norwegian opera singer. I identify as Irish, though. But so I don't know if there is any feng shui in Scandinavia. But their designs are so clean. I would suspect so. Yes, feng shui is huge in Asia, Taiwan, Singapore, Hong Kong. I believe it's practiced widely in mainland China, even though it's officially frowned upon as a superstition. But it's also huge here in the U.S., no less than the Donald. Donald Trump doesn't make a move without it. He would no more start working on a building project without a feng shui master than he would without, you know, if it was L.A., without . . . a seismologist to tell him that the building would stay up in an earthquake. Umm. That's because . . . these observations that amount to feng shui have developed over thousands of years and they work as Donald Trump says. I do love to quote Donald Trump, not that I've ever talked to him, but . . .

ST: A famous feng shui expert, as we all know. I know for instance that people in San Francisco, if a one-way street sign is put up pointing toward a house where there are some Chinese living, they can approach the city traffic sign department and have the sign removed . . . not necessarily pointed back in the opposite direction, but have the sign removed or at least not pointing at their house.

KL: You know, I didn't know that. But thanks, that's a great little anecdote for the rest of my book tour.

ST: Did you choose your home because of feng shui? How did you set it out?

KL: We didn't choose our home because of feng shui. . . . I arranged my office at home according to feng shui . . . and it's a real basic example that illustrates a couple of principles. I am lucky enough to have a great view out the window at the far end of my office. And I was going to put my desk facing out the window, and . . . uh . . . but I would've had my back to the door which is such . . . you know . . . it's not just old west saloons and feng shui, it's also a bad idea to sit with your back to the door. Anybody who comes into your office can surprise you. They surprise you with the things they have to say. You're constantly off guard. So I turned my desk, so that I still had the view at one hand and I had the door and the rest of the room at the other hand, and then I kind of put the other furniture in the office where it worked around that. I've got a better floor plan than I would've figured out for myself.

Part Two

ST: What's the role of mirrors?

KL: Well, mirrors in the bedroom. That's about the only room where mirrors are not wonderful. You don't want a mirror to reflect your bed in the bedroom because that could scare the heck out of you when you wake up at night. It also could frighten your spirit. You know, there's always a common sense and the transcendent explanation. So, it'll either scare your spirit, or if you prefer, it'll scare you. In every other room in the house, mirrors are terrific. They reflect ch'i, which is the basic principle of feng shui . . . this energy. It's like electricity. We

can't see it, but boy is it there doing things. So, mirrors will reflect ch'i, help it circulate in a more healthy way, and they also say in the dining room or kitchen they double your abundance. Suddenly, you have twice as much food, twice as many friends sitting at the dining room table.

ST: That is true. . . . Um . . . how did you develop your interest in feng shui?

KL: I came at this topic pretty skeptically as a journalist, hard-bitten journalist that I was. I did a piece for the Los Angeles Times a few years ago on feng shui as real estate phenomena, because major deals rise or fall on good or bad feng shui. That was kind of that. And, so then, I really got more deeply into it, started to study it. I was still at the . . . you know . . . my friends would sort of lean in, look at me with one eyebrow up, and say, "Yeah, but do you believe this stuff?" And I would say, "Oh no! But don't quote me." Now, based on just simple things I've done and also lots and lots of people I talked to for the book, I'd have to say, it works and at the very least, it couldn't hurt.

ST: When you walk into a building, are you able to sort of immediately sense whether it has good feng shui or not . . . a good flow of the ch'i?

KL: Yes, and so are you. Anytime you walk into any room, you get a feeling about it, whether you feel good about being there or not so good. So everyone has experienced good feng shui. Anytime they've walked into anybody's home or even an office where suddenly they think, "Oh, this is pleasant. I feel good." You know, maybe their mood's a little peppier or maybe they're more relaxed . . . whatever. It's just a positive reaction that you get when you're in the midst of good feng shui.

LISTENING FOR DETAILS

(*Repeat Listening for Main Ideas*)

REACTING TO THE LISTENING

Exercise 1

Excerpt One

ST: So, feng shui is exactly, what, a way of ordering buildings, rooms, corridors in your life to keep out evil spirits?

KL: Well, I wouldn't say to keep out evil spirits. That sounds so superstitious.

Excerpt Two

KL: But it's also huge here in the U.S., no less than the Donald. Donald Trump doesn't make a move without it. He would no more start working on a building project without a feng shui master than he would without, you know, if it was L.A., without . . . a seismologist to tell him that the building would stay up in an earthquake. Umm. That's because . . . these observations that amount to feng shui have developed over thousands of years and they work as Donald Trump says. I do love to quote Donald Trump, not that I've ever talked to him, but . . .

ST: A famous feng shui excerpt, as we all know.

Excerpt Three

KL: I really got more deeply into it, started to study it. I was still at the . . . you know . . . my friends would sort of lean in, look at me with one eyebrow up, and say, "Yeah, but do you believe this stuff?" And I would say, "Oh no! But don't quote me."

2B LISTENING TWO: *Feng Shui in the Newsroom*

Steve Scher: Kirsten Lagatree is our guest. Her book is *Feng Shui: Arranging Your Home to Change Your Life—A Room by Room Guide to the Ancient Chinese Art of Placement.* OK, so, I would like to walk into our newsroom, if we can, and have you just quickly look at it and figure out what we can do for some of the people here who need a little help in their careers or their happiness. Any initial thoughts you have looking at this room?

Kirsten Lagatree: Umm . . . There are some very good things about this newsroom. For one thing, some of the writers are facing northeast. Northeast is the direction that governs mental ability, acuteness of thinking, scholarly success. So, those people in this newsroom, who are facing this, they not only get an extraordinarily peaceful and beautiful view out the window, they are facing in the direction that's going to make them sharp, and make their writing better.

SS: OK, so this is my desk, over here, scattered with a barrel of monkeys, and they're red, so that's good . . . I'm facing east here, right? I'm facing east, almost to the southeast. Am I blocked up a little bit?

KL: Yeah, well, facing east, actually . . . when you face east you are facing the direction of growth, vitality, the color green. Health, vitality, youth: Those are the things that come with the direction. So maybe that's what makes you so peppy, Steve, and so young at heart. I'd like to say something about this southeast wall right here. That is your money corner. Southeast is the direction that governs money. You haven't done anything with this direction. You've got lots of equipment there . . . what you should have is the color purple, the number 4.

SS: And a fish tank.

KL: Well, one thing at a time. The color purple and the number 4 go with that one direction, with the southeast. I'm glad you mentioned a fish tank . . . water flow symbolizes cash flow. There's a lot in feng shui that does word play, both in the Chinese language and in the English language, so, water flow equals cash flow. You walk in to some major corporate buildings nowadays, in New York or Los Angeles or Hong Kong, you are going to see fountains in the lobby. A lot of that. The fish that are in the tank . . . they symbolize abundance, as in "there are always more fish in the sea." What's your goal? You know . . . if your goal is to be a better writer, talk somebody into changing places with you here so that you can face northeast. If your goal is to become wealthy, do some enhancement there on your southeast wall, or do it at home. Say you want to get in a relationship in your life . . . at home, enhance a southwest wall with the color yellow and the number 2. The southwest corner governs marriage, partnerships, motherhood. You pay attention to what, umm you know what, you can do to make something happen, and then you work with these outward symbols.

4A PRONUNCIATION

And I was going to put my desk facing out the window, and . . . uh . . . but I would have had my back to the door . . .

I've got a better floor plan than I would have figured out for myself.

could have done, would have done, should have done, might have done, must have done

couldn't have done, wouldn't have done, shouldn't have done, mustn't have done

Exercise 1

Listen to my tale of a true tragedy that occurred in Hong Kong several years ago. Most people say Bruce Lee, the famous kung fu actor, shouldn't have bought the house in the valley. The wind in the valley can destroy the ch'i. People didn't understand why he chose that particular area, since the wealthy actor could have lived anywhere in Hong Kong. Rumor has it, though, that in order to change his feng shui, he put a mirror on a tree in the backyard. This might have worked if there hadn't been an accident.

The tree was destroyed in a storm, and he never replaced the tree or the mirror. If he had, most people say he wouldn't have died. It is said that the unfavorable feng shui must have caused his death. Replacing the tree and the mirror immediately could have saved his life.

4C STYLE

Exercise 1

Well, I wouldn't say to keep out evil spirits. But I would say it's a system of arranging all the objects around you at home or at work.

He would no more start working on a building project without a feng shui master than he would, you know, if it was L.A., without a seismologist.

The new Regency Hotel in Singapore just opened with two beautiful fountains in the lobby. Talk about great feng shui! The hotel is booked solid for the next two months!

Now, based on just simple things I've done, and also lots and lots of people I talked to for the book, I'd have to say it works . . . and at the very least it couldn't hurt.

We can't see it, but boy is it there doing things.

UNIT 6: Spiritual Renewal

2A LISTENING ONE: *The Religious Tradition of Fasting*

Duncan Moon, reporting: But while there are differences in approach and style, those who fast are most often hoping to increase spirituality and come closer to the divine. Dr. Diana Eck, professor of comparative religion at Harvard Divinity School, says fasting accomplishes this in part by breaking an attachment to material things.

LISTENING FOR MAIN IDEAS

Duncan Moon, reporting: Fasting is an ancient tradition. The three Abrahamic religions, Judaism, Christianity and Islam, all trace it back to the prophets of the Old Testament. For example, many people believe the prophet Mohammed's first fast was probably Yom Kippur. Many Eastern religions trace their roots of fasting to ancient yogic and ascetic traditions. But while there are differences in approach and style, those who fast are most often hoping to increase spirituality and come closer to the divine. Dr. Diana Eck, professor of comparative religion at Harvard Divinity School, says fasting accomplishes this in part by breaking an attachment to material things.

Dr. Diana Eck: And of course the most repetitive attachment to earthly things is that that we enact every day by our desire for food. So there is a way in which breaking that, even in a symbolic way, speaks against the consumption, the materialism that is so pervasive in our world.

DM: Professor Barbara Patterson of Emory University is an Episcopal priest. She says fasting is similar to the discipline displayed by an athlete in a gym, although in the case of fasting, it's a spiritual gym.

Professor Barbara Patterson: There is a celebration itself in establishing a discipline for oneself and actually working, making decisions, forming the will, if you would say, intention to be able to move through a time where there's a certain amount of stress that's not undoing but that gives you a sense of your capacities. It's very much a way of sharpening the heart's capacities.

DM: The Church of Jesus Christ of Latter Day Saints, the Mormons, fast the first Sunday of every month. They skip two meals and take the money they would have spent on those meals and give it to the poor. Mormon Bart Marcoy says fasting helps to foster humility and gratitude, allowing him to put aside his human competitiveness.

DM: In Islam during the holy month of Ramadan, Muslims fast from sunrise to sunset, refraining from food, water, smoking and sex. Dr. Ahbar Ahmed, a professor of Islamic studies at American University, says in this time of rapid change and fear, fasting is vital to spiritual well being.

Dr. Ahbar Ahmed: Because if you do not withdraw during the day, then the replenishment of the soul is not being affected, and when that does not happen, then over time the individual begins to become exhausted, spiritually exhausted.

DM: Dr. Ahmed says the rhythm of life has become so hectic, so fast moving, that finding time to pull back from our daily lives, even temporarily, has become more difficult than ever. But he says that only means the need for it has never been greater, and that the ancient tradition of fasting is still necessary, even in the twenty-first century. Duncan Moon, NPR News, Washington.

LISTENING FOR DETAILS

(*Repeat Listening for Main Ideas*)

REACTING TO THE LISTENING

Exercise 1

Excerpt One

DM: . . . Dr. Diana Eck, professor of comparative religion at Harvard Divinity School says fasting accomplishes this in part by breaking an attachment to material things.

Dr. Diana Eck: And, of course, the most repetitive attachment to earthly things is that that we enact every day by our desire for food. So there is a way in which breaking that, even in a symbolic way, speaks against the consumption, the materialism that is so pervasive in our world.

Excerpt Two

DM: Dr. Barbara Patterson of Emory University is an Episcopal priest. She says fasting is a similar to the discipline displayed by an athlete in a gym, although in the case of fasting, it's a spiritual gym.

Dr. Barbara Patterson: There is a celebration itself in establishing a discipline for oneself and actually working, making decisions, forming the will, . . . it's very much a way of sharpening the heart's capacities.

Excerpt Three

DM: Dr. Ahbar Ahmed says in this time of rapid change and fear, fasting is vital to spiritual well-being.

Dr. Ahbar Ahmed: Because if you do not withdraw during the day, then the replenishment of the soul is not being affected, and when that does not happen, then over time the individual begins to become exhausted, spiritually exhausted.

2B LISTENING TWO: *Describing Monastic Life*

Alex Beam: Was this an . . . Was this an . . . sort of an intellectual fact-finding journey or was this a spiritual quest for you?

Willam Claassen, author: It was a number of things. It was a . . . certainly it was a project that I took on as a journalist, as a writer. It was also a spiritual journey for me because it allowed me to continue my journey in monastic traditions, uh, and what I might find there and how that might apply to my life and what I could communicate about what I had witnessed in these various communities.

AB: I want to draw you out on the subject of the work of the Wat Tham Krabok monastery. Why don't you briefly talk about the work of Wat Tham Krabok monastery which is in a sense the easiest to illustrate.

WC: Sure. Although Wat Tham Krabok is part of this forest monastic tradition, it was different in the sense that they were working on issues that were outside of the monastery. They had taken on efforts of working with AIDS patients and also providing assistance with Hmong villagers who were refugees out of Laos who had begun gathering in that area where the monastery was located. So, actually, a great deal of their time was spent in this work, the AIDS work, and also the work with the refugees, which, uh, created a little different situation in terms of their daily schedule, in terms of how rigorous their chanting schedule was, in terms of the solitude of the community because there were a lot of people coming in, children as well as adults, as well as Westerners, coming in to view this program for the AIDS patients, also for drug addicts. They also worked in that area. So, there was a lot of movement in and out of the community which made it a different situation than what I experienced in other forest monasteries.

AB: What um . . . were you ever . . . um . . . I am going to use a term—not totally flattering, but this notion of the monastic day tripper—the visitor—were you . . . I know that at some times you were sort of greeted with a bit of suspicion. Isn't that fair to say?

WC: I think so. I talk in the book about a term that I learned on Mt. Athos—the two legged wolf, the idea of an individual being on pilgrimage, but really more interested in the uniqueness of what this community is . . . and sort of the temporary visitor. There were certainly times when there was suspicion about my time in those communities.

AB: The two-legged wolf obviously refers to sort of tourists who are kind of visiting the beaches in Thailand and the monks of Mt. Athos, kind of joy riders. But what specific impact have the two-legged wolves, had, say, on Mt. Athos?

WC: Well, on Mt. Athos, for example, at one time, there was maybe a seven or ten day period that men could make a pilgrimage on the peninsula. Because of the numbers of men that are wanting to be on Mt. Athos, they've reduced that period of time to four days. Actually, four days was five or six years ago, so they may have even reduced it further than that. But it creates a demand on the land, and it also creates a time demand on the part of the communities.

AB: You also visited another monastery that's well known and from your description, too well known to our listeners. That's the monastery of the Santo Domingo in Spain which has gained international notoriety. Tell us why, please, and what impact that's had.

WC: Well, as you may remember, there was a very popular album of Gregorian chants called the Chant Album that was produced back in the early 90s and that was a recording made by the monks, made by the Benedictine monks, El Monasterio de Santo Domingo which is in Silos, Spain. Although they had been making recordings for the last 20 years, this particular recording happened to catch on internationally. So that's actually one of their cottage industries . . . uh . . . there at the monastery. This is one of the ways that they are able to survive, by making their recordings.

AB: But what impact . . . I mean . . . celebrity and going platinum isn't like the greatest thing that's ever happened to them, is it?

WC: No, I mean, it's one of many ways that they do make a living and they see it as an extension of their work, of their spirituality, of their hospitality, really, of sharing their music with the world.

AB: Did you ever get a sense of—I mean—there must be some sort of excess revenues there. What does that particular monastery do with the royalties from the CD?

WC: All I know is that the money goes back into their work, the community work.

4A PRONUNCIATION

divine–divinity

grateful–gratitude

heal–health

Exercise 1

1. /ay/ div**i**ne   /ɪ/ div**i**nity
   - a. r**i**te   r**i**tual
   - b. dec**i**de   dec**i**sion
   - c. wr**i**te   wr**i**tten
2. /ey/ gr**a**teful   /æ/ gr**a**titude
   - a. expl**ai**n   expl**a**natory
   - b. Sp**ai**n   Sp**a**nish
   - c. n**a**tion   n**a**tional
3. /iy/ comp**e**te   /e/ comp**e**titiveness
   - a. k**ee**p   k**e**pt
   - b. st**ea**l   st**ea**lth
   - c. pl**ea**se   pl**ea**sure

4C STYLE

Exercise 1

Mary Tilotson, host: Give me an idea of, William, as a guest—and your experiences were varied enough that there's not gonna be one schedule that applied to every monastery, but more or less how would the day start, when would it start, how would it unfold for you when you are in retreat?

William Claassen, author: Well, I'll pull in an example first from Thailand where I spent time in a forest monastery in the northeast part of the country near the Laotian border. It's an old tradition . . . the forest monastic tradition in Thailand. We would wake up at 3:30 in the morning. We would gather as community to chant for approximately an hour and a half to two hours. We would chant, we would also sit meditation, we would also walk meditation. From there, each individual would return to their living space and focus on their meditation. They would then come back together again. In this tradition, the monks would go out and collect food in the morning. They would go out in the community. So, that was an important daily ritual to collect food for their one meal of the day. They would go out to collect the food in the various villages that surrounded the community, come back, deliver the food, the food would then be served to the community. Then there would be a separation of the members of the community to again return to their meditation. A little later there would be a work period, late in the morning and a work period in the afternoon. The community would come back together again for at least two more chanting sessions before the evening chant, but usually the evening chant would end about 8:30 or 9:00 and then the individuals were permitted to study, return to their living quarters to meditate. It was independent in time.

UNIT 7: Workplace Privacy

2A LISTENING ONE: *Interview on Workplace Surveillance*

Elaine Korry: And the practice is on the rise. According to the ACLU Workplace Rights Project, the number of employees being monitored has doubled in the last five years.

What's driving this increase? Partly, it's competition. If everyone else in an industry is keeping tabs on their workers, there's pressure to join in.

But, to a large extent, companies have stepped up monitoring simply because it could be done, cheaply and efficiently.

LISTENING FOR MAIN IDEAS

Part One

Scott Simon, host: Many employees can assume that they're being watched while they work during the day. The majority of U.S. companies keep watch on their workers with video cameras, tape recorders, computer surveillance.

Most employers insist that these are legitimate and even necessary business practices. But as NPR's Elaine Korry reports, many attorneys are arguing that employees do not give up their privacy rights when they show up for work.

Elaine Korry: If you send personal e-mail on your office computer, there's a good chance the boss is keeping an eye on you. In a new survey of more than 900 major U.S. companies, nearly two-thirds of them acknowledged using a range of surveillance methods to monitor their employees.

Eric Greenberg directed the survey for the American Management Association.

Eric Greenberg: Employees should know that any employee at any time may be under watch, and that any employee's communications, be they on the phone or via the Internet, may be subject to review.

EK: Greenberg issues that warning. But some employers do not. In what he calls the most worrisome finding of the survey, up to a quarter of the companies that monitor their workforce do it secretly.

And the practice is on the rise. According to the ACLU Workplace Rights Project, the number of employees being monitored has doubled in the last five years.

What's driving this increase? Partly, it's competition. If everyone else in an industry is keeping tabs on their workers, there's pressure to join in.

But, to a large extent, companies have stepped up monitoring simply because it could be done, cheaply and efficiently. Yet, Greenberg says, even as surveillance becomes more widespread, there's nothing sinister about the practice itself.

EG: When you read data like this, there's a certain tendency to do a Big Brother metaphor . . . Big Brother is watching and whatever. But really, I think that's a cheap shot. What we're talking about for the most part are very legitimate forms of performance monitoring.

EK: Greenberg says employers have a right to know how equipment they provide is being used on the job, if rules are being obeyed, if employees are getting the job done. That helps explain why banks routinely tape customer service calls, and why the U.S. Postal Service is testing a satellite system to track how long it takes to get the mail delivered.

Part Two

EK: But Larry Finneran, with the National Association of Manufacturers, says companies are using technology to accomplish other important goals. Video cameras were recently installed in his building to deter theft. And the Association keeps a log of all phone calls so employees can pay the company for their personal calls.

According to Finneran, monitoring can be used for the workers' own protection.

Larry Finneran: If an employee is sending pornography from an employer's computer, obviously the employer would be expected to go through there. If somebody complains about sexual harassment, that somebody's sending out racial slurs over the e-mail, the employer has a right to take action.

EK: In fact, the Chevron Corporation was sued by female employees who said they were sexually harassed through company e-mail.

That's all well and good, says Rebecca Locketz, the legal director of the ACLU's Workplace Rights Project. She concedes there are legitimate uses of monitoring programs. But too often, says Locketz, surveillance practices demean workers for no good reason.

Rebecca Locketz: You certainly do not need to monitor key strokes. When you give someone fifty reports to key into a computer, and you see that they have only completed twenty by day's end, you don't need to count key strokes. They only finished two-fifths.

EK: Locketz argues that employees should not have to leave their human dignity at the workplace door. And she says they're entitled to a few safeguards in this area.

First, the ACLU says employees should always be informed when they're monitored. And second . . .

RL: There should be no monitoring whatsoever in purely private areas.

Part Three

EK: Yet, so far there is only one state—Connecticut—that forbids surveillance in areas such as locker rooms or the employee lounge. In other states, employers do secretly videotape private places if they suspect theft or criminal activities such as drug dealing.

There's only one federal statute, the 1986 Electronic Communications Privacy Act, that safeguards employee privacy. But according to Larry Finneran with the National Association of Manufacturers, the scope of the act is limited to eavesdropping on private telephone calls.

LF: There are specific rules. An employer listening for content of personal phone calls . . . an employer can . . . can limit duration of personal phone calls. An employer can say, "no personal phone calls." But under the Electronic Communications Privacy Act, an employer cannot listen for content. And that . . . they are already protected to that degree.

EK: Employee rights attorney Penny Nathan Cahn is involved in a case over this very issue. She says as companies continue to expand employee monitoring, workers are turning to the courts to protect their rights.

Penny Nathan Cahn: Then unless there is a substantial interest to be served by the employer, I don't think the juries are going to look at the . . . the willy-nilly surveillance and monitoring very sympathetically.

EK: There may even be good business reasons for companies to think twice about increased surveillance. Studies link electronic monitoring to higher levels of worker stress, which can lead to lower productivity. I'm Elaine Korry reporting.

LISTENING FOR DETAILS

(*Repeat Listening for Main Ideas*)

REACTING TO THE LISTENING

Exercise 1

Excerpt One

Eric Greenberg: Employees should know that any employee at any time may be under watch, and that any employee's communications, be they on the phone or via the Internet, may be subject to review.

Excerpt Two

EG: When you read data like this, there's a certain tendency to do a Big Brother metaphor . . . Big Brother is watching and whatever. But really, I think that's a cheap shot. What we're talking about for the most part are very legitimate forms of performance monitoring.

Excerpt Three

Rebecca Locketz: You certainly do not need to monitor key strokes. When you give someone fifty reports to key into a computer, and you see that they have only completed twenty by day's end, you don't need to count key strokes. They only finished two-fifths.

Excerpt Four

RL: There should be no monitoring whatsoever in purely private areas.

2B LISTENING TWO: *Managers and Employees Speak Out*

Speaker 1: I own a small data-processing company in which I employ about eight to ten workers. The point I want to make has to do with trust. Listen, I know it's possible to force people to be 100 percent efficient. But when you do that you lose morale, confidence, trust. I let my employees use our equipment, computers, make personal phone calls, whatever. They are more than welcome to decide what is right and wrong. You can't run a company by just issuing orders to robots and watching them like Big Brother. You have to trust people, respect them, and give them a little freedom. Also, as far as phone calls and all that go, I want my people to call home and check on their children, and know their children are OK, because then they can refocus on the job . . . and their work is better. As a result, I have dedicated employees who are willing to go that extra mile . . . to show up at work smiling. I get more satisfaction and rewards by trusting my employees than by suspecting them of doing something wrong.

Speaker 2: I'm an attorney in a large law firm in Seattle. In my firm, there's a capability, sure, of monitoring my performance. I input a lot of my work into computer systems with limited security. And you know what? I'm not bothered in the least. The real question is, if we're not doing anything wrong, what do we have to worry about? I think employers have the right to keep an eye on what goes on in their businesses, just like home owners have the right to use video and audio surveillance to protect their own homes. I mean, you would have to agree that when you're in the office, you're not conducting your private life. You're conducting business. In some cases, such as lounge areas at work, there's a fine line; but mostly I believe it's OK for, you know, an employer to actually listen and watch while you're working. They're just safeguarding their businesses.

Speaker 3: I'm a chemist in a large pharmaceutical company. I would like to say specifically that private communication that doesn't relate to my job shouldn't be an open book just because it happens to occur between nine and five. I've got a right to talk privately even on the job. It's impossible to totally separate my job from my home. Let me just pose a question here. Isn't it a fact that we all take work home every once in a while? And every once in a while you've got to have a communication at work, on the phone, on your computer, or your e-mail that isn't work related. You know, if I were making forty-seven long-distance calls to Honolulu for no real reason, sure . . . my boss would want to know why I'm running up all these long-distance phone bills. Maybe something sinister is going on. But . . . a handful of local phone calls that everybody has to make once in a while? I don't get why any employer would or should object to that! I don't see why an employer has any legitimate reason to bug my phone to find out who I just called. . . . It's an invasion of my privacy, and it's just not fair.

Speaker 4: I run a video production company and employ about fifty professionals. The point I want to make is this . . . even though I trust my employees, the company is still mine. Stuff on their desk, their work product and other things . . . while it may be inappropriate for me to look at it or even remove it, the fact of the matter is . . . it's not private stuff. I have a right to know the materials in the workplace. If it's a work product, I may need access to it. And one more thing I want to say . . . I could also go into their computers after they leave and read all sorts of business-related documents. It's my right.

4A PRONUNCIATION

Exercise 1

Companies recórd service calls.

They keep récords of personal phone calls made by employees.

The óbject of installing the surveillance equipment was to create a top-notch security system.

I don't understand why any employee would or should objéct to that.

Exercise 2

1. The ACLU director was shocked by the íncrease in monitoring and was afraid that willy-nilly surveillance would continue to increáse.
2. We decided to condúct a comprehensive survey to measure employee cónduct.
3. The óbject of my presentation is simply to objéct to the use of secret surveillance.
4. The boss suspécts that she is the only súspect in the case involving the stolen computer files.
5. She got a special pérmit that would permít her to see confidential employee information.
6. We all had to keep a special récord in order to recórd all personal phone calls.
7. Why do you always insúlt me with all those ínsults? Just tell me how to fix the mistakes.
8. We're pleased with your prógress in the job so far, but you'll have to progréss even further before getting promoted.
9. As hard as I tried to settle the cónflict with my boss, our opinions continued to conflíct over certain key issues.
10. The company projécts big profits from these prójects.

4D SPEAKING TOPIC

Ann Riley: Governor, I appreciate your taking the time to meet with me.

Governor: My pleasure.

AR: The employee monitoring law has received a great deal of media attention recently. However, many Illinois citizens are still very confused. What exactly does the new law allow?

Governor: The law permits employers to listen in on their workers' phone conversations. The law permits any listening that serves educational, training, or research purposes. It allows for both computer and phone monitoring.

AR: How did this law come about?

Governor: Well, it was originally conceived by the telemarketing industry. This industry, which uses the telephone to sell its products and services, needed a way to monitor its employees' sales performance. The retail industry is also a big proponent of the law. Recently, I spoke with the president of the Illinois Retail Merchants Association. He told me the law is helping to make sure that Mrs. Smith gets the red dress in size 6 rather than size 16, which may have been entered into the computer by mistake.

AR: So, in other words, the law is meant to monitor the quality of customer service calls.

Governor: Yes, for courtesy, efficiency, and overall service.

AR: Well then, why all the opposition? I hear that many groups—from unions to the ACLU—are clearly furious about this law.

Governor: Yes, I know. Our office has been flooded with calls and letters. The problem is, the law does not specify whether or not employers must tell employees each time they are being monitored, or just issue a one-time blanket warning. Also, only one person must agree to the monitoring, but the law does not state who must agree—the employee or the supervisor. The scope of the law is so broad that some people find it frightening.

AR: Yes, it sounds like there are many unanswered questions. I appreciate your speaking with me, Governor. Thank you very much.

Governor: You're welcome.

UNIT 8: Warriors without Weapons

2A LISTENING ONE: *Warriors without Weapons*

Terry Gross, host: This is *Fresh Air*, I'm Terry Gross. Journalist Michael Ignatieff spent a year traveling to the sites of volatile regional wars. He wanted to learn how war is changing, and what that means for the safety of relief workers. In a recent *New Yorker* article called "Unarmed Warriors," he wrote about the international committee of the Red Cross, the new risks its unarmed members face in war zones, and the new controversies surrounding the group's position of neutrality. I asked him why he wanted to write about the Red Cross.

LISTENING FOR MAIN IDEAS

Part One

Terry Gross, host: This is *Fresh Air*, I'm Terry Gross. Journalist Michael Ignatieff spent a year traveling to the sites of volatile regional wars. He wanted to learn how war is changing, and what that means for the safety of relief workers. In a recent *New Yorker* article called "Unarmed Warriors," he wrote about the International Committee of the Red Cross, the new risks its unarmed members face in war zones, and the new controversies surrounding the group's position of neutrality. I asked him why he wanted to write about the Red Cross.

Michael Ignatieff: . . . As a group I was very drawn to them because I thought they could take me into the whole world of what involves people in that kind of humanitarian relief work. . . . From being interested in the Red Cross, I then became interested in the laws of war and came to see that the laws of war are a very different moral tradition than, say, the human rights tradition. And I began to see that there are two traditions at work out there in the humanitarian movement: One of them is international human rights, which most Americans can identify with, and then there's this very different tradition called the laws of war tradition, which is basically trying to make sure that if people are going to fight, conduct

the fighting according to certain rules . . . and that's what the Red Cross is trying to do.

Part Two

TG: The international committee of the Red Cross is trying to disseminate information about the Geneva Conventions, about the International Laws of War. What are they trying to do? How are they trying to educate people who are fighting, about these codes?

MI: Well, I think first of all we need to back up a little and just understand what the codes are. They're these things called the Geneva Conventions, which were ratified by hundreds of countries and the basic document dates to 1864 and then it was revised in 1949. They're a bunch of rules that are quite simple . . . they simply say, "Don't fire on ambulances, don't shoot on non-combatants, don't torture prisoners, allow prisoners to communicate with their families, allow the Red Cross to visit you if you're a prisoner of war, spare civilians . . ."

I mean, they're very house-and-garden common rules, and in lots of combat situations they function more or less adequately. In the Gulf War, for example, when a hundred thousand Iraqi prisoners were taken, the United States subscribed to the Geneva Conventions, released them according to those conventions. So it's a system that . . . it's easy to laugh at . . . people say, you know, "You can't wage a war that's civilized." Well, in fact, the Geneva Conventions have done a lot to civilize certain aspects of war, and so they have a lot of legitimacy. . . .

I think something very interesting is going on there . . . an attempt to say, "The standards of decency that ought to prevail in the world are not white, western European values; they're human universals, and if you look deeply enough into your own traditions of warrior culture, you will find them." And that's what the Red Cross is trying to do . . . they're just beginning that work, but they're putting out comic books that tell the story, they're running radio soap operas to tell the story. They're not just sitting there reading out the Geneva Conventions; they're trying to translate them into new languages, and it's one of the most interesting bits of work that's going on.

Part Three

MI: . . . Yes, I think what I'm trying to get at here is that . . . it's a sort of counterintuitive thought. One of the oldest moral traditions, that all human societies have, is the warrior tradition. The tradition of warriors' honor. The idea that a warrior has a very dangerous and therefore sacred responsibility; that is, his job is to protect the community and to engage in the infliction of death. Because that's a very dangerous and a very serious task, men have to be trained for it, and they're trained not to simply unleash their aggression, but to control it and—you know and—to discipline it, and use it for the benefit of the community. And those traditions then mean that there are certain people you can kill and there are certain people it's wrong to kill. There's certain ways of waging war that are honorable, and certain ways of waging war that are dishonorable. Most modern military—most modern military forces attempt in some way or the other to subscribe to those very ancient codes; and I think we forget . . . I think . . . partly because war has become so awful and so horrible and so devastating, we've come to equate war with pure barbarism and pure savagery. It seems to us to be a zone where morality cannot prevail at all. And so it's a rather counterintuitive thought that in fact the warrior's honor is one of the oldest moral traditions in the world, and the Red Cross is trying in a way to simply institutionalize that culture . . . remind people that in their own cultures they can find elements of the warrior's honor which should restrain their people.

LISTENING FOR DETAILS

(Repeat Listening for Main Ideas)

REACTING TO THE LISTENING

Exercise 1

Excerpt One

Michael Ignatieff: And I began to see that there are two traditions at work out there in the humanitarian movement: One of them is, you know, international human rights, which most Americans can identify with . . .

Excerpt Two

MI: I think something very interesting is going on there . . . an attempt to say, "The standards of decency that ought to prevail in the world are not white, western European values; they're human universals . . ."

Excerpt Three

MI: And so it's a rather counterintuitive thought that in fact the warrior's honor is one of the oldest moral traditions in the world, and the Red Cross is trying in a way to simply institutionalize that culture . . . remind people that in their own cultures they can find elements of the warrior's honor which should restrain their people.

2B LISTENING TWO: *Michael Ignatieff's Views on War*

Part One

Terry Gross: In your article about the Red Cross in *The New Yorker,* you wrote that witnessing the Red Cross, and traveling to all these war zones, challenged your views on antiwar culture. What do you mean by that?

Michael Ignatieff: Well, I'm a Canadian; I was very involved in the anti-war, anti-Vietnam protests that were centered in Toronto during the 60's because Toronto was an antiwar center because so many draft evaders and draft resisters ended up there. I grew up in the anti-war culture of my generation . . . I think what I discovered in the Red Cross's approach is an alternative ethic, which is that, you know, you cannot abolish war, you can't do without war.

Part Two

MI: And war in fact is a natural, necessary, and sometimes, dare I say it, even desirable way to solve certain social conflicts between ethnic groups. Oppressed groups sometimes can only use war to free themselves. Well, if that's the case, if we can't abolish war from human culture, then we'd better find some way to tame it.

Part Three

MI: And that's the ethic that the Red Cross lives by, and I think the simple rules that the Red Cross tries to enforce, which is: You don't shoot prisoners, you don't make war on noncombatants, you try and stay away from civilian targets, you kill people, you don't torture or degrade their bodies.

Part Four

MI: You know, just very very simple rules of humanity are an important addition to civilization. And there is no necessary reason . . . I suppose that this is what I've learned . . . to equate war with barbarism. There's a distinction between war and barbarism. And we should keep to that distinction and struggle to ensure it, and that's what the Red Cross tries to do. And . . . I don't want to sound like a recruiting sergeant from the Red Cross; I'm critical of some of the things they do . . . but I did learn that from them. And I respect this morality.

TG: Michael Ignatieff, I want to thank you very much for talking with us.

MI: A pleasure.

3 FOCUS ON VOCABULARY

Exercise 1

1. accept/except
2. access/excess
3. advice/advise
4. affect/effect
5. assure/ensure
6. council/counsel
7. disinterested/uninterested
8. eminent/imminent
9. imply/infer
10. principal/principle

4A PRONUNCIATION

Exercise 1

| cat | cot | cut |

Exercise 2

1. cat	cot	cut
2. cap	cop	cup
3. lack	lock	luck
4. Nat	not	nut
5. hat	hot	hut
6. lag	lock	lug

Exercise 3

(Repeat Exercise 2)

Exercise 5

government funding	gun shots	a practical discovery
public controversy	a bloody struggle	love of country
natural disasters	floods and famines	a challenging task
Cultural values	a bloody battle	a tough job
lack of money	savage attack	combatants' conduct

Exercise 6

1. A block from the gun battle, the cops found a black bottle full of gasoline.
2. A lack of love and trust made him lock the clock in the closet.
3. Nat did not eat the nuts.
4. The big black bug bled black blood.

4D SPEAKING TOPIC

Exercise 1

Ever give a gift that didn't go over real big—one that ended up in a closet the second you left the room? There is a gift that's guaranteed to be well received, because it will save someone's life. The gift is blood. And the need for it is desperate. Over 20 thousand people must choose to give this gift every day. We need your help. Please give blood. There's a life to be saved right now. Call the American Red Cross at 1-800-GIVE LIFE. This public service message brought to you by the Advertising Council and the American Red Cross.

Exercise 2

(*Repeat Exercise 1*)

UNIT 9: Boosting Brain Power through the Arts

1B SHARING INFORMATION

Mozart's Sonata for Piano in F Major, 1st Movement, Allegro. Pianist: Bora Kim, a 14-year-old student at Ichimura Music School in Englewood Cliffs, NJ. [music]

2A LISTENING ONE: *Does Music Enhance Math Skills?*

Michelle Trudeau, reporter: Just how music enhances mathematical skills is unknown. It may be by the more general effect of increasing self-esteem, or maybe something neurological happens in the brain, or maybe, psychologist Andrea Halpern from Bucknell University suggests, these children are learning how to learn.

LISTENING FOR MAIN IDEAS

Part One

Linda Wertheimer, host: This is *All Things Considered*. I'm Linda Wertheimer.

Noah Adams, host: And I'm Noah Adams. Most schools offer music and art classes to give students a well-rounded education. New research indicates those classes may do more for students than just give them an appreciation of the arts. According to a study in tomorrow's issue of the journal Nature, studying music and art can significantly advance a child's reading skills and especially boost math proficiency. Michelle Trudeau reports.

Michelle Trudeau, reporter: A class of six-year-olds getting a special music lesson, part of a special arts program that researcher Martin Gardiner and his colleagues at the music school in Rhode Island designed for several elementary schools in the state.

Martin Gardiner: We started out wanting to see the impact of arts training in some first- and second-grade kids.

MT: So, some classrooms had an extra hour of this special arts curriculum incorporated into their normal school week.

MG: And other classrooms getting the standard curriculum in the arts, which was pretty standard for Rhode Island and rather representative of the country as a whole.

MT: The standard curriculum, say the researchers, gave students music lessons twice a month and art lessons twice a month. The typical music lesson tended to be somewhat passive, says Gardiner. Students listened to tapes and concerts and talked about music in class. In contrast, the special arts classes met twice weekly and got students actively involved as a way to teach them the basic building blocks.

MG: The kinds of skills that they are learning in these grades are . . . in music, they're learning to sing together properly, sing together on pitch, sing together in rhythm, sing together songs; and, in the visual arts, they're learning to draw shapes and deal with colors and forms, and so forth.

MT: A very interactive, experiential approach that took advantage of children's natural inclination to master enjoyable tasks and build upon sequential skills.

MG: And at the end of seven months, all the kids in the school took standardized tests, and we looked not only at how these teachers rated the kids on attitude and so forth, but also how the kids scored on their tests.

MT: And here's what the researchers found. First of all, those kids who'd entered the first grade toward the bottom of the class in reading and then received the special arts program for the year had now caught up to the average in reading.

MG: And that in itself is wonderful. But, in addition, they were now statistically ahead in learning math.

MT: Dramatically ahead in math, compared to the kids who had not received the special arts classes throughout the year. The researchers found also that the kids who continued their special arts classes for a second year continued to improve in math.

Part Two

MT: Psychologist Frances Rauscher, from the University of Wisconsin at Oshkosh, says this is an important study showing that a group of typical children, regardless of talent or parental involvement, can reap benefits from arts training that affects other academic areas, especially math.

Frances Rauscher: It's getting as close as is absolutely possible to the real world. You know, this . . . these are kids that already enrolled in schools that are just simply assigned to these different groups, this test group and this control group. And what they're finding is a strong effect in the improvement of mathematical ability as measured by school standards. So, this has real general . . . real world appeal.

MT: Rauscher's own recent research could help explain why arts education might have this additional benefit. In her study, a group of three-year-olds were given music lessons in preschool—piano and singing. Rauscher found they scored significantly higher on a particular IQ test that measures abstract reasoning—a skill, adds Rauscher, essential to mathematics.

FR: Training in the arts, and particularly training in music, enhances the ability for children to understand proportions and ratios, and that's obviously a skill that's very important for mathematical reasoning.

MT: Just how music enhances mathematical skills is unknown. It may be by the more general effect of increasing self-esteem, or maybe something neurological happens in the brain, or maybe, psychologist Andrea Halpern from Bucknell University suggests, these children are learning how to learn.

Andrea Halpern: In other words, you can learn skills, but you can also learn about how you learn things. And that seems to be a hallmark of the true mature learner, that they know how to learn things. And it's possible that these early interventions might be having some effect in children knowing how to attack new material.

MT: Whatever may be going on in the growing brains of children, both psychological and biological, these new findings underscore an increasing awareness among scientists and educators that a rich learning environment can significantly enhance children's intellectual development in unexpected ways. I'm Michelle Trudeau reporting.

LISTENING FOR DETAILS

(*Repeat Listening for Main Ideas*)

REACTING TO THE LISTENING

Exercise 1

Excerpt One

MT: The standard curriculum, say the researchers, gave students music lessons twice a month and art lessons twice a month. The typical music lesson tended to be somewhat passive, says Gardiner. Students listened to tapes and concerts and talked about music in class. In contrast, the special arts classes met twice weekly and got students actively involved as a way to teach them the basic building blocks.

MG: The kinds of skills that they are learning in these grades are . . . in music, they're learning to sing together properly, sing together on pitch, sing together in rhythm, sing together songs; and, in the visual arts, they're learning to draw shapes and deal with colors and forms, and so forth.

Excerpt Two

MT: Rauscher's own recent research could help explain why arts education might have this additional benefit. In her study, a group of three-year-olds were given music lessons in preschool—piano and singing. Rauscher found they scored significantly higher on a particular IQ test that measures abstract reasoning—a skill, adds Rauscher, essential to mathematics.

FR: Training in the arts, and particularly training in music, enhances the ability for children to understand proportions and ratios, and that's obviously a skill that's very important for mathematical reasoning.

2B LISTENING TWO: *Music, Art, and the Brain*

Part One

Warren Levinson: "Your Child's Brain" is the subject of this week's cover story in *Newsweek*. To discuss it we have science editor Sharon Begley. Thanks for joining us again, Sharon.

Sharon Begley: Hi, Warren.

WL: What parts of an infant's brain are already physically set at birth?

SB: Really the only things that a baby is born with are the circuits that do things absolutely crucial for life . . . keeping the heart beating . . . breathing . . . controlling temperature . . . reflexes . . . things like that . . . and of course a baby can see and hear. A baby has the primary senses when he or she comes into the world. But the rest of it is still a "work in progress."

Part Two

WL: I was fascinated by some of the research on music and the relationship to other kinds of reasoning, particularly mathematics. I had always assumed that musical talent and mathematics kind of went together because they had something to do with each other . . . um . . . in terms of filling puzzles . . . and in terms of . . . you have mathematics involved in setting out the beats to various kinds of music.

SB: That's right. Yes . . . music itself is highly mathematical, and that made some neuroscientists think that somehow the patterns of firing in neural cells were similar, as in mathematical abilities and logical thinking and spatial reasoning. So what they did is give two- and three-year-old little preschoolers lessons in singing and piano, and after several weeks of this the children were much better at solving mazes on pieces of paper and copying geometric shapes, so it seems again that these circuits were sort of primed to be wired up, and music somehow did it.

WL: But it also turns out that they tend . . . the wiring for both of those things tend to be right next to each other . . .

SB: They're in the same part of the brain . . . this old right side of the brain that we've heard about for years . . . yeah.

Part Three

WL: I have to say, though, that in your reporting . . . there . . . as a father of children, I get two reactions: One fills me with excitement that I really have a very significant role to play in how my children grow up to be able to solve things and to be able to live their lives, but the other reaction . . . and it's a little bigger . . . it's sort of scary . . . the notion that so many windows are closed so early, that by the ages of three and seven, I may have already blown it in so many areas.

SB: Well I feel the same way . . . mine are ten and seven . . . and I look at all these missed opportunities and think . . . Oh God . . . I should've been doing this or that . . . or whatever. You know, I think we should not panic parents.

Part Four

SB: If you love your child . . . if you do very simple things . . . we are not talking about the crazy superbaby stuff from the 1980s. This is really paying attention to your child . . . playing the kind of games that your grandmother played with your parents . . . you know, "peek-a-boo" and "Where did the object go?" It's paying attention and trying, and you know, if you blow up at your kid . . . whatever . . . you're not going to scar the kid for life. We're talking about repeated patterns of how you play with and interact with your child. But yeah, I felt the same way.

4A PRONUNCIATION

Exercise 1

1. music appreciation	7. math theories
2. art education	8. abstract topics
3. critical ingredients	9. math proficiency
4. parental involvement	10. reap benefits
5. music class	11. research findings
6. top performance	12. geometric shapes

Exercise 2

standard curriculum	typical lesson
a critical ingredient	an interactive approach
art classes	logical thinking
boost brain power	self esteem
research challenge	

UNIT 10: Television and Freedom of Expression

2A LISTENING ONE: *Interview with* Newsweek *Entertainment Editor*

David Alpern: The president got what he wanted out of the television industry last week . . . a pledge to develop the rating system necessary to program electronic V-chips that could automatically block sex and violence from individual home screens . . . at least in the hours children are watching.

LISTENING FOR MAIN IDEAS

Part One

David Alpern: The president got what he wanted out of the television industry last week . . . a pledge to develop the rating system necessary to program electronic V-chips that could automatically block sex and violence from individual home screens . . . at least in the hours children are watching. Clearly the industry was responding to pressure from the government and a disgusted if somewhat hypocritical public. And even the president conceded that the ratings/V-chip combo would not itself end the trashy tidal waves sweeping American society or American culture. It's only a panacea if you promise a panacea, but it will help.

Newsweek television editor Rick Marin looked into the debate over TV ratings and the V-chip, and he's with us now. Rick, thanks for being with us again.

Rick Marin: Thank you.

Part Two

DA: We hear the ratings won't cover news or sports, but what about raunchy news magazines . . . talk shows?

RM: That's unclear. I think talk shows would fall under the category of entertainment. Ummm . . . I'm not sure whether like *A Current Affair, Hard Copy,* trashy news stories would be considered news or entertainment . . . since often they have neither news nor entertainment in them. But uh . . . the focus of it is . . . is just the bread-and-butter programming of television . . . the TV shows, the prime-time series, and also movies that TV picks up from Hollywood.

DA: Will the ratings and V-chip combination block out whole shows, or just offensive parts?

RM: They'll block out the whole show. Umm . . . so you could presumably program your TV to just pick up shows that were either G or PG rated, and you could lock it and unlock it as you wanted . . . so when your kids are watching they couldn't see anything except wholesome stuff, and then when you're ready to sit down and watch, you flip a button and then you could watch, you know, *NYPD Blue* or whatever you want.

Part Three

DA: Some researchers last week reported that adult ratings actually attract young audiences, but isn't that exactly what the V-chip is supposed to counteract?

RM: Yeah, the problem is that, I mean, the V-chip technology is going to take a while to penetrate the culture . . . If you buy a new set, you've got one; but if you stick with your old set for another ten years, you're not going to have one . . . so before you have the V-chip, you're going to have this rating system.

And yes, studies have shown that, you know, just as any of us who were kids remember, that if you put a forbidden fruit label on something, that just makes us want it even more. There was one study where some kid said the cooler the movie, the higher the rating.

DA: But Canada is already experimenting with some form of this. What are the results there so far?

RM: The Canadian results have been encouraging for people who want this kind of stuff. They did an experiment with 250 families in four cities in Canada, and all the families that tried it out loved it. It was a very elaborate system built into the cable boxes, and it was very successful. That said, you know, we've got to remember that the Canadians are . . . have always loved violence less than Americans and regulation less than Americans. So who knows if it'll take here as well as it has there.

LISTENING FOR DETAILS

(*Repeat Listening for Main Ideas*)

REACTING TO THE LISTENING

Exercise 1

Excerpt One

Rick Marin: That's unclear. I think talk shows would fall under the category of entertainment. Umm . . . I'm not sure whether like *A Current Affair, Hard Copy,* trashy news stories would be considered news or entertainment . . . since often they have neither news nor entertainment.

David Alpern: Gaffaw/sigh

Excerpt Two

RM: . . . so when your kids are watching, they couldn't see anything except wholesome stuff, and then when you're ready to sit down and watch, you flip a button and then you would watch, you know, *NYPD Blue* or whatever you want.

Excerpt Three

RM: And, yes, studies have shown that, you know, just as any of us who were kids remember, that if you put a forbidden fruit label on something, that just makes us want it even more. There was one study where some kid said "the cooler the movie, the higher the rating."

DA: (Laugh, guffaw.)

2B LISTENING TWO: *Interview with Former Chairman of MPAA Ratings Board*

David Alpern: Next we turn to Richard Heffner, distinguished Professor of Communications and Public Policy at Rutgers University . . . we caught up with him in Sydney, Australia, at the Office of Film and Literature Classification. Dick, welcome to *Newsweek on Air.*

Richard Heffner: Thank you for inviting me.

DA: You should be flattered that TV is taking up your model, but in fact you are opposed to voluntary ratings even with a V-chip to lock them into family viewing. Why do voluntary ratings work for movies, but not TV?

RH: To me, the most important thing was that the glory of the movie rating system and the genius of it was that it incorporated a box office intermediary between children and harsher media content . . . harsher movie content. It incorporated that into the rating system, and my concern about today . . . with its incredible number of media inputs in the home . . . uh . . . means that there is no box office intermediary.

DA: You say that society would benefit from nonvoluntary regulation and that it might actually save the entertainment industry from full-fledged censorship. How would regulation work and not be censorship?

RH: Well, censorship means that someone has told you, "You may not do this!" And that someone is almost invariably government. I'm too much of a Jeffersonian . . . I'm too much of a civil libertarian to be able to swallow the notion of censorship. I don't want it, David. I don't want it at all. But I do think that regulation by blue-chip entities, not by putting the fox in charge of the hen house, but by putting public-spirited, clearly identified individuals . . . whether it's the head of the PTA, whether it's the head of the American Psychological Association. I'm thinking now of a system in which almost by statute . . . your leadership is concerned essentially with the public interest.

DA: Richard Heffner, thank you very much.

RH: Thanks, David.

4A PRONUNCIATION

Exercise 1

1. Will the ratings and electronic blocking devices block out whole shows, or just offensive parts?

2. So you could presumably program your TV to pick up shows that were either G or PG rated.

3. . . . but if you stick with your old set for another ten years . . .

4. All the families that tried it out, loved it.

5. We caught up with him in Sydney, Australia.

6. You should be flattered that TV is taking up your model.

7. Rick Marin, a magazine editor, looked into the debate over TV ratings.

8. Manufacturers are reluctantly putting them in.

The Phonetic Alphabet

Consonant Symbols

/b/	**b**e		/t/	**t**o
/d/	**d**o		/v/	**v**an
/f/	**f**ather		/w/	**w**ill
/g/	**g**et		/y/	**y**es
/h/	**h**e		/z/	**z**oo, bu**s**y
/k/	**k**eep, **c**an		/θ/	**th**anks
/l/	**l**et		/ð/	**th**en
/m/	**m**ay		/ʃ/	**sh**e
/n/	**n**o		/ʒ/	vi**s**ion, A**s**ia
/p/	**p**en		/tʃ/	**ch**ild
/r/	**r**ain		/dʒ/	**j**oin
/s/	**s**o, **c**ircle		/ŋ/	lo**ng**

Vowel Symbols

/ɑ/	f**ar**, h**o**t		/iy/	w**e**, m**ea**n, f**ee**t
/ɛ/	m**e**t, s**ai**d		/ey/	d**ay**, l**a**te, r**ai**n
/ɔ/	t**a**ll, b**ou**ght		/ow/	g**o**, l**ow**, c**oa**t
/ə/	s**o**n, **u**nder		/uw/	t**oo**, bl**ue**
/æ/	c**a**t		/ay/	t**i**me, b**uy**
/ɪ/	sh**i**p		/aw/	h**ou**se, n**ow**
/ʊ/	g**oo**d, c**oul**d, p**u**t		/oy/	b**oy**, c**oi**n

Credits

Photo credits: Page 1 The New Yorker Collection 2001 David Sipress from cartoonbank.com. All rights reserved; **9** Copyright 1995, Boston Globe. Distributed by Los Angeles Times Syndicate. Reprinted with permission; **23** (left) Sherry Preiss, (right) Preston C. Mack/Getty Images; **26** (top) Preston C. Mack/Getty Images, (bottom) David Toase/Getty Images; **27** (left) Sherry Preiss, (right) Sherry Preiss; **76** Courtesy of Hush Puppies; **81** Bettmann/Corbis; **92** Geoffrey Clements/Corbis; **99** The New Yorker Collection 1995 Donald Reilly from cartoonbank.com. All rights reserved; **118** The White House; **121** Tom Nebbia/Corbis; **124** (top) maps.com, (bottom) Chris Hellier/Corbis; **130** AP/Wide World Photos; **145** Signe Wilkinson/Cartoonists & Writers Syndicate; **169, 170, 172** Copyright International Committee of the Red Cross; **193** The New Yorker Collection 1997 Leo Cullum from cartoonbank.com. All rights reserved; **219** Bob Gorrell, Richmond Times-Dispatch, Creators Syndicate.

Listening credits: Page 4, *Talk of the Nation: Science Friday,* interview with Jonathan Kandell, February 2, 1996. Reproduced with permission of Talk of the Nation; **Pages 52, 150** © Copyright National Public Radio 1995, 1996. **Page 6,** from *Newsweek on Air,* April 30, 2001 © 2001, Newsweek Inc. and The Associated Press. All rights reserved. Used with permission. **Page 28,** from Disney's Utopian Experiment, and interview with Andrew Ross on *Marketplace,* as aired on National Public Radio. Reproduced with permission of Minnesota Public Radio. **Page 31,** interview with Douglas Frantz and Catherine Collins, September 9, 1999. As heard on *Fresh Air,* produced at WHYY in Philadelphia, PA USA, and distributed by National Public Radio. Reproduced with permission of WHYY. **Page 55,** *Tales from the Workplace: Making Lemonade* by Julie Danis, May 30, 1996. Reproduced with the permission of Marketplace Radio. **Page 68,** *Left of Center* by Suzanne Vega and Stephen Addabbo © 1986 WB Music Corp. (ASCAP), Waifersongs Ltd. (ASCAP) and Famous Music Corporation (ASCAP). All Rights o/b/o Waifersongs Ltd. administered by WB Music Corp. Warner Bros. Publications U.S. Inc., Miami, FL 33014. **Page 78,** from an interview with Malcolm Gladwell on *The Connection* on April 13, 2000. Reproduced with permission of WBUR, Boston University Radio. **Page 81,** an interview with Malcolm Gladwell on the Todd Mundt Show, January 3, 2001. Reproduced with the permission of Michigan Radio, © Copyright, 2001. **Page 104,** *West Coast Live,* interview with Kirsten Lagatree by Sedge Thomson, February 10, 1996. Reproduced with the permission of West Coast Live. **Page 107,** interview with Kirsten Lagatree and Steve Scher on JUOW Public Radio, February 6, 1996. Reproduced with the permission of KUOW Radio. **Page 128,** Monks & Monasteries, June 18, 2001. Reproduced with the permission of WAMU, American University Radio. **Pages 173, 177,** interview with Terry Gross and Michael Ignatieff, March 31, 1977. As heard on *Fresh Air with Terry Gross,* produced at WHYY in Philadelphia, PA USA, and distributed by National Public Radio. Reproduced with permission of WHYY. **Page 200,** Bora Kim, 14 years old, a student at the Ichimura Music School in Englewood Cliffs, NJ. The piece is Mozart's Sonata for Piano in F Major, 1st Movement, Allegro, K-332. **Page 204,** from *Newsweek On Air,* February 25, 1996, © 1996, Newsweek, Inc. and AP Network News. All rights reserved. Used with permission. **Pages 225, 228,** from *Newsweek On Air,* March 3, 1996, © 1996, Newsweek, Inc., and AP Network News. All rights reserved. Used with permission.

NorthStar CD Tracking Guide

CD 1

1. Audio Program Introduction

UNIT 1

2. 2A. Listening One
3. Listening for Main Ideas
4. Listening for Details
5. Reacting to the Listening
   Exercise 1
   Excerpt One
6. Excerpt Two
7. Excerpt Three
8. 2B. Listening Two
   Exercise 1
9. 4A. Pronunciation
10. Exercise 1
11. Exercise 2

UNIT 2

12. 2A. Listening One
13. Listening for Main Ideas
14. Listening for Details
15. Reacting to the Listening
    Exercise 1
    Excerpt One
16. Excerpt Two
17. Excerpt Three
18. Excerpt Four
19. 2B. Listening Two

20. 4A. Pronunciation
21. Exercise 1

UNIT 3

22. 2A. Listening One
23. Listening for Main Ideas
    Part One
24. Part Two
25. Listening for Details
26. Reacting to the Listening
    Exercise 1
    Excerpt One
27. Excerpt Two
28. Excerpt Three
29. 2B. Listening Two
    Exercise 1
30. 4A. Pronunciation
    Exercise 1
31. Exercise 2
32. 4D. Speaking Topic
    Exercise 1

UNIT 4

33. 2A. Listening One
34. Listening for Main Ideas
35. Listening for Details
36. Reacting to the Listening
    Exercise 1
    Excerpt One

37. Excerpt Two
38. Excerpt Three
39. Excerpt Four
40. 2B. Listening Two
    Exercise 1
41. 4A. Pronunciation
    Exercise 1
42. Exercise 2
43. 4D. Speaking Topic
    Exercise 1
44. Exercise 2

UNIT 5

45. 2A. Listening One
46. Listening for Main Ideas
    Part One
47. Part Two
48. Listening for Details
49. Reacting to the Listening
    Exercise 1
    Excerpt One
50. Excerpt Two
51. Excerpt Three
52. 2B. Listening Two
53. 4A. Pronunciation
54. Exercise 1
55. 4C. Style
    Exercise 1

CD 2

1. Audio Program Introduction

UNIT 6

2. 2A. Listening One
3. Listening for Main Ideas
4. Listening for Details
5. Reacting to the Listening
   Exercise 1
   Excerpt One
6. Excerpt Two
7. Excerpt Three
8. 2B. Listening Two
9. 4A. Pronunciation
10. Exercise 1
11. 4C. Style
    Exercise 1

UNIT 7

12. 2A. Listening One
13. Listening for Main Ideas
    Part One
14. Part Two
15. Part Three
16. Listening for Details
17. Reacting to the Listening
    Exercise 1
    Excerpt One
18. Excerpt Two
19. Excerpt Three
20. Excerpt Four
21. 2B. Listening Two
22. 4A. Pronunciation
    Exercise 1

23. Exercise 2
24. 4D. Speaking Topic

UNIT 8

25. 2A. Listening One
26. Listening for Main Ideas
    Part One
27. Part Two
28. Part Three
29. Listening for Details
30. Reacting to the Listening
    Exercise 1
    Excerpt One
31. Excerpt Two
32. Excerpt Three
33. 2B. Listening Two
    Part One
34. Part Two
35. Part Three
36. Part Four
37. 3 Focus on Vocabulary
    Exercise 1
38. 4A. Pronunciation
    Exercise 1
39. Exercise 2
40. Exercise 3
41. Exercise 5
42. Exercise 6
43. 4D. Speaking Topic
    Exercise 1
44. Exercise 2

UNIT 9

45. 1B. Sharing Information
    Exercise 1

46. 2A. Listening One
47. Listening for Main Ideas
    Part One
48. Part Two
49. Listening for Details
50. Reacting to the Listening
    Exercise 1
    Excerpt One
51. Excerpt Two
52. 2B. Listening Two
    Part One
53. Part Two
54. Part Three
55. Part Four
56. 4A. Pronunciation
    Exercise 1
57. Exercise 2

UNIT 10

58. 2A. Listening One
59. Listening for Main Ideas
    Part One
60. Part Two
61. Part Three
62. Listening for Details
63. Reacting to the Listening
    Exercise 1
    Excerpt One
64. Excerpt Two
65. Excerpt Three
66. 2B. Listening Two
67. 4A. Pronunciation
    Exercise 1